# RIGHT ACTIONS
# IN SPORT

## Ethics for Contestants

**WARREN P. FRALEIGH, PhD**

State University of New York
College at Brockport

*17942*

**HUMAN KINETICS PUBLISHERS, INC.**
Champaign, IL 61820

Production Director: Kathryn Gollin Marshak
Copy Editor: Peg Goyette
Typesetting: Yvonne Sergent and Sandra Meier
Text Layout: Lezli Harris
Cover Layout: Precision Graphics

Library of Congress Catalog Number: 83-083165
ISBN: 0-931250-55-2

Printed in the United States of America
10  9  8  7  6  5  4  3  2  1

Human Kinetics Publishers, Inc.
Box 5076, Champaign, IL 61820

*On sport, for Sondra*

# Contents

**PART 3     Introduction to the Guides and Ends
of Right Action for the Good Sports Contest**               **107**

CHAPTER 8     The Primary Guides
and Ends of Right Action                                            113

CHAPTER 9     The Supererogatory Guides
and Ends of Right Action                                           126

CHAPTER 10     Secondary Guides and Ends of Right Action     136

# Preface

Many decades of association with sport as an athlete, as a coach, as a teacher, as a spectator, and as a scholar make one well aware of the lack of articulated and comprehensive guides for morally right actions. Usually the guides available are sweeping generalizations such as "play fair," or specific expectancies such as "shake hands with your opponent." Some of these guides and conventional expectancies advise actions that are morally right. Others are simply socially accepted advice that has not been submitted to moral evaluation. This book attempts to provide a systematic, comprehensive normative ethic that reveals which existing guides are substantiated and which are not. Additional nontraditional guides will be stated to fill in obvious gaps. However, it is not sufficient merely to state guides regardless of their comprehensiveness and unity. They must be supported with rational argument. Intelligent readers are persuaded by guides based upon good reasons.

Most discriminating readers like to know the logic behind such a treatment. This allows ready access to the scope of the work and yet provides the framework that reveals the relationships of particulars. This work has a basic logic with three major divisions. First, an adequate normative ethic needs a foundation which relates it to moral decision making in life. That foundation here is the particular kind of event called the good sports contest. The sports contest is called good when it meets a set of dual standards. Initially, a contest is good when it fulfills its nature as a sports contest to a high degree; it is outstanding *qua* contest. Then, a contest is good when it fulfills the substantive characteristics of the moral point of view.

Second, knowledge and agreement on the characterization of the good sports contest will provide the basis for identifying guides for our actions. Such guides, when adhered to by all contestants, will increase the probability of more good sports contests. In short, the guides are practical in identifying actions which will enhance achieving that particular kind of event.

Third, having these practical guides, we must know how to use them correctly and know how to overcome seeming incongruence or to resolve conflicts among the guides.

To understand the structure of this book, it is also helpful to know what it does not try to do. Certain crucial concerns in the philosophy of sport are not essential to argue here. One is the general question, "What is sport?" a question that is neither asked nor answered, although a narrower one, "What is a sport contest?" is. Accordingly, whether or not noncontest activities such as hiking, surfing, or mountain climbing are sport is not a concern here. Neither is there direct concern for the sport status—or lack of it—of bull fighting, dog fighting, dog racing, turtle racing, or other nonhuman "contests."

Also not discussed here are problems of right action external to the sports contest, which nonetheless often have an impact upon the contest. Questions and problems of academic eligibility of school and college athletes are not discussed, and the same is true regarding problems of amateurs and professionals. These issues, and others, are filled with questions of morally right actions but will not be discussed here. Rather, the focus is upon the sports contest as contest, and an ethic for contestants.

# Acknowledgments

One's conclusions in any complex area of study are formed over decades and influenced by diverse people and events. I am indebted to many people for their contributions to this study; however, I am responsible for the conclusions reached. It would be impossible to identify every influential person or event, but I would like to identify a few persons who have contributed in different ways.

For their contributions to presenting this material to the public, sincere thanks to Diane Glidden who typed the manuscript, to Peg Goyette for her editorial skills, and to Kathryn Marshak, who guided this book through production.

My high school and (later) college football coach, Herb Smith, helped me comprehend as a sports participant how intense competitiveness can be paired with courtesy, friendship, and humility, although I have yet to master the latter.

As a 32-year-old coach, I learned that the safety of others is more important than technical competence, thanks to 18-year-old college baseball pitcher Dick Holden. In response to my encouragement of the brush back pitch he responded, "Coach, I can't do that—I might hurt someone!"

During my formal education, three persons increased my existing interest in moral concerns—Delbert Oberteuffer and Everett Kircher at The Ohio State University, and Joseph Fletcher at the Episcopal Theological School.

Many colleagues and friends have given generous advice on this study. Professors Ken Ravizza, Scott Kretchmar, and Francis Keenan all reacted to an early outline. Professor Joseph Gilbert, then director of the Center for Philosophic Exchange, SUNY College at Brockport, spent valuable time in discussing my ideas and in referring me to some useful works in moral philosophy. I am very grateful to Professors Luther

Binkley and Scott Kretchmar for their careful reading of and insightful reactions to the original manuscript. They helped me to correct some serious errors and will perhaps recognize some remaining problems whose treatment, although forewarned, I prefer to modify rather than avoid.

Over decades of teaching undergraduate and graduate students, the demands of communication have forced me to clarify my thinking in some crucial areas. Teaching remains a productive enterprise for the scholar to test ideas, to hear innocent but penetrating questions, and to find ways to say it better. I am thankful to thousands of students who, perhaps unwittingly, have contributed to this study.

*Warren Fraleigh*
*December 1983*

# PART ONE

## INTRODUCTION TO THE PROBLEM OF RIGHT ACTIONS AND A STRUCTURE TO ESTABLISH GUIDES

Persons associated with sports contests for a significant length of time are aware of many instances in which questions arise about morally right actions. Chapter 1 illustrates this basic problem by describing five cases in which different and conflicting answers are proposed. Also, it examines two different sources for right answers and notes their deficiencies. The recognition of such deficiencies results in the need for a different kind of source for answers, namely, a moral basis.

Chapter 2 outlines a structure for establishing guides for morally right actions in sports contests. This structure has three elements which are discussed briefly for clarification. The elements are: establishing a point of view, developing the guides, and specifying ends consistent with the point of view.

By identifying the problem for study and the structure for pursuing the study, Part I lays the foundation for tasks to be taken up in greater detail in Parts II and III of the book.

# Chapter One

# The Problem
# of Right Actions
# in the Sports Contest

Involvement in sports contests often leads to differences regarding appropriate actions in diverse circumstances. It is reasonable to expect diverse views on appropriate actions because different individuals bring varying perspectives to sports contests. Varied perspectives arise from differing purposes of participants, geographically distinct customs and expectancies, and variations in sports contest rules and their interpretations. Diverse views on actions appropriate within sports contests, however, does not eliminate the need to seek guides applicable to thousands of specific cases over time. Indeed, sports participants often ask, "What shall I do?" when confronted with problematical situations or, even after performing a certain action, "What should I have done?" or, when asked for advice, "What should be done?" The bewildering differences may be clarified by illustrating a few cases.

## ILLUSTRATIVE CASES

*The Case of the Faked Injury.*     In 1953, two American universities were playing a football game which, at the time, was crucial to the relative national rankings of each team. In the closing seconds of the first half and having previously used all of its legal time-outs, Team B was inside the 5-yard line of Team A with the clock running and only enough time for one more play *if* the clock could be stopped. Team B was behind by one touchdown and one extra point. A player from Team B fell to the ground as if injured, and the officials quickly called a time-out so that the "injured" player could receive attention. While the clock was stopped, the quarterback of Team B was able to call a play, a substitution was made for the injured player, and the members of Team B were able to line up to run a play. The play was run, Team B scored a touchdown, successfully kicked the extra point, and went to the locker room at the half with the score now tied. Oddly enough, a nearly identical situation occurred at the end of the second half with Team B again behind by one touchdown and one extra point. Again, a Team B player feigned an injury and his team was able to score a touchdown and an extra point to end the game in a tie.

This contest was nationally televised and the action of feigned injury was discussed vigorously in newspapers and magazines. Several commentators, sports fans, and coaches branded the faked injury play as unethical; but many others, including the coach of Team B who had instructed his team in this action, defended the faked injury as smart strategy. This case shows a clear conflict between those who say such action is unethical and those who support it as smart strategy. Is it possible to find a guide for action that will provide an answer to such conflicts — a guide supported by good reasons? Or, must sports contestants refer only to their own purposes, geographic customs, or rules interpretations?

*The Case of the Intentional Foul.*     In basketball, soccer, or American football, it occurs not infrequently that a defensive player intentionally fouls an offensive player. Sometimes, this intentional foul occurs after the offensive player has legally and skillfully outmaneuvered the fouling defensive player and has gained the advantage. What is the appropriate action in such circumstances? Should the defensive player deliberately foul in order to prevent what appears to be a sure score, or should that person leave the offensive player unhindered after the latter has attained the advantage? Does the score of the contest and the time left to play influence right action? Does the type and severity of penalty for intentional fouling make a difference? This situation again leads to conflicts between those who would judge such an action as unethical and those who would claim it to be the only intelligent thing to do in such circumstances. Is there a guide for action applicable to such a case that will provide an answer supported by relevant reasons?

*The Case of the Tennis Linesman's Error.*     In tournament tennis sometimes a player, observing the landing point of the ball on his or her side of the net and seeing it hit on or inside the court line, deliberately faults on the next serve in order to neutralize an advantage attained when the official called the opponent's stroke out of court. Is this the best action to take? Some would say the official's decision ought to be final here. They further assert that such errors will, over time, equal themselves. Others maintain that this particular contest cannot be equated with any other and that the accurate determination must be made here and not by some hypothetically accurate law of averages. What relevant guide for action can be cited in such a conflict?

***The Case of Anabolic Steroids.*** In sports events in which competitive superiority is directly related to the weight and size of the athletes, such as shot putting, the use of anabolic steroids to develop muscular bulk has become highly controversial. It appears that a significant number of world-class athletes do, in fact, take anabolic steroids as part of their training regimen. The scientific data regarding harmful side effects of steroids appear to be mixed but some potential danger is cited; some athletic control groups prohibit the use of steroids and some do not, and some say that such drugs are artificial training aids. Others claim that an athlete cannot effectively compete at the world-class level without steroids, that rules prohibiting such drugs infringe upon an individual's right to choose, and that drugs are no more artificial than diet or other kinds of conventional training routines. Is there a principled answer to the question of drug use in sports?

***The Case of the Uneven Contest.*** At times, a thoroughly unequal contest occurs wherein one contestant or team has so completely dominated the other and has attained such a substantial lead in the score that it is almost impossible for the opponent to win. What ought to be done in such circumstances? Should the presently superior contestant or team increase the advantage as far as possible by vigorously using their normal style of play? Should the superior contestant or team play deliberately to the opponent's strength? Adherents to one point of view say that advantage must be pressed to its fullest, and if the situation were reversed they would expect likewise from opponents. The conflicting view would argue that aggressive pressing of the advantage is undesirable because it humiliates opponents deliberately. Again, can guides for action be brought to bear upon such circumstances and provide a reasoned answer?

## THE SOURCES OF ANSWERS

Obviously, persons who participate in sports contests do find answers to the kinds of questions raised in these few examples and in numerous other specific contexts. Individuals faced with such specific problems do act in one way or another, which is to say that they have by their actions implicitly answered the inherent questions. Whether or not such actions indicate any conscious and reflective response to the questions cannot be ascertained from the actions themselves. As sports participants act in ways that indicate an implicit though nonreflectively based answer to the questions inherent in such situations, it is obvious that their actions issue out of some sources.

*Convention and Custom.* Perhaps the most obvious source which tacitly answers the vexing questions raised is that of custom and convention. In short, actions often issue from a conventional and customary conception of what *is* done in such situations. For example, the basketball player, who has been skillfully outmaneuvered by an opponent who is now about to score an easy basket, will in many instances deliberately foul in order to void the easy basket. The player may have been coached to do just that or, after observing other respected players foul deliberately, may follow their lead. English professional soccer provides another example, in the practice of tackling from behind, now apparently conventionally done. Robert Armstrong writes:[1]

> It should be remembered that, before the beginning of this season...portentous warnings were issued, via referee's training seminars, of the penalties that would befall any player rash enough to persist with this particular method of interrupting an attack. The tackle from behind, it was said, constituted a *proven* menace to our national game...and was...an unfair and provocative technique for gaining possession.

Despite recognition of such "official" attitudes toward the practice, Armstrong continues by saying,

> Whatever its long term effects, though, *nine times out of 10 the tackle from behind is every defender's fail-safe device* — if he fails to retrieve the ball, he will certainly bring down the forward and halt an attack. Even if the defender does win the ball, he will almost inevitably take the legs of his opponent and thus remove him temporarily from the flow or play. Either way, the defender wins — and in almost every case, by a technique that involves an unavoidable trip.

Examples of actions performed in accord with what is done conventionally are numerous. The use of "grapevining" and other underwater defensive techniques in water polo is practiced by almost all players even though such techniques are clearly against the rules. Illegal or not, such practices are conventionally accepted and practiced by most coaches and players. In fact, players who do not use and/or expect such techniques are often less effective.

But surely an action based on what is done conventionally is not "right" because it is consistent with what is conventional. Even though conventional acceptance may sanction a certain action as the right thing to do, rather than simply the thing to do, it does not follow that such "baptism" is legitimate. For as Baier[2] says, "embodiment in the morality of the group is no final guarantee of the morality or immorality of the type of conduct in question. The morality of the group may be wrong. The moral convictions of the group may be mistaken." And as Richards[3] observes, "one of the most important marks of an intellectually satisfying moral theory is that it enables us to see...what is justifiably part of our moral beliefs, and what is introduced by other assumptions which may be the residue of shibboleth and arbitrary convention." Notwithstanding the conclusion that conventional group standards may or may not be moral expectancies, when it comes time for standards to be acted upon Hare[4] reminds us that it is the individual who must answer the problem:

> ...a man who is faced with such a problem knows that it is his own problem, and that nobody can answer it for him. He may, it is true, ask the advice of the people [*or simply act upon the conventional morality of the group*]; and he may also ascertain more facts about the circumstances and consequences of a proposed action, and other facts of this sort. But there will come a time when he does not hope to find out anything else of relevance by factual inquiry, and when he knows that, whatever others may say about the answer to his problem, *he* has to answer it.

To this point, we can see that reference to convention and custom as the authoritative source for answers to the action questions in sport situations is inadequate. Even though answers are available there, they may not be authoritative answers. This is not to say that convention never provides a correct answer, but only that such answers are not guaranteed by convention and that the answers thus provided may be correct because of the authority of something other than convention.

*Self-Interest.* A second major source for answers to the action questions inherent in sport situations is self-interest. Broadly speaking, self-interested actions are those taken because they are believed to be in the interest of the agent who is acting. There can be concepts of long-term self-interested actions because such actions, in Baier's words, satisfy or help in the agent's, "realization of his life plan or the satisfaction of his ambitions, aspirations, and ideals." There can also be concepts of short-term self-interested actions in which such actions are enjoyable or wanted by the acting agent. If we apply Baier's analysis, a golfer's enjoyment of playing slowly may be classified as a *self*-regarding individual rule of reason in support of the action. However, an agent may enjoy providing pleasure, such as making someone else laugh. In such, the action leading to the laughter can be supported by an *other*-regarding individual rule of reason. But, even considering the benefit of another is supported by the acting agent's reasoning, at times, because it contributes to the enjoyment of the acting agent — and not because of primary concern for the other's welfare. An agent may want to prevent the opponent from scoring in basketball, soccer, or football and, because of that, deliberately foul a player on the offense who has skillfully outmaneuvered him or her. Such an action can be supported by a short-range, self-regarding individual rule of reason, according to Baier.[5]

When we examine each case discussed earlier, it is easy to identify many reasons supporting a particular idea of the appropriate action. Perhaps the most easily identified kinds of reasons are those of self-interest. For example, the player faking the injury has a reason to do so because he wants to stop the clock. Furthermore, stopping the clock is supported both by a self-regarding individual reason because it enhances his possibilities of winning the game, and by his long-term, self-interested aspirations (supposedly) of attaining or maintaining a higher national ranking. In the case of the linesman's error, the tennis player may deliberately fault on the next serve in order *not* to win a contest due to an error that gives him/her an advantage. Such advantage would contradict the ideal of the sportsman who seeks advantage gained solely by the exercise of skill. Here, the reason for regarding the welfare of the opponent is that the sportsman would be displeased if his or her own ideal image were tarnished because of the official's error. Thus, another illustration of an other-regarding individual rule of reason.

If we analyzed all the reasons that could support all the actions possible, we would probably find that most of them stem from self-interest, some from convention, and a few are of a third type which will be discussed in the next section. Reasons of self-interest might predominate, at least numerically, because actions of any kind are characteristically performed for some purpose of the agent, and when the agent's purpose is identified the action is explained; we know "*why* he acted as he did."[6] When we examine the purposes identified by acting agents we often see them expressed in terms of the agent's own interest, such as: "I faked the injury to stop the clock so that my team would have a chance for a touchdown and a tie game," or, "I double faulted on that serve to correct the linesman's error so that I would not be known as someone who won unfairly."

Also, when agents explain actions in terms of their purposes such explanations carry, directly or tacitly, an expression and justification that what was attempted by the action, its purpose, was good. As Gewirth[7] observes:

> The purpose for which the agent acts, since it is something which seems to him to be good, not only explains the action but also, *from his standpoint*, it justifies the action. For it provides the rationale which gives the action its point, appropriateness, or correctness for him. And since it is the agent's own action whose appropriateness or correctness is established through what he takes to be the goodness of the purpose for which he performs the action, he regards himself justified in performing it. His attitude toward his action, hence takes the logical form of a normative judgement of endorsement.

So if most purposes of an agent's actions are due to self-interest, and if those agents think those purposes are good, then the agents feel that their actions are the right thing to do. In such an analysis the "right" thing to do is what is in the agent's self-interest.

However, arriving at conclusions on the right sports action based on reasons of self-interest, like reasons based on custom and convention, also has serious difficulties. For instance, if two players from opposing basketball teams each want to occupy exactly the same geographical position at the same time, it is obvious that what each wants, although the same in this instance, contradicts what the other wants. Likewise, if one tennis player believes the linesman's calls to be authoritative but the other tennis player thinks it necessary to negate the linesman's call by deliberately double faulting, then satisfying one player necessarily negates satisfying the other.

So it appears that reference to the base of self-interest as the source for authoritative answers is, like convention, not effective. For often sports participants may have wants that contradict each other, like the two basketball opponents who want to be in the same place at the same time. Or the players may receive enjoyment in ways that are incompatible with each other, like the two golfers who enjoy fast play and slow play individually. Or the players may find contradictory actions supporting each of their different aspirations, ambitions, or ideals, like the tennis players — one of whom has an interest in clearly defined third-person decision authority for the linesman and one of whom has an interest in achieving advantage by skill alone and not by officiating errors. Inasmuch as agents act in accord with their individual purposes, whether for want, enjoyment, or long-term self-interest, the performance of such actions comes with, as Gewirth[8] has observed from the agent's standpoint "a normative judgement of endorsement," and "for an agent to regard his action as justified is for him to regard himself as having a right to perform the action."[9]

In a specific sports situation, as in all of life, assuming that reasons of self-interest are authoritative in determining appropriate action is dangerous precisely because it carries the inherent, inevitable reality of conflict. Further, it does not provide the possibility for the reasoned resolution of such conflict. Two golfers, one of whom enjoys fast play and the second of whom enjoys slow play, cannot resolve this difference reasonably by each appealing to his or her own kind of self-interested enjoyment. Baier[10] clearly and eloquently states why self-interest cannot dictate the appropriate action for resolving conflict.

> Let us begin with a state of affairs in which reasons of self-interest are supreme. In such a state, everyone keeps his impulses and inclinations in check when and only

when they would lead him into behavior detrimental to his own interest. Everyone who follows reason will discipline himself to rise early, to do his exercises...and so on. However, it will often happen that people's interests conflict. In such a case, they will have to resort to ruses or force to get their own way. As this becomes known, men will become suspicious, for they will regard one another as scheming competitors for the good things in life. The universal supremacy of the rules of self-interest must lead to what Hobbes called the state of nature.

## Summary

In this brief analysis of questions about the most appropriate action to take in specific sport contexts I have tried, by citing five cases, to illustrate examples of different actions considered most appropriate in each case. I have asked whether guides for action, supported by good reasons, are available to provide an authoritative answer to the question about the most appropriate action. I have then briefly examined convention and self-interest as the potential sources for guides for action. It turns out that neither convention nor self-interest can be adequate guides. With regard to convention, what is done and approved is not itself a guarantor of its rightness; it may even be wrong. Or, because the conventions of different societies sometimes differ, this may lead to conflict based in different conventions. With regard to self-interest, it is logically impossible to base guides for action there because reasons of self-interest in support of particular actions often lead inevitably to conflict, and such conflict cannot be resolved by guides that are themselves based in self-interest. It appears necessary, therefore, to seek some other basis for guides for action.

## NEED FOR A MORAL BASIS

In all the cases discussed so far, the implicit general question is "What shall I do?" (or, "What shall be done?" or "What should have been done?"). As we have seen, the specific actions that agents take are sometimes those supported by the reasons (rules) of convention or, most frequently, by the reasons (rules) of self-interest. However, when there is a choice of actions, agents are able to ask, "Shall I act this way or that way?" And it is in deliberating this question that agents ask the further, related question, "Ought I to do this or that?"[11] This question brings us to the need for a moral basis to ascertain which actions are the best. To provide a firm base for dealing with thousands of situations in sports contests, says Baier, "The crucial moral question...will therefore be the agent's questions 'What ought I to do?' asked before acting, asked in order to obtain guidance by moral reasons, asked in order to be put in a position to decide on what is the morally right thing to do."[12]

Moral reasons are the best kind when compared to other kinds of reasons. We prefer reasons of self-interest to reasons of simple pleasure; we consider reasons of long-range interest superior to reasons of short-range interest, and we consider reasons of law, religion, and morality as outweighing reasons of self-interest. Additionally, Baier observes, moral reasons exist to adjudicate the conflict that is inherently created by following reasons of self-interest as superior. Further, moral reasons are the best reasons because moral rules (reasons) exist, "for the good of everyone alike."[13]

It is quite easy to assert that moral reasons are better than those of self-interest and even to say that moral reasons are the best kinds of reasons. But we must support such an assertion. On the one hand, we can support it by the explanation "We have been trained to regard moral reasons as superior to all others, and have accepted that."[14] Although such a statement may explain a belief in the superiority of moral reasons over self-interest, it does not justify such a belief because, as we discovered earlier, the existence of a conventional belief is not the guarantor of its moral superiority. Furthermore, if faced with two different and incompatible possible actions in a specific sports contest, each supported by reasons of the self-interests of two different sports participants, then it is clear, if we apply the best moral reasons to the case, that the self-interest of one participant will not be served.[15] Recall the contradictory self-interests of the tennis players, one of whom sees the final and effective decision making as being the linesman's while the other sees it as being the player's when the linesman has made an error unfair to the player's opponent. We see here that a superior moral reason will support one's self-interest and will negate the other.[16] This raises a difficult question: Why should we accept moral reasons as superior when they, in a particular case, may be detrimental to one's own self-interest? For clearly, "Moral rules are not designed to serve the agent's interest directly."[17]

The question we now face was raised by instances in which sports agents chose from alternative actions. Thus, questions such as "What shall I do?" or "What shall be done?" or "What should have been done?" then become questions like "What ought I to do?" or "What ought to be done?" or "What ought to have been done?" These latter questions then lead us to identify the actions supported by the best reasons—the moral reasons. And what does it mean to say moral reasons are superior reasons?

> If you offer reasons of self interest, you are arguing in a circle. Moreover, it cannot be true that it is always in my interest to treat moral reasons as superior to reasons of self-interest. If it were, self interest and morality could never conflict, but they notoriously do. It is equally circular to argue that there are moral reasons for saying

that one ought to treat moral reasons as superior to reasons of self interest. And what other reasons are there?

The answer is that we are now looking at the world from the point of view of *anyone.* We are not examining particular alternative courses of action before this or that person; we are examining two alternative worlds, one in which moral reasons are always treated by everyone as superior to reasons of self-interest and one in which the reverse is the practice. And we can see that the first world is the better world, because we can see that the second world would be the sort which Hobbes describes as the state of nature.[18]

We can now see that we are choosing the better of two possible worlds for everyone, including ourselves. In the sports world we can see that everyone is better off if everyone follows moral rules rather than rules of self-interest. The latter would invite chaos, distrust, fear, and rampant disregard of one participant for other participants. Now when we adopt the position that we ought to be moral in its more general sense because it is consistent with a world that is better for everyone, we establish a general recipe for guidance in specific sports situations. Our general recipe becomes, "We ought to act in the way supported by the best moral reasons." Then, when faced with the ought questions in specific sports situations, we can best answer them by finding the actions(s) supported by the best moral reasons. In using moral reasons to support our answers we are saying such things as:

I ought to do X because....

X ought to be done because....

X ought to have been done because....

Here the statements following "because" are the moral reasons justifying what ought to be done.

As we shall see in Chapter 2, it is necessary to characterize what kind of sports world is better for everyone so that we can understand the source from which we derive our general moral rules. For it is these general rules that will guide us in finding the answers to our specific questions.

A general "ought" rule is a rule for answering questions of the form "What shall I do"—a recipe for the production of particular pieces of advice. Singular "ought" sentences are means of instructing in or instantiating general "ought" rules.[19]

## NOTES

[1]Robert Armstrong, "Tackling From Behind," *The Guardian* (February 1, 1977), p. 18. (Italics mine.)

[2]Kurt Baier, *The Moral Point of View* (Ithaca & London: Cornell University Press, 1958), p. 179.

[3]David A. J. Richards, *A Theory of Reasons for Action* (Oxford: Oxford University Press, 1971), p. 226.

[4]R.M. Hare, *Freedom and Reason* (Oxford: Oxford University Press, 1963), p. 2. (Material in brackets and italics mine.)

[5]Baier, *Moral Point of View*, pp. 101-118.

[6]Richard Taylor, *Action and Purpose* (Englewood Cliffs, NJ: Prentice-Hall, 1966), p. 151.

[7]Alan Gewirth, "The Normative Structure of Action," *The Review of Metaphysics* XXV, No. 2 (December, 1971), p. 244. (Italics mine.)

[8]Gewirth, "Normative Structure," p. 244.

[9]Ibid., p. 250.

[10]Baier, *Moral Point of View*, p. 309. (The state of nature according to Hobbes is characterized by conditions of life which are "poor, nasty, brutish, and short").

[11]Hare, *Freedom and Reason*, p. 51.

[12]Baier, *Moral Point of View*, p. 46.

[13]Ibid., pp. 99, 190, 200.

[14]Ibid., p. 297.

[15]Kurt Baier, "Why Should We be Moral?" in *Morality and Rational Self Interest*, ed. David P. Gauthier (Englewood Cliffs, NJ: Prentice-Hall, 1970), p. 164.

[16]Some might argue that the self-interest of each player can be supported simultaneously by the simple "solution" that the one player acts appropriately when following his or her own self-interest and that the other player acts appropriately when doing likewise. I am fully aware of this possibility, but reject it for two reasons. First, it simply avoids the question at hand, "How *ought* I act?" Second, the potential consequences of such a determination would be to the detriment, in principle, of only one of the the participants and thus raise the problem of unfairness. For, if player A *alone* acts to double fault deliberately when the linesman calls the opponent's shot out when it is clearly in, then player A could never have the negative effect of the linesman's errant calls on his or her score removed while player B would usually have the negative effects of the linesman's errant calls neutralized by the score. In principle, then, each player following his or her own reason of self-interest would be absolving himself or herself from the *consequences* of obeying that reason. This would be, according to Hare, "cutting off morality at its roots" (*Freedom and Reason*, p. 135).

[17]Baier, "Why Should We Be Moral," p. 164.

[18]Baier, *Moral Point of View*, p. 310.

[19]R.M. Hare, *Essays in the Moral Concepts* (Berkeley and Los Angeles, CA: The University of California Press, 1972), p. 2.

# Chapter Two

# A Structure
# to Establish Guides
# for Right Actions

We have seen that the best kinds of reasons supporting one particular action over another are moral reasons. But how do we recognize moral reasons? For don't we often believe that the reasons we offer in support of our actions are not only in our self-interest but also justifiable? Doesn't each adherent to the different actions suggested in the five cases think that his/her view on the most appropriate action is superior to the others? When we debate the merits of the different actions, doesn't the discussion often become impassioned and even heated?

In general, we care deeply about our actions. We do not perform actions that we do not care about; it may be said that "there are no indifferent actions."[1] Human action necessarily is always done by an agent, is something over which an agent exercises control, is not something that merely happens to the agent, and is an activity and not the achievement resulting from activity. Finally, because of all the foregoing, an action always involves the person.[2] Metaphorically, our actions are our offspring — they issue forth from us like babies from the mother's womb to take their place in the community of actions that issue from other persons. Is it any wonder that we do care so very much about our own actions as mothers and fathers care about their offspring?

This deep regard for our own actions is probably the result of our desire to do the right actions. For at the least, we desire to do the right things because we wish to be favorably regarded and respected by others. At the most, we desire to do the right things because we wish to be good.

In any case, we wish to be good in some sense of that word. Our wish to be good motivates us to justify, and justification requires reasons to support the actions we prefer. But some kinds of reasons are justificatory and others are only explanatory.[3] For example, the "injured" player in the first case might have said, "I faked the injury because the coach told us to do so in such a situation" or "I faked the injury to stop the clock so that my team would have a chance for a touchdown and a tie game." Both statements give us some explanation of why the injury was faked but cannot constitute justifications except in the player's own mind. For whether or not the action in question is justifiable is precisely the issue at hand. An explanation of an action which justifies that action solely with respect to the acting agent's desires, wishes, or self-interests may be a reason for that action but not a morally justifiable reason.[4]

## THE ELEMENTS IN THE STRUCTURE
## TO ESTABLISH GUIDES

We must describe a structure for determining the guides for right actions in sports contests. What basic process will establish the guides to right actions supported by moral reasons? This process must establish general guides that will be applicable to diverse sport situations — sports participants living within different systems of convention and in many different sports. Like the rules of sport that provide the structure within which individual players and teams strive to determine who is better in performing, we need to describe and explain a framework for our reasoning process. Such a framework will dictate the form of our reasoning process. But like the rules of sport which do not themselves determine who will win any particular sports contest, it will not itself predispose an answer in any particular sport situation to any particular moral opinion.[5]

A structure for moral reasoning will not eliminate the need for individual sports participants to exercise their own intelligence and judgment when answering specific moral questions. For as is well understood, any person as a moral agent must face real alternative action possibilities among which he or she must make the specific decision. Nonetheless, moral philosophy can help by showing us where our convictions stem from our parochial conventions[6] and by clarifying the calculus and general rules for moral deliberation.[7] It is not the function of moral philosophy to answer all moral questions before they appear in specific situations,[8] nor should we expect that the description and explanation of a moral theory will induce people to think morally. For those who already wish to do so, a moral theory will be very helpful, but those who influence public opinion must persuade people to think morally.[9] In the sports world, such persuasion is the responsibility of coaches, physical education teachers, parents, sports journalists, sports administrators and agents who make sports rules, officiate sports contests, and adjudicate conflicts arising in them.

### Establish a Point of View

The first element in the proposed framework for establishing guides for right action is the establishment of a point of view. Discussion here will focus upon what establishing a point of view means, how a point of view functions in moral reasoning and which characteristics certify that it is a moral point of view rather than some other. In following chapters, discussion will turn to establishing a moral point of view for sport.

*The Meaning of a Point of View.*    A point of view is the perspective from which we look at our object of inquiry. The problem we are concerned with is, "How shall we look at sport to ascertain guides for right action that are supported by moral reasons?" Our ability to ask such a question presupposes the possibility of more than one point of view as our perspective. But as we shall see, not just any point of view is acceptable.

*The Function of the Point of View.*    We must establish a structure for moral reasoning, which is a form of practical reasoning. It is directly applicable to the questions arising in life situations. As Baier[10] observes:

> Answers to practical considerations can be arrived at by reference to a point of view, which may be defined by a principle. When we adopt a point of view, we adopt its defining principle. To look at practical problems from that point of view is to be prepared to answer practical questions of the form "What shall I do?" "What should be done?" by reference to its defining principle.

Accordingly, the designated point of view functions as the reference for answering our practical questions. Without the reference provided by the point of view, we will not find consistent answers to questions about appropriate actions in sports situations which, although occurring at different times and places with different participants, are nonetheless the same in their moral aspects.

*Characteristics of the Moral Point of View.*    There are many candidates for our possible adoption as the point of view in our practical reasoning. For instance, we could look at sport from the economics point of view and, in so doing, our resulting guides for right actions would be dominated by economic criteria of right. One economic criterion of right action might focus on whether an action increases or decreases monetary profit. Or we could look at sport from the health point of view and our guides for right actions would reflect health criteria. One health criterion of right action would be whether or not an action presents unnecessary physical risks for the participants. Or, we have examined in Chapter 1 the possibilities of adopting the points of view of convention and self-interest. We rejected both and found that a moral basis, or a moral point of view, was necessary for our practical deliberations. Let us now identify and explain what characterizes the moral point of view. We will not focus upon arguments in support of these characteristics because that is properly done by those who are concerned with ethics as distinguished from moral questions.[11] Also, these arguments are both lengthy and complex and have been well presented in several sources referred to in this work.[12] This work itself is primarily concerned with moral questions of the form "What ought I do?", "What ought to be done?", or "What ought to have been done?" as they appear in sport contests and in the guides to the morally right answers.

Characteristics of the moral point of view differ somewhat in the writings of several philosophers. But with apology in advance for any misinterpretation or oversimplification, some will be combined here for the sake of the brevity consistent with the primary function of this treatise. The characteristics of the moral point of view are four in number, according to Baier in *The Moral Point of View.*

*The resolution of conflicts of interest* is a procedural characteristic of the moral point of view in that the moral point of view exists to perform such a function. It is the supreme court to which appeals based in conflicts of interest can be made.[13] Indeed, "The very *raison d'etre* of a morality is to yield reasons which overrule the reasons of self interest in those cases when everyone's following self interest would be harmful to everyone."[14] Thus, our guides for action must be procedurally useful in resolving the conflicting self-interests of different sports participants who recommend or do actions that are contradictory in the same situation. Conversely, a guide that does not help resolve conflicts of interest cannot fulfill this characteristic of the moral point of view. However, this does not mean that a moral point of view useful in resolving conflicts of interest may not be congruent with one of the self-interested points of view that is in conflict. It does say that the moral point of view is not, before the specific case arises and before the conflict of interest occurs, congruent with any particular self-interested reason or any particular conventional reason. In principle, the moral point of view is neutral and does not favor the self-interests of one person over another or the conventions of one social group over another.

*Meant for everybody* is a substantive characteristic of the moral point of view. It means that the view taken can apply, logically, to everybody and that a view which cannot apply to everybody is not meant for everybody. It means that everybody is subject to the superiority of the moral point of view regardless of an individual's particular goals.[15] The moral guides for action that reflect the moral point of view are prescriptive for everybody; each person wills that his or her actions will be prescribed by the guides.[16] These guides must be universalizable in a particular sense. That is, if an agent judges an action to be morally right in a given situation and if there is another agent in another situation in which the morally relevant characteristics are the same, then the judgment on a morally right action must be the same.[17] For instance, if it is judged morally right to decrease the possibility of injury in football by teaching defensive linemen to avoid contact with a passer after he has released the ball, then it must be judged as morally right in basketball to teach defensive players to avoid undercutting offensive players on driving leaps to score. Universalizable does not mean that a substantive moral guide for action is accepted by everyone, or that commitment to such a guide justifies intolerance of someone who thinks differently. Such difference on moral convictions is a base for discussion — not suppression of different views.[18] Thus, it can be seen that this sense of universalizable fulfills the need for moral consistency in different cases sharing similar moral aspects.

*For the good of everyone alike* is a substantive characteristic of the moral point of view. This means that the substance of the moral guides adopted "should be 'reversible,' that is, not merely for the good of the agent, but at least not detrimental to the persons who are affected by the agent's behavior."[19] Further, it means that action which is nonreversible is wrong. Also, the principle of reversibility means that it is "wrong an omission — not to help another person when he is in need and when we are in a position to help him."[20] To illustrate, suppose an athlete thinks it is right to injure an opponent intentionally to get the opponent out of the contest and thus increase the chances of winning. That same athlete would not think it right if the opponent injured him or her intentionally. Accordingly, such an act is not reversible. Thus, we can see that reversible means that what I consider right action when I am the acting agent, I must be able, rationally, to consider right action when I am the recipient of another agent's act under the same circumstances.

Next, for the good of everyone alike means the guides must advise actions that are good for the beneficiaries in the same way. For instances, the guides could prescribe such goods as equal opportunity, nonharassment, noninjurious action, courtesy, and appropriate compensation, to name a few, for everyone affected by the actions.

Finally, for the good of everyone alike means everyone is better off if everyone adheres to this characteristic of the moral point of view,[21] even though such adherence may sometimes require a sacrifice of self-interest. Nonetheless, says Baier, "The best possible life for *everyone* is possible only by everyone's following the rules of morality."[22,23]

*Acting on principle* is a procedural characteristic of the moral point of view. It means that one determines one's action in relation to a moral guide rather than upon some rule of thumb that operates only to promote one's aim.[24] According to Hare, the adoption of moral guides which are universalizable ensures that actions are not based only upon opportunistic reasons.[25] Adopting guides and acting upon them consistently helps assure that we do not, because of the influence of wants, desire, and self-interests, act in ways not supported by moral reasons. Acting upon principle more often assures the long-term and widespread benefits of the moral action as against the immediate or narrowly confined benefits of the self-interested action. Finally, the guides are meant for everybody, are for the good of everyone alike, and are useful in resolving conflicts.

Upon completing this element in this structure, we will have characterized sport from the moral point of view. This characterization will establish the basis for the second element — the development of guides for right actions.

### Developing the Guides from the Moral Point of View

The second element in this structure for moral reasoning is developing the guides for right action from the moral point of view. To clarify this element, we will attempt to clarify the general nature of these guides and to state what kind of human agents, under what conditions, would establish such guides.

*General Nature of the Guides.* These guides are statements that, taken together, function in three ways. First, they declare the substance of the rules of action drawn from the moral point of view of the type of human action being considered. They lay out rule-like generalizations regarding certain actions under consideration in language germane to those actions. For example, guides from the moral point of view in sport use language that is sport relevant. Second, these guides help sports participants select the appropriate ends to pursue.[26,27] For instance, the guides would help participants decide whether the end sought by the player who faked the injury in the first case was appropriate or whether the end sought by the basketball, football, or soccer player in the case of intentional fouling was appropriate. Third, these guides if adhered to will influence the practical state of affairs in the action area so that it becomes congruent with the moral point of view.

These guides for moral action will embody the substantive characteristics of being meant for everybody and being for the good of everyone alike. They will be stated as procedural guides useful in resolving conflicts of interest in thousands of specific situations involving thousands of participants in hundreds of sports in dozens of societies with different conventions.

*Development of the Guides.*    Together, the guides are a set of moral guides, a morality. Developing a morality is rationalizing, giving reasons that are universalizable,[28] a system to provide advance guidance for sports situations in which different actions are possible, to guide advice to others, and to appraise past actions. The characterization of sport from the moral point of view is a given for developing this set of guides. By itself it is not a morality but only a basis from which the set of guides may be derived. Therefore, something besides the characterization is needed—a way of examining the characterization of the moral point of view in sport to designate the moral guides needed to make more of the actions performed moral actions.

We could look at the moral point of view in sport as an ideal observer who, according to Brandt, is fully informed and vividly imaginative, impartial, and in a calm frame of mind and otherwise normal, and thus capable of accurate designation of the necessary moral guides for action.[29] But since we are concerned with a system of moral guides useful for many people in the process of moral judgments, we would risk developing a set of guides understood and accepted by only an elite minority of intellectuals. This in principle would eliminate the effectiveness of the guides in resolving conflicts of interest because they would not be comprehensible to persons in conflict. Such is not the best approach for our task here.

To avoid this difficulty we will look at the moral point of view in sport as rational contractors would. More specifically, we will adopt the rational contractor's concept in a way specific to our present task and these specific adaptations will be discussed in the introduction to Part III. Here it is sufficient to say that the rational contractor's concept is the development of a set of moral guides by all persons who have certain things in common.

As explained by Richards:[30]

> The concept of morality and moral principles is equivalent to the concept of those ultimate standards of conduct which, if publicly known and generally acted on, perfectly rational egoistic men (consisting of all persons), from a position of equal liberty, and in the absence of any knowledge of their own particular desires, nature, and circumstances, but with knowledge of all other circumstances of human life and desire, would agree to as standards to be used in regulating their actual relations to one another, whether in their common institutions or apart from them.

One must understand that this concept establishes a hypothetical position occupied by certain agents who have the responsibility to examine the description and explanation of sport from the moral point of view and, from that hypothetical position, to identify, state, and explain the moral guides for action to which they can agree. In the hypothetical position each agent is free, equal, rational, and wishing to pursue general human interests. From that hypothetical original position, the rational contractors must attempt to state the agreed-upon moral guides *without* any individual rational contractor's knowledge of his/her own particular ability, status, and circumstances, but knowing in general the meaning of being a person and the facts relevant to personal well-being and desire satisfaction.[31] Upon completing this second element in this structure, we will have stated a set of guides for action drawn from the characterization of sport from the moral point of view.

### Specifying Ends Consistent With the Moral Point of View

The third element in this structure for moral reasoning is the identification of ends appropriate for sports agents to pursue because these ends are consistent with the moral point of view. Specifying ends that are consistent with the moral point of view will provide a key to the appraisal of specific actions of sports agents in achieving their ends. Appropriate ends are those general ends consistent with the substantive characteristics of the moral point of view, namely, meant for everybody and for the good of everyone alike. Such general ends also mean those ends consistent with the procedural characteristics of the moral point of view. These ends, if pursued, can overcome conflicts of interest and are the ends in principle toward which the more specific ends of specific actions act as instrumentally effective means. This specification of appropriate ends makes the moral point of view and the moral guides operational: It provides useful judgments about what ends *ought* to be pursued.

*Intended Ends.* Intended ends are states of affairs that a human agent consciously intends to effect as the result of his or her actions in a situation.[32] For example, if I were the tennis player benefitting from the tennis linesman's error described in Chapter 1, I could indicate to the linesman that my opponent's shot was in court by pointing with my racket. If I did that I would expect the linesman to reconsider the call and possibly change it. That would be my specific intended end. In this work we want to identify those general intended ends toward which an agent's specific intended ends are effective instrumental means. Thus, when the general intended ends consistent with the moral point of view are established, sports participants will have the best ends to bring about by their specific intended ends. They will have some standard to evaluate which, among conflicting specific intended ends, is most consistent with the moral point of view.

However, persons sometimes do things, the outcomes of which they did not or could not forsee or may not have intended.[33] Also, a particular action often has multiple results, some intended and some not intended by the agent. For instance, I may open a door to see if my daughter is in the room (my intended end). At the same time I may also do many other things. I may hit someone on the other side of the door, causing the person to fall down and sprain a wrist; I may admit an unwanted animal into the room; or I may distract someone else in the room who is reading or contemplating. This indicates that complex actions are purposive: They are, as actions, understood by referring to the agent's intended end.[34]

So if we wish to appraise the actions of agents in specific situations, we need to know what they intend to bring about.[35] Because the agents know what they are trying to bring about or prevent and believe it is possible to do so, these agents will also know if they have succeeded. Thus, another understanding of the concept of intended end is that it is something which can be gained or failed and, for this reason, is distinguished from a principle which is not something that can be gained or failed but rather is upheld or broken.[36] In further distinguishing end from principle, a principle is a rule guiding the selection of ends.[37,38]

The achievable, concrete nature of an intended end is emphasized further by contrasting it with an ideal. An ideal "is to think of some kind of thing as pre-eminently good within some larger class."[39] In contrast to intended ends, ideals are long-range goals and are so general as to be unattainable. Despite this unattainability, "We know what it is to come closer to or to drift away from our ideal while knowing all the time that we cannot reach it."[40]

I have tried to clarify the concept of an intended end carefully so that we understand we are not now discussing some esoteric thing beyond human ability to achieve. I am interested in establishing the best general, but achievable, ends that sport agents pursue when they choose certain actions over others. For our intended end admits some means and eliminates other means for its most effective realization. Thus, if we are clear about the best ends to pursue, we have already established some selectivity of appropriate actions (means). As is readily evident, these best intended ends, like the moral guides for action, will be expressed in language that is sports relevant. Specifying ends consistent with the moral guides for action will make them useful regarding the kinds of situational problems in the cases set forth in Chapter 1.

*Types of Intended Ends and Institutional Purposes.*     Let us now examine and compare different kinds of intended ends. We should also discuss the idea of institutional purposes.

*A personal intended end* is one that a person has accepted as his/her own in performing an action. People may adopt a particular intended end for different reasons. For our purposes here, the most important are moral reasons, self-interested reasons, and conventional reasons.

*Self-interested intended ends* are those personal intended ends an agent adopts because of self-interested reasons. In brief, the agent intends a certain state of affairs because its existence is in his/her self-interest without regard to the interests of others.[41] The reasons for adopting a self-interested, personal intended end do not take into account the interests and claims of others. An example of a self-interested intended end would be:

> Person A says: "I ought to play fair in sports."
>
> Person B asks: "Why should you play fair?"
>
> Person A responds: "Because if I do not play fair, I will be penalized."

It does not follow that a self-interested, personal intended end must contradict the interests of others. Whether or not it is contradictory can be ascertained only by taking into account the interests of others. It is clear that most intended ends, adopted because they are in the self-interest of the agent, are also the agent's personal intended end. People seldom offer a self-interested reason for an intended end which they have not accepted as their own. This may be precisely because self-interested reasons are by nature personal—they are relevant to that particular person.

*Conventional intended ends* are those personal intended ends the agent adopts because of conventional reasons—reasons sanctioned by some social group. Social groups support "rules" such as regulations, mores, customs, manners, and etiquette.[42] These conventionally accepted rules supply the reasons for certain personal intended ends, that is, "Do X because it is polite," "Do X because the regulation says so," "Do X because that is the way we do it." Following is an example of a conventional intended end:

> Person A says: "I ought to play fair in sports."
>
> Person B asks: "Why should you play fair?"
>
> Person A responds: "Because the regulations of my sports organizations state that playing fair is expected."

Conventional reasons for a personal intended end, unlike self-interested, personal intended ends, take into account the interests of *some* others. However, since conventions and customs are by nature rules for limited social groups (e.g., they are not universal), it is obvious that conventional reasons in principle cannot take into account the interests of all others. Since the conventions of social groups vary, conflicting personal intended ends in the same situation can be pursued by agents who adopt conflicting ends for divergent conventional reasons. For example, women have been excluded from long-distance races because sports organizations have had rules against it; professional atheletes in one sport have been excluded from other intercollegiate sports in the United States because the NCAA had rules against it; blacks have been excluded from sports in South Africa because of that country's customs. Although these things apparently change over time, differing rules supported by social groups give reasons for conflicting actions.

*Moral intended ends* are those personal intended ends the agent adopts for moral reasons — reasons in support of a personal intended end because that end is meant for everybody and for the good of everyone alike. An example of a moral intended end would be:

Person A says: "I ought to play fair in sports."

Person B asks: "Why should you play fair?"

Person A responds: "Because playing fair fulfills the tacit promise everybody makes in agreeing to play a sport, and playing fair is absolutely necessary for everyone to have equal access to the value of sport itself."

Inasmuch as moral reasoning is a form of practical reasoning, the latter constituted by value comparisons of various actions and their intended ends, moral reasoning is responding to "the value question 'Which is *the best* course open to me?' "[43] when I consider everybody and the good of everyone alike.

> The best course of action is not the course which most quickly, least painfully, least expensively, etc., leads to the gaining of our ends, but *it is the course of action which is supported by the best reasons.* And the best reasons may require us to abandon the aim [the intended end] we actually have set our heart on.[44]

As stated in Chapter 1, moral reasons are superior to the reasons of self-interest and convention. When an agent adopts a moral intended end as a personal intended end, it may mean that the agent will not like the intended end because it is contrary to his/her felt desire in the situation, or adopting the moral intended end may be uncomfortable because it is contrary to a conventional intended end. Nonetheless, a moral intended end can be a personal intended end because the agent realizes that the moral intended end is for everybody, is for the good of everyone alike, is effective in resolving conflicting intended ends, and is consistent with moral guides for action. A moral intended end can also be consistent with a self-interested intended end and/or a conventional intended end.

In comparing the concept of a personal intended end to the concepts of self-interested and conventional intended ends, I have indicated how we use various kinds of reasons to support the personal intended ends adopted. Clearly it is much easier to adopt a self-interested intended end for it is always more personal because it does not have to consider the real interests of others and because, says Baier, "by and large, everyone is himself the best judge of what is in his own best interest, since everyone usually knows best what his plans, aims, ambitions, or aspirations are."[45] Also, it is easier to adopt a conventional intended end because this keeps us in harmony with social groups with which we share our daily lives. It may be concluded, then, for reasons of ease of knowing—I know what is in my self-interest, immediately, personally, and authoritatively, or for reasons of harmony with the social groups with which I identify (my social group tells me to do X and will accept me if I do X), that adopting a moral intended end is inherently more difficult. Inasmuch as the ends we intend immediately circumscribe those actions (means) which are practical in their attainment, it is a small wonder, indeed, that we frequently have serious conflicts of interest. For it is clear that we most often adopt as our personal intended end those intended ends that are easier and more comfortable to adopt, and these are self-interested and/or conventional intended ends.

*An institutional purpose* is related to, but not exactly equivalent to, the concept of an intended end. The intended end is the projected and expected consequence of one agent's specific action. Institutions do not themselves act, however, but are invested with a purpose, or a reason for existence, by the corporate intended ends of numerous individual agents who voluntarily constitute the institution. The basic purpose of human institutions, manifested in a variety of purposes for each institution, is to provide some beneficial intended end that would not be available to each of the individual agents without the institution. An institution's intended end, or purpose, cannot be brought about by the actions of a single agent but is dependent for its very existence upon the mutual participation of many agents. For example, individuals engage in the institution (the act) of promising, and its benefits would be unattainable unless other individuals engaged in that same institution. For instance, if a business salesperson promises to deliver some goods I need, then I depend upon that business and its agent, through the institution of promising, to deliver the goods. At the same time, the business and its agent depend upon me, again through the institution of promising, to deliver some goods. In both cases, each of us could not receive the goods and be free to pursue other intended ends without investing considerably more personal time and energy. As we shall see, sport involves human agents in the institution of promising in such a way that no one agent can receive, at least on any continuing basis, the goods available without entering into promising and the relationships with other human agents that such promising demands.

In summary then, human institutions such as sport each have an institutional purpose which is a collective version of an intended end. By its very nature, however, this intended end cannot be achieved at all, at least not efficiently, by a single agent but exists through the institution itself to provide mutual access to the intended end by all the agents who participate.

***Intended Ends Consistent With the Moral Point of View.***     From these examples of self-interested intended end, conventional intended end, and moral intended end, it is evident that the same end, such as to "play fair," may be intended for different reasons. Assuming that the end to play fair may be established by the view of sport from the moral point of view, agents can choose specific actions which are effective means to that general end for reasons other than moral reasons. This means that a personal intended end adopted by an agent for self-interested or conventional reasons may be consistent with a morally intended end – the agent's intended end is the same but the reasons are different.

In our structure for moral reasoning, we are now attempting to identify the general ends of action that are consistent with the moral point of view in sport. Section IV will further discuss the relationships of reasons to ends after sport has been described from the moral point of view, after the rational contractors have stated their agreed-upon guides for actions, and after the general ends of action consistent with the moral point of view have been identified. The general ends of action will be stated in the title supplied for each guide for action that is agreeable to the rational contractors. The titles will suggest the general ends of action consistent with the moral point of view in sport. For instance, one such title in Chapter 8, The Guide of Noninjurious Action, suggests that one of the general ends consistent with the moral point of view in sport is noninjurious action. We can also see how identifying this general end functions in a structure for determining right action. For, identifying a general end of noninjurious action provides a clear criterion by which many possible actions in the sports contest may be evaluated and judged right or wrong. That is, if an action is performed to avoid injury it is right, and if an action is performed to inflict injury it is wrong.

## NOTES

[1]Alan Gewirth, "The Normative Structure of Action," *The Review of Metaphysics* XXV, No. 2 (December 1971), p. 240.

[2]Nicholas Rescher, "On the Characterization of Action," in *The Nature of Human Action*, ed. Myles Brand (Glenview, IL: Scott, Foresman & Co., 1970), p. 248.

[3]Kurt Baier, *The Moral Point of View* (Ithaca & London: Cornell University Press, 1958), pp. 150, 265-266.

[4]David A. J. Richards, *A Theory of Reasons for Action* (Oxford: Oxford University Press, 1971), pp. 219-221, 280.

[5]R. M. Hare, *Freedom and Reason* (Oxford: Oxford University Press, 1963), p. 89.

[6]Richards, *Theory of Reasons*, p. 226.

[7]Baier, *Moral Point of View*, p. 172.

[8]Ibid., p. 172.

[9]Hare, *Freedom and Reason*, p. 224.

[10]Baier, *Moral Point of View*, p. 184.

[11]For a concise and clear differentiation of moral questions, descriptive ethics, and ethics see R. M. Hare, "Ethics," in *Essays in the Moral Concepts* (Berkeley and Los Angeles: The University of California Press, 1972), pp. 39-54.

[12]Those of the greatest help to me have been: Kurt Baier, *The Moral Point of View*; Eric D'Arcy, *Human Acts: An Essay in Their Moral Evaluation* (Oxford: Oxford University Press, 1963); William K. Frankena, *Ethics* (2nd ed.) (Englewood Cliffs, NJ: Prentice-Hall, 1973); R. M. Hare, *Freedom and Reason*; David A. J. Richards, *A Theory of Reasons for Action*; and Paul W. Taylor, *Normative Discourse* (Englewood Cliffs, NJ: Prentice-Hall, 1961).

[13]Baier, *Moral Point of View*, p. 190.

[14]Ibid., p. 309.

[15]Ibid., p. 195.

[16]Hare, *Freedom and Reason*, pp. 47, 89.

[17]Ibid., pp. 48-49, 139-140.

[18]Ibid., pp. 49-50.

[19]Baier, *Moral Point of View*, p. 208.

[20]Ibid., pp. 202-203.

[21]Ibid., p. 164.

[22]Ibid., pp. 314-315.

[23]This formulation raises still another problem which so far as I can tell has not been dealt with satisfactorily. If everyone acts in accord with the moral point of view, then a single agent acting primarily from enlightened self-interest can achieve the benefits of moral treatment by all others *without* making any sacrifices the moral point of view requires. For example, if all tennis players, upon perceiving a linesman's errant call of "out" to an opponent's stroke that was clearly in, deliberately double faulted in their next serve to neutralize the linesman's error—but *one* player *never* double faulted for that reason, then that one player would profit by everyone's following morality but himself or herself.

[24]Baier, *Moral Point of View*, p. 191.

[25]Hare, *Freedom and Reason*, p. 47.

[26]Ibid., p. 267.

[27]Richards, *Theory of Reasons*, pp. 76, 230.

[28]Hare, *Freedom and Reason*, p. 5.

[29]Richard R. Brandt, *Ethical Theory* (Englewood Cliffs, NJ: Prentice-Hall, 1959), p. 173.

[30]Richards, *Theory of Reasons*, p. 80.

[31]For a complete exposition of the concept of rational contractors upon which this statement is based, see: John Rawls, *A Theory of Justice* (Cambridge, MA: The Harvard University Press, 1971), and Richards, *Theory of Reasons*.

[32]Glenn Langford, *Human Action* (Garden City, NJ: Anchor Books, 1971), pp. 96-97.

[33]Anthony Kenny, "Intention and Purpose," *Journal of Philosophy* LXIII, No. 20 (October 27, 1966), p. 644.

[34]Bernard Berofsky, "Purposive Action," *American Philosophical Quarterly* 7, No. 4 (October 1970), pp. 276-277.

[35]Roderick M. Chisholm, "Freedom and Action," in *The Nature of Human Action*, ed. Myles Brand (Glenview, IL: Scott, Foresman & Co., 1970), p. 291.

[36]Baier, *Moral Point of View*, p. 267.

[37]Ibid, p. 267.

[38]Richards, *Theory of Reasons*, p. 230.

[39]Hare, *Freedom and Reason*, p. 159.

[40]Baier, *Moral Point of View*, pp. 262-263.

[41]Hare, *Freedom and Reason*, p. 94.

[42]Baier, *Moral Point of View*, pp. 123-124.

[43]Ibid., p. 84.

[44]Ibid., p. 88. (Material in brackets mine.)

[45]Kurt Baier, "Why Should We Be Moral?" in *Morality and Rational Self Interest*, ed. David P. Gauthier (Englewood Cliffs, NJ: Prentice-Hall, 1970), p. 157.

# PART TWO

# INTRODUCTION
# TO THE CHARACTERIZATION
# OF SPORT FROM THE
# MORAL POINT OF VIEW

The first element in our structure of reasoning is to describe sport from the moral point of view. Therefore, the basic thrust of this section is to characterize sport when we view it with respect to the characteristics of the moral point of view. To make this description more comprehensible, we must identify the format of our description. First, the phrase "describe sport" here means to focus our attention on the sports contest, which we will do for several reasons important to the task of establishing guides to right action.

1. The institution of sport most frequently manifests itself in the form of the sports contest.
2. The sports contest is precisely where many conflicting ideas of right action occur. That is, because the sports contest necessarily involves two or more opponents it has the inherent possibility of conflicts arising from either self-interest or convention.
3. By circumscribing our description to the sports contest, we will focus upon the problems of right actions between human beings as differing from the problems of right action between, say, humans and natural environment or humans and animals. Such a focus will better clarify what this description is and what it is not.
4. Focusing upon the sport contest will make our description more accessible and meaningful to those who will most need our

guides for right action, namely those who participate in sport contests and would value help in responding to the questions "What ought I to do?", "What ought to be done?", or "What ought to have been done?"

Second, we are attempting to establish what the good sports contest is from a dual view. One of these is what the good contest is when viewed from the nature of contest itself. The other is the substantive characteristics of the moral point of view, which means the good sports contest is that event which is meant for all participants and is for the good of everyone alike. This dual characterization sheds light on the kind of event at which the participants' actions ought to aim. Such a comprehension helps determine what kinds of actions will bring that kind of event about. It is the basis for our guides for action.

Third, in describing and explaining the good sports contest, we will be examining different and even conflicting views of certain elements within the contest. To describe and explain what that sports contest is, which is meant for everybody and for the good of everyone alike, we must examine alternative possibilities to see which is more compatible with those standards. The ones chosen will be more clearly comprehensible, then, because they will be more defined by contrast to those not chosen.

Finally, the characterization of the good sports contest will use several categories of analysis, chosen to illuminate the characteristics of the good sports contest. In each category, alternative conceptions will be examined and one will be identified, described, and explained as normative for the good sports contest. In one sense the categories to be used are necessary: They must be capable of illuminating the characteristics of the good sports contest from the moral point of view. In another sense the categories are arbitrary: Their labels could be worded differently or their content could be placed differently. The important point is whether the substance that appears does indeed describe and explain the good sports contest clearly and comprehensively. The categories of analysis will be (a) the ends of the sports contest, (b) winning-losing and quality of play, (c) rules and their functions, (d) relationship of opponents, and (e) value of the sports contest.

## DESCRIPTION OF ONE GOOD SPORTS CONTEST

To exemplify the concept of the good sports contest, a specific contest will be described here. This will capture the feel of the good sports contest and help introduce a discussion of the elements implicit in it.

Bob and John were members of a local badminton club which met once a week to play. Each had been playing the game for about 2 years.

Most of the club members played doubles only and the doubles matches were usually completed by 9:30 p.m., one-half hour before the gymnasium was to close. Bob and John usually agreed to play each other one game of singles after the doubles games.

They spun a racket for service and Bob won and chose to serve, while John chose the side of net he preferred. Bob's first serve was high and deep toward the middle of John's court. John returned with an offensive clear to Bob's backhand deep corner. The accuracy and power of John's return forced Bob to play a weak backhand drop shot which barely cleared the net. John anticipated a weak return and was there as the shuttle dropped close to the net on his side, so close that he could not risk intercepting it above the net for fear of reaching over. He could see Bob charging toward the net to cover his imminent "hair pin" shot and, holding his shot until the last instant, flicked the shuttle on a low trajectory to Bob's forehand backcourt corner. Bob reversed quickly and pursued the shuttle toward his backcourt. With a last second stretch and a violent stroke which intercepted the shuttle about two feet from the floor, he executed a clear toward John's almost deep backhand corner. John meanwhile had moved toward his backhand forecourt anticipating a second weak return by Bob. He was very surprised when Bob executed the clear so well, and found himself playing a defensive, desperate leaping block of the shuttle on the backhand side and sending a weak return directly at Bob. Bob promptly smashed the shuttle to the floor at John's midcourt while John could not offer any reaction. John retrieved the shuttle and as he was returning it to Bob for his serve said, "Well done, Bob."

Both players positioned themselves for Bob's next serve. Bob observed that John was stationed well over toward the sideline on his service court and well back from the short service line. The possibility of a short serve to John's forehand occurred and he executed a fine serve which barely cleared the net and dropped rapidly. John lunged toward the falling shuttle and with a delicate return placed it barely over the net and descending close to the net. John's return was so well placed that Bob had only two choices for return, either try a hair pin at the net or attempt to clear the shuttle deep. Bob rejected the hair pin as too risky for setting up an easy smash for John. He tried to clear the shuttle high and deep but succeeded only in placing it high to midcourt. Perceiving this as a "set-up" for John to smash, Bob retreated hurriedly and raised his racket in a defensive position ahead of his head. The smash came and, without further effort on Bob's part, rebounded fortuitously off his racket and across the net. The shuttle again was in a set-up position and John raised his racket high, appearing to ready for a second smash, while Bob kept his own racket raised in anticipation and preparation for the smash. But the smash never came, for John, after completing all the moves preparatory to a smash, executed a delicately placed drop shot which dropped to the floor on Bob's side while Bob rocked back on his heels anticipating the threatening smash. Bob broke into a soft chuckle at the ludicrous combination of his fortuitious return of the smash for which he could not prepare and his preparation for the second smash which never came. He glanced over the net at John, smiling and nodding his approval of John's excellent execution of a fine tactic.

The game see-saws back and forth with a preponderance of long rallies in which each player, by determined effort, keeps the shuttle in the air and, on occasion, completes a stroke effectively which the opponent does not anticipate. The score is now 13-12, John's favor, with Bob serving. Still another long and demanding rally takes place and the final stroke in the rally is a smash by Bob which lands on the sideline on John's side. From his perspective Bob cannot be sure whether the bird was in or out. John, however, has no doubt as he clearly saw the shuttle land on the sideline and immediately signaled "good." Bob asks, "Are you sure?" John replies, "Definitely!" On two previous and similar situations neither player was sure if the shot in question was in or out. On both of these occasions they had agreed to play the point over. This time, however, John was sure and so Bob won the point that tied the game 13-13. At this junction John "sets" the game at 18 points, reasoning that inasmuch as Bob is now holding the serve and appears to be tiring, a longer game is to his own advantage. Bob is exhilarated at tying the game and, whereas a moment earlier he was aware of a slight leadenness of the legs and a little shortness of breath, he now feels a flood of fresh energy.

The serve shifts back and forth with a continuation of long rallies in which each successive shot creates a slightly higher level of tension as to the outcome of that particular point. The score is now 17-17 with Bob serving. He delivers a drive serve to John's backhand which returns crisply down toward Bob's forehand. Bob is forced to scoop the shuttle and his return hits the tape at the top of the net and trickles to the floor on John's side. His momentary elation at seeing the "winning" point is accompanied by the realization that his return was thrown by his racket rather than clearly hit. He acknowledges his illegal shot and the serve now goes to John.

John serves high but the shuttle is dropping about two thirds back in Bob's court. Bob smashes to John's forehand and John raises the bird again. Bob smashes directly at John's racket shoulder and John blocks the smash and the shuttle returns just over the net to Bob's forecourt backhand below the net. Bob attempts to clear to John's deep backcourt forehand but the bird is high and short. John smashes to Bob's forehand and Bob drops the shuttle softly over the net and down to John's forecourt backhand. John executes a difficult and dangerous cross-court hair pin from his backhand and appears to have a winner until Bob, with an all out stretch, contacts the bird about two feet off the floor on his backhand and attempts to clear it deep. His clear is short, however, and he retreats hastily once more anticipating the smash that he has set up. John settles into position and raises his racket in preparation for the smash while Bob readies himself for the seemingly inevitable. John begins his racket swinging forward violently, then, at the point before contact, slows the racket and contacts the shuttle lightly. The shuttle drops softly to the floor on Bob's side while Bob rocks back on his heels. Once again Bob grins and nods assent to John's excellent tactic.

The two men walk to the locker room together to cool off. They discuss some of the events of the game and recount some of the many fine rallies and shots. Both are pleased to have engaged in such a fine contest and engage in some good natured bantering about making it easy for one another. They cool off and enter a tingling shower which feels especially cleansing to their now-tired bodies. They dress and leave the gymnasium together. Their last words for that night are — "Thank you very much." "See you next week, then?" "Yes, let's do it again!"

# Chapter Three

# The Ends
# of the Sports Contest

Certain ends must be pursued to have the sports contest. These ends are therefore necessary for the good sports contest when the reference point of view is the nature of the sports contest. Sports participants pursue different personal intended ends which may or may not be supportive of the ends necessary for the good sports contest. Also, the sports contest has an institutionalized purpose, which is a common understanding of the nature of the event called the sports contest. These three kinds of ends and their relationships will be examined to see which are necessary for, which are consistent with, and which are inconsistent or incongruent with the good sports contest. Finally, a certain set of relationships between these ends is necessary for all participants and is for the good of everyone alike. Thus, this set of relationhips is necessary for the good sports contest from the moral point of view.

## THE ENDS IN THE SPORTS CONTEST

The ends in the sports contest are those that exist because of the contest itself; in fact, no contest can occur without them. Therefore, sports participants must adopt some of these ends as their personal intended ends or a contest cannot exist – good or not. Suits[1] identifies these ends as the end of achieving a specific state of affairs, the end of winning, and the end of playing the game. This last end will be called the end of contesting, since we are now restricting its use to the sports contest.

Achieving a specific state of affairs may be understood, in the language used previously, as bringing about a change in a state of affairs as a result of an agent's action. In the present context this means realizing some specific result for an action — a result which the sport so specifies. For instance, as Suits provides, the specific state of affairs achieved in any race is having the racers reach a designated point. The designated point is common to all race contests and includes many variations such as crossing a finish line drawn on a track, touching a wall at the end of a swimming pool, or rowing under a certain bridge on the river Thames. In a badminton game the specific state of affairs sought by both players is hitting the shuttlecock in the air with the racket.

The end of winning, a necessary end of any sports contest and therefore of the good sports contest, is constituted by achieving the specific state of affairs adopted using the means specified and within the restrictions set by the accepted rules of the sport. If I am to achieve the end of winning a race, I must arrive at the designated point, not necessarily by the shortest and the most efficient means, but certainly by those defined by the rules. For instance, to win a running race of 200 meters around a curved track I must start on a given signal from point A, run within marked lanes around the track to the designated point B 200 meters away, and arrive there before anyone else who follows the same regulations. If I am interested only in arriving at the designated point B, I could run across the infield to get there, or ride a turtle, or use any means and routes that suit my fancy. But if I am interested in achieving the end of winning I must adopt, at the least, the mode of transport and the route specified. Furthermore, I must achieve the same state of affairs, the means and routes to which are rule-determined, by engaging an opponent and achieving that same state of affairs better than the opponent.[2] Accordingly, in our description of a good sports contest in badminton, John alone wins because he has hit the shuttlecock with his racket legally in the air more often, over the net within the prescribed boundaries, against the opposition of Bob, who was also attempting to hit the shuttle more often and within the rule-determined prescriptions.

In the good sports contest, all participants must achieve the end of the specific state of affairs. Yet it is clearly not necessary to the sports contest, good or bad, that all participants achieve the end of winning. As a matter of fact, in zero sum or negative sum games, only one of the opponents can win. Thus, the end of winning is a constitutive feature of any sports contest but cannot be a necessary personal intended end of all participants.

If the above statement appears to be contradictory, it is because of an unfortunate conflation of our common language about winning. But this may be clarified by discussing the third end in the sports contest, namely, the end of contesting or trying to win. This end means exerting one's best effort in the requisite ways toward the specific state of affairs. Exerting one's best effort is trying to win better than an opponent is winning. Please note that there is a real difference between the end of winning as a factual condition, which is achieved by only one participant, and the end of trying to win, or contesting, which is necessary for all participants. Thus all participants must adopt, as their personal intended end, the end of trying to win—the end of contesting.

We may summarize the ends in the sports contest in a way that will anticipate further discussion, and three generalizations are appropriate. In order for the good sports contest to occur:

1. The ends of achieving a specific state of affairs, of winning and of trying to win, or contesting, are all necessary.

2. All participants must adopt as personal intended ends the end of achieving a specific state of affairs and the end of trying to win.

3. It is not necessary that all participants adopt the end of winning as their personal intended end.

## THE INTENDED ENDS OF THE PARTICIPANTS

The intended ends of participants in sports contests range from very specific states of affairs intended as ends within the contest to states of affairs intended as ends resulting from the contest. In the badminton game one participant executes a smash and the intended end of this action is to hit the shuttle to the floor on the opponent's side and to score the point or to win the serve. One action is often instrumental in achieving an end which helps achieve another end. Thus, smashing the shuttle with the intended end of scoring the point is useful, along with other actions, in pursuing the end of trying to win or contesting. The action of smashing and its intended end of scoring the point is congruent (alike in characteristics) with the end of trying to win, or contesting. Now it is conceivable that any sports participant may adopt, as a personal intended end of actions, an intended end that does not anticipate any state of affairs beyond itself. This is to say that we can, in Chisholm's words, "define an *ultimate end* as one that is intended but not intended in order that some *other* end be realized."[3] In short, trying to win can be all that a participant is doing in the sports contest and, accordingly, intended ends are contained wholly within the sports contest itself. As indicated, a sports participant does not need to adopt the end of winning as a personal intended end.

This understanding is important. First, it is important to distinguish between winning and trying to win in the sense of what agent participants in sports contests do, that is, the actions which they perform. Agent participants perform actions that intend the end of trying to win—they do not perform winning. Winning is not an action; it is an achievement verb, whereas trying to win or contesting is an activity verb for an action.[4] Second, the end of winning is properly understood, not as the personal intended end of an agent participant but as the description of the point of termination of the sports contest, good or bad. In other words, winning is a constitutive element of the complete sports contest,[5] as is its opposite, losing. As terms describing termination, winning and losing are the partners of those terms that describe the beginning of the sports contest such as serving, where we have servers and receivers.

Trying to win can be a sports participant's personal intended end, adopted not because it is sufficient in itself but because it is instrumental in achieving a state of affairs outside the contest. Trying to win becomes a means to another intended end such as earning money or prizes, achieving social recognition, or improving one's physical fitness. These are not ends within the sports contest itself but are external ends. The adoption of personal intended ends external to a sports contest sometimes effectively negates one of the ends which must be intended by all participants, namely, the end of trying to win. For example, in American college football we observe situations in which the participants have chosen an action that intended an end of trying to achieve a tie game, or even avoiding a defeat, both of which negate the end of trying to win. Kicking a point after a touchdown rather than trying a two-point conversion by the losing team in the last seconds of a 7-6 game is trying to achieve a tie, not trying to win. Trying to tie negates exerting one's best effort except in unusual circumstances. For instance, if a basketball player whose team is behind by two points attempts a field goal in the last second of a contest, he/she is exerting the best effort.

Spectators react negatively to an action that intends the end of trying to tie but they cheer an action that intends an end of trying to win, such as trying to run for two points in the football game. The reason is evident. Choosing to tie negates the end of trying to win—and trying to win is an end that all participants must intend in order for the contest to be the good contest. But the "experts" among the sports participants, the athletes, or coaches, always claim good reasons for trying to tie. The reasons they give are that achieving a tie is instrumental for some external intended end such as attaining or maintaining a national ranking, maintaining their standing in an athletic league, or qualifying for a postseason bowl game. When such intended ends predominate over the end of trying to win, this is not a good sports contest.[6] Exerting one's best effort is essential to determining who is better in a contest; such a determination is what the contest is about.

Sports participants may also adopt intended ends external to the sports contest that do not negate the end of trying to win but reduce its significance so that the good sports contest cannot occur. For instance, entertaining spectators with unusual and indirect clowning methods of trying to win may emphasize the external end of entertainment. Exhibitions by organizations such as the Harlem Globetrotters is a good illustration of this. Clearly, the intended end of these actions is to entertain the audience by obviously hilarious antics, not to determine which team plays better basketball. No aspersion on the basketball skills of these players is intended; obviously they are well-skilled. The point is that these skills are used to provide laughs for the audience, not for good sports contests.

Individual sports participants can also adopt personal intended ends that are external to the contest and reduce the significance of trying to win so that the good sports contest cannot occur. For instance, a tennis player may deliberately play in a haphazard or a less skillful manner, or perhaps deliberately and unnecessarily execute unusual strokes such as hitting the ball between the legs, behind his/her back, or with the racket held by the nondominant hand. Such actions may be taken for the fun of it, to embarrass the opponent, to get the game over with, and so on, all of which indicate a personal intended end external to the contest itself. By assuming priority, these actions reduce the significance of the end of trying to win so that the contest is not the good sports contest but is a farce instead.

Finally, sports participants may intend personal ends external to the contest but yet consistent with the personal intended end of trying to win or contesting. This occurs when the personal intended end can be realized only by trying to win. For instance, when the external end is a consequence of a participant being declared a winner because he or she has tried to win, that external end can happen only if the participant indeed does try to win. A golfer who adopts the personal intended external end of earning a $60,000 first-place prize in a tournament, for example, must adopt the end of trying to win as a personal intended end. Inasmuch as intending one of these ends entails intending the other end as its necessary instrumental means, the two intended ends are consistent with one another.

In summary, we may now make some general conclusions about the various possible relationships of the participants' own intended ends to those constituted by the sports contest.

1. If a participant intends ends that are realized wholly within the sports contest, such as trying to win, then personal intended ends are congruent with the ends in the good sports contest.

2. If a participant intends ends that are realized externally to the contest, but are realized only if the participant intends the end of trying to win the contest, then his/her external personal intended ends are consistent with the ends in the good sports contest.

3. If a participant intends ends that are realized externally to the contest, but are realized by the participant intending an end which negates the end of trying to win, then his/her external personal intended ends are incongruent with the ends in the good sports contest.

4. If a participant intends ends that are realized externally to the contest, but are realized by the participant intending an end which assumes priority over the end of trying to win, then his/her external personal intended ends are inconsistent with the ends in the good sports contest.

## THE PURPOSE OF THE SPORTS CONTEST

The purpose of the sports contest is the reason for its existence.[7] As indicated in Chapter 2 in discussing an institutional purpose, the purpose of the sport contest can be understood as the collective intended end of those participants who voluntarily enter into the institution of sport. As a collective intended end it is an institutionalized purpose, the establishment of and maintenance or destruction of which can occur only through the actions of many agent participants. The ends in the sports contest are those that occur within a specific sports contest, while the purpose of the sports contest is the reason why any sports contest exists.

I have stated elsewhere that if sport has an institutional purpose, it comes from someone or somewhere. There seem to be three logical possibilities: the existential thesis, the metaphysical thesis, and the historical thesis. The existential thesis contends that each individual who engages in the sports contest is the source of the purpose of the contest. "This view considers purpose as the conscious choice of what the participant wants to get out of his participation. Sport becomes an instrumentality to a diversity of individual purposes."[8] The metaphysical thesis contends that, "the purpose of sport is supplied by God, or whatever agent you wish, who is the originator of all that is. In short, there is a metaphysical essence of sport which contains a true purpose in its given structure."[9] The historic thesis states that "the purpose of sport is supplied by the historic institutionalized structure of sport as it has developed over thousands of years by millions of individuals and by hundreds of societies. That is to say that the structure of sport itself as it has evolved carries within itself a sense of purpose."[10]

In viewing these three possibilities I have chosen the historical purpose, for it seems to me that historical human consciousness intends a phenomenal structure for sport that includes an awareness of the purpose of the institution of sport. Sport has been initiated and developed by humans through history so that, as with all human institutions, value may be available to human beings that would not be available to individuals in a state of nature—that is, without institutions. A historical phenomenal structure for sport may not give us the clear and precise definitions of sport that the language analyst would prefer,[11] but it can provide, rather, a description of what the substantial content of human consciousness of sport carries. Since our primary focus is to establish a moral point of view for sport which will be the reference source for moral actions in the sports contest, that reference point must portray what human consciousness intends as sport so that the result may make sense to sports participants.

We may describe the purpose of a sports contest by first providing a phenomenal description of what the sports contest is.

> A sports contest is a voluntary, agreed upon, human event in which one or more human participants opposes at least one human other to seek the mutual appraisal of the relative abilities of all participants to move mass in space and time by utilizing bodily moves which exhibit developed motor skill, physiological and psychological endurance and socially approved tactics and strategy.[12]

It is the claim here that when human consciousness focuses upon the concept of the sports contest (not sport), this description, or something very near to it, has been embodied in our collective, historical consciousness. In short, this phenomenal structure of the sports contest has become institutionalized. Given the description above, we may readily describe the sports contest's purpose, remembering that purpose is understood to mean the reason for the existence of the sports contest. It follows that:

> The purpose of the sports contest is to provide equitable opportunity for mutual contesting of the relative abilities of the participants to move mass in space and time within the confines prescribed by an agreed-upon set of rules.[13]

This is what sport participants are about, in common, when they enter the sports contest. It is the common purpose, shared by its institutionalization, which provides for value that would be otherwise unattainable for agents acting without sports contests. It is the specification of the reason for the sports contest's existence, as distinguished from the personal intended ends of the participants and from the ends in the sports contest.

This normative concept of the purpose of the sports contest is helpful in several ways. First, "it allows us to conceive of the activity itself as having a purpose as distinct from whatever intentions individuals or societies bring to the activity."[14] In this book such a conception will allow the necessary moral perspective, which is in principle superior to either the perspective of self-interest or that of convention. "Second, this description of purpose serves to individuate sport from other human activities which appear to be at the same level of generalization...Third, because this individuation of purpose occurs at less than the cosmological level of generalization, it allows for possibilities of relating the purpose of sport to other more general purposes without confusing levels of generality."[15] In differentiating the purpose of the sports contest from that of, say, the dance performance, we have a reference point that allows us to differentiate actions appropriate in one context from the same actions as less or not appropriate in the other. This allows us to appraise actions concerning sport itself without, in certain cases, importing external standards that are inappropriate at least and misleading at worst. On the other hand, differentiating the purpose of sports contests from broader conceptions allows the application of general concepts of purpose to sport which are appropriate to all human activities, and to realize that such occurs precisely because some broader conceptions of purpose are relevant to all human activity and not simply to sport.

Finally, establishing the concept of the sports contest's purpose, along with the idea of the participants' intended ends and the ends in the sports contest, allows us to relate these three distinct conceptions of the ends of the sports contest to ascertain, in particular conflict situations, which idea is of highest priority. Furthermore, these three concepts may be related to each other in sports-relevant language that is necessary in developing the moral guides for action.

Notwithstanding the above perspective, that the purpose of the sport contest is best expressed as the reason for its existence, some other views relevant to this discussion have appeared. In an earlier work[16] I reviewed briefly the ideas of Vanderzwaag in his *Toward a Philosophy of Sport*, Slusher in *Man, Sport and Existence*, Metheny in *Movement and Meaning*, and Weiss in *Sport, a Philosophic Inquiry*. Vanderzwaag interprets purpose in sport by discussing it as the motive that impels individuals to participate. Slusher states that sport is not purposeful itself but that human beings have purpose, and their entry into the purposeless activity of a sport can be understood as a way of pursuing their purpose of actualization. Metheny speaks of the intention of sport performers as directed at moving mass in space and time in a specified way, and appears to conceive of purpose as the intention of the performer within sport. She also says sports rules provide an opportunity for concentration of the performer's energies into performing a self-chosen task or the actions of sport. Finally, Weiss interprets sport purpose in terms of the deep satisfaction it provides humans in their realization of the desire to be self-complete through testing and extension of the body.

All these explanations of sports purpose are interesting and illuminating but, with the exception of Metheny, are not too useful for developing moral guides for the sports contest. Except for Metheny, the ideas of the purpose of sport are not derived from the nature of the sports contest and do not speak directly to sports actions. Also, the motive or the pursuit of actualization does not necessarily consider other sports participants and is probably similar to what was discussed earlier here as the intended ends of the participants. Because such intended ends are for individual participants, they do not in principle meet the characteristic of being for the good of everyone alike. Accordingly, although Weiss, Slusher, or Vanderzwaag do not necessarily contradict the concept of the sports contest's purpose stated here, none of them speaks directly to sport itself nor pays specific attention to the characteristics of the moral point of view. Metheny's ideas and the purpose of the sports contest presented by this work focus upon sport as sport and provide a base for moral principles of action that are sports relevant.

The purpose of the sports contest as stated here qualifies as the purpose of a just institution. First, it embodies a collective intended end which guarantees that sport's unique value is available to all participants. It does so by prescribing equitable opportunity for contesting to all participants. Prescribing such opportunity guarantees that the unique value is available to all participants because, as we shall see in the Chapter 8 description of the value(s) of the good sports contest, these goods are a direct result of contesting; and equitable opportunity for contesting therefore guarantees access to those things which are a direct result of contesting.

In the description of a good sports contest we can see manifestations of the normative purpose of the sports contest, discussion of which will serve two important functions. First, it will show different instances in how such an institutional purpose becomes evident in the actions of sports participants. Second, it will illustrate the earlier claim that this institutional purpose is a result of historic human consciousness of the purpose of sports contests in that the actions taken in the badminton game are not unusual but normal. John and Bob act in the certain ways because they, as sports participants, already know that the purpose of the sports contest is to provide equitable opportunity for mutual contesting of the relative abilities of the participants to move mass in space and time within the confines prescribed by an agreed upon set of rules, as stated earlier.

First we notice that John and Bob have agreed to play a game of singles and, following their game, reiterate their agreement by the brief interchange "See you next week, then?" "Yes, let's do it again!" This agreement has two aspects relevant to the normative concept of the purpose of the sports contest: first, to pursue the purpose of the contest together by both adhering to the rules of badminton; second, to choose an opponent of one's own caliber to try to guarantee an even contest so that the relative abilities of the participants will be contested in this particular contest. Indeed, in examining what occurs in sport where participants have a choice of opponent, we find almost invariably that they choose opponents who will provide an equal contest. Sport is replete with examples of the attempt to assure equal opportunity for contesting of the participants' relative abilities. Within sports we specify weight classes, novice or open competitive groups, age groups, and all other divisions which intend to equalize the contest before it occurs. In American professional football, a player draft is one way of trying to develop more equal opponents by allowing the poorer teams earlier player choices.[17] American professional football also attempts to equate competition by its scheduling policy.

The next thing we note is the action of spinning the racket to determine who will serve and who will occupy which court. This is so each player has equal opportunity to have the slight advantage of serving first, a slight advantage not given by a procedure that provides a better chance to one player. Rather, the opportunity is 50% for each player. This assures equal opportunity to all participants so that the contest is between their relative performance abilities, and the determination of who displays better relative ability is not unduly influenced by arbitrary and privileged advantage. Normal sports actions illustrate this: Coins are flipped to determine who will kick off and who will receive. Captains of opposing teams guess odd or even number of fingers that the official conceals. And in some instances, a player earns the right to serve first by winning a rally for service or by throwing a ball to see who will come closer to a predetermined mark.

To strengthen the case, we see that if one player loses the spin of the racket or the coin flip, that player is compensated by having the right to choose which half of the badminton or tennis court he/she will play on, or which goal he will defend in American football. These actions illustrate the continued effort of trying to maintain equal opportunity for all participants; they are not simply conventional actions but are actions exhibiting the historic consciousness of the purpose of the sports contest.

A third thing to be noted in the badminton game is what occurs when Bob, who is the server and is behind 12-13 at the time, executes a smash that lands very close to the sideline on John's side. John, who saw the shuttle clearly land on the line, immediately calls the shot "good." Bob asks "are you sure?", to which John replies affirmatively. John calls the shot good because he knows that Bob has earned a point within the agreed rules, and if he were to deny Bob that earned point, then he would be putting Bob into an unfair disadvantageous position that would contradict the purpose of the sports contest. The same kind of consciousness is illustrated in those two previous occasions when neither player was sure whether the shuttle was in or out. In those instances, they agreed to play the point over. This illustrates consciousness of contesting the participants' relative abilities, which refers to ability to perform the skills of the sport itself and not the players' abilities to guess at the landing point of the shuttle or for either player to use the situation to his/her own advantage.

One more illustration will reinforce the argument that human consciousness in the sports contest displays awareness of the purpose of the sports contest. The option of setting or not setting the badminton game when a tie occurs at either 13 or 14 points indicates this consciousness at work in the rules. Badminton rules provide this option because in any contest that becomes tied either one or two points away from its normal completion, it is obvious that neither player has demonstrated markedly greater ability to that point and, since only the server may score points in badminton, being the server is a distinct advantage. Therefore, the option is available to extend the contest by either two or three points in order to diminish the advantage which the server has at this time. If I am the player who has an option, I will now calculate what choice is to my advantage since my opponent has the advantage of service. If I choose to set the game at five points I must then play a longer contest which, if my endurance is less than my opponent's, could work to my disadvantage. If I set the game at five points and my endurance is greater than my opponent's (of which I cannot be positive), I nonetheless still must overcome the opponent's advantage of having the service and being able to score several points quickly. This will diminish the chance of my being able to score five before my opponent does. If I choose not to set the game because my opponent now appears exhausted and I believe I can win the service quickly, I run the risk that my opponent may summon a reserve of perseverance and win two points by sheer determination. These points show that the consciousness displayed in the rules and in the player's calculations show awareness of the purpose of equitable opportunity for contesting the relative abilities of the participants.

Let us now summarize the major points on the purpose of the sports contest. This will anticipate the task of relating the purpose of the sports contest to the personal intended ends of participants and to the ends in the sports contest. Relating these three will then allow for a clear and normative exposition of the ends of the good sports contest.

1. The purpose of the sports contest, when conceived as the reason for its existence, is to provide equitable opportunity for mutual contesting of the participants' relative abilities to move mass in space and time within the confines prescribed by an agreed-upon set of rules.

2. This purpose of the sports contest is understood as the collective intended end established by historic human consciousness of why sports contests exist.

3. This purpose of the sports contest is specific to sport as a distinct form of human action but may be related to general human purposes that are applicable to all human activities.

4. Establishing this purpose indicates that, as an institution, sport has a purpose distinguishing it from the personal intended ends of participants and the conventional ends established within any particular social group.

5. This stated purpose of the sports contest is a just purpose because it guarantees equal opportunity to the good(s) of the institution of sport by all participants.

## THE ENDS OF THE GOOD SPORTS CONTEST

The ends of the good sports contest may now be established by describing the necessary relationships among the ends in the sports contest, the personal intended ends of the participants, and the purpose of the sports contest, and by giving reasons why such relationships are necessary.

The ends of the good sports contest are a composite of certain relationships of those ends of the sports contest that must exist in order for the good sports contest to be possible. Such a condition does not guarantee that the good sports contest will occur, but only that it is now possible because the ends pursued will allow it. As we shall see in subsequent chapters of this section, elements other than the ends pursued are necessary for the good sports contest. Those kinds of ends needed for the good sports contest to occur are summarized as:

1. The institutionalized purpose of the sports contest expressed as the reason for the existence of any sports contest;

2. The ends in the sports contest, namely, the end of achieving a certain state of affairs, the end of winning, and the end of trying to win or contesting;

3. Those personal intended ends of the participants which are, at best, congruent, and at the least, consistent with both the institutional purpose of the sports contest and with the ends in a sports contest of achieving a certain state of affairs and of trying to win, or contesting.

The purpose of the sports contest is necessary for a good sports contest for several reasons. It is that goal which the participants have in common and which guarantees access to the value(s) of the sports contest for all participants. It is what binds people together in a common endeavor; the sports contest cannot have any social meaning without it. For if a person wants to have a sports contest and a sports contest necessarily involves at least one other person, neither can have the sports contest unless the other is guaranteed equal opportunity to do the task. Neither John nor Bob can have a badminton game unless the other is there to hit the shuttle over the net. Furthermore, there is no contest, no test which is shared,[18] unless both have equal opportunity to hit the shuttle over the net. Equal opportunity to perform that task is the presupposition of satisfying the desire to contest relative ability. So, the purpose of the sports contest is not only necessary for the good sports contest but has priority over the ends in a contest or the personal intended ends of the participants.

The ends in the sports contest come into being when the participants begin a particular contest that is constituted by the purpose of the sports contest. Achieving a specific state of affairs, such as arriving at a designated point in a race, has no relevant sports meaning independent of the purpose of the sports contest. Without the purpose of the sports contest, arriving at a designated point remains just that. Arriving at a designated point, however, when observed in relation to the purpose of the sports contest, is now either crossing the finish line or completing the race. Likewise, the ends of winning and of contesting derive their sports-relevant meaning from the purpose of the sports contest. The term winning cannot be sports meaningful until it is seen in relation to equitable opportunity for mutual contesting of the participants' relative abilities within the confines prescribed by an agreed-upon set of rules, since winning means the result of the mutual contesting. Also, contesting as an end receives its meaning from the purpose of the sports contest since contesting means testing the relative abilities of the participants to do the same task.

The ends in the sports contest then come into being and depend for meaning upon the existence of a sports contest, which itself comes into being when the participants accept the purpose of the sports contest. However, the personal intended ends of the participants need careful analysis in relation to both the ends in the sports contest and the purpose of the sports contest. We have seen earlier in this chapter that participants may adopt ends either within the contest or external to the contest. If a participant adopts as his/her final ends the achievement of a state of affairs relevant to that sport and trying to win in that contest, his/her personal intended ends are wholly within a sports contest. In our badminton game John and Bob may both adopt as their final ends the achievement of hitting the shuttle in the air and trying to win, or contesting, by hitting the shuttle in such a way that it falls to the floor on the opponent's side. The adoption of these as personal intended ends by John and Bob means that their personal intended ends are meaningful only in relation to the purpose of the sports contest.

In such cases, the personal intended ends of these participants are congruent with the purpose of the sports contest since they are exactly equivalent to ends which participants must pursue in any contest and because their meaning as ends depends upon the purpose of the sports contest. Personal intended ends that are congruent with the purpose of the sports contest are one way to enhance the possibility of the good sports contest because what the participants intend is for the sake of the contest alone. Accordingly, the particular actions actually performed are most likely to be actions that will sustain the good sports contest. If all the participants in the sports contest intend nothing more than contesting, it is most likely that the actions they choose will result in the good sports contest, along with other elements yet to be discussed, since their practical reasoning will select the most appropriate actions (means) to those ends.

The personal intended ends of participants may be consistent with the purpose of the sports contest when they adopt as a personal intended end trying to win in order to achieve an end external to the specific sports contest. For instance, either John or Bob can intend the ends of hitting the shuttle in the air in such a way that it falls to the floor on the opponent's side in order to win a beer or increase cardiovascular endurance. If all the participants adopt personal intended ends external to the sports contest, ends that, however, may only be achieved by adopting the end in the contest of contesting, then it is more likely that the actions they choose, along with other elements yet to be discussed, will result in the good sports contest.

Participants' personal intended ends may be inconsistent with the purpose of the sports contest if they adopt an external end that reduces the significance of contesting to a level whereby it is not deemed necessary. For example, either John or Bob could try hitting the shuttle over the net by striking it consistently behind the back, even though the opponent struck the shuttle with normal badminton strokes. The participant who performs in this way is not pursuing the end of contesting as a necessary end. Hitting the shuttle consistently behind one's back, after all, is not the kind of action which ensures a contest but, rather, decreases its possibility. A participant who acts in this way may be pursuing a personal intended end of being funny, which relegates the end of contesting to a subordinate role. And since such an end is a necessary one that all participants must pursue, the actions thus performed are less likely to produce the good sports contest.

Finally, the personal intended ends of the participants may be incongruent with the purpose of the sports contest. This occurs when a participant adopts an external personal intended end that negates pursuit of the end in the contest of contesting. Trying to tie a football game in order to achieve the external end of attaining or maintaining a national rating is a good illustration here. Again, the pursuit of this end negates the necessary end in the game of trying to win, and trying to win derives its meaning from that part of the sports contest's purpose which mentions contesting. Contesting is by nature "a commitment...made by each side to attempt to better the other's performance"[19] and trying to tie is one form of denial of trying to better the other's performance. Thus, a personal intended end that is incongruent with the purpose of the sports contest is the source of those actions which, if performed, are unlikely to produce the good sports contest.

We may now see that those personal intended ends which participants adopt may foster actions that maintain the integrity of the sports contest by being either congruent or consistent with the purpose of the sports contest. Conversely, those personal intended ends that are inconsistent or incongruent with the purpose of the sports contest compromise its integrity by detracting from it or negating it.

In conclusion, the good sports contest is one in which the personal intended ends of actions are congruent with or consistent with the purpose of the sports contest and necessary for the establishment of one condition from which a good sports contest may grow. Other conditions are also necessary foundations for a good sports contest.

## NOTES

[1] Bernard Suits, "What is a Game?" *Philosophy of Science* 34 (June 1967), pp. 148-156.

[2] R. Scott Kretchmar, "From Test to Contest: An Analysis of Two Kinds of Counterpoint in Sport," *Journal of the Philosophy of Sport* II (September 1975), pp. 28-29.

[3] Roderick Chisholm, "The Structure of Intention," *Journal of Philosophy* LXVII, No. 19 (October 8, 1970), p. 639.

[4] Nicholas Rescher, "On the Characterization of Actions," in *The Nature of Human Action*, ed. Myles Brand (Glenview, IL: Scott, Foresman & Co., 1970), p. 248.

[5] A tie describes the incomplete sports contest, and the lack of general human satisfaction with a tie is probably why various means have been adopted to complete tie contests: tie breakers, overtimes, sudden death, sudden victory, and so on.

[6] In some sports, the constitutive rules virtually prevent the problem of trying to tie. The rules prescribe either that winning is always achieved at a specific time, such as in badminton, volleyball, or handball, or that if the game is tied at the end, winning will be achieved by using overtimes, tie breakers, and so forth. Those who formulate the constitutive rules of a sport should note that rules against trying to achieve a tie would benefit that sport by producing more good sports contests.

[7]Warren P. Fraleigh, "Sport-Purpose," *Journal of the Philosophy of Sport* II (September 1975), p. 78.

[8]Ibid., p. 76.

[9]Ibid., p. 77.

[10]Ibid., p. 77.

[11]See Frank McBride, "Toward a Non-Definition of Sport," *Journal of the Philosophy of Sport* II, (September 1975), pp. 4-11.

[12]Adapted from an earlier version in Fraleigh, "Sport-Purpose," p. 78.

[13]Ibid., p. 78.

[14]Ibid., p. 79.

[15]Ibid., p. 79.

[16]Ibid., pp. 74-76.

[17]The idea of trying to guarantee more equal contests before any particular sports contest occurs is very important and will be discussed below in relation to the element of winning/losing and of quality of play.

[18]Kretchmar, "From Test to Contest," pp. 28-30.

[19]Ibid., pp. 27-29.

# Chapter Four

# Winning/Losing
# and Quality of Play

As we shall see, various meanings are carried by the terms winning and losing, and by the phrases playing well and playing poorly. It must be ascertained what meanings are normative in relation to the good sports contest, especially with respect to winning, losing, playing well, or playing poorly, precisely because our conventional rhetoric in this area is seldom analyzed carefully. Popular discussion of sport is filled with such cliches as, "Winning isn't the most important thing, it's the only thing"; "Winning sure beats whatever comes in second"; "Defeat is worse than death because you have to live with defeat"; "Winning isn't everything, it's nothing"; or "It matters not whether you win or lose, but how you play the game." Such flights of hyperbole may be useful for encapsulating bits of conventional "wisdom" but they do not help clarify the meanings normative to the good sports contest. Yet these same cliches, when carefully analyzed, can help establish normative meanings.

## THE NORMATIVE MEANINGS
## OF THE TERMS WINNING AND LOSING

The meanings of winning and losing normative for the good sports contest can be identified and explained after analyzing five different meanings that are somewhat common.

***Winning and Losing as a Functional Aspect of the Complete Sports Contest.***    This means that the complete sports contest has a point of closure, an end; in terms of the complete sports contest, the idea of winning and losing is one necessary facet of its existence. This idea may be characterized as winning and losing for the sports contest and is one meaning that is essential in comprehending the sports contest. Accordingly, winning and losing for the sports contest is part of the normative meaning of winning and losing in the good sports contest.

***Winning and Losing as a Specified End State of Affairs.***    In the sports contest wherein one participant becomes the winner and the other becomes the loser, this meaning indicates that one participant achieves the particular end state of affairs prescribed by the rules better than the other participant. Furthermore, achieving the particular end better cannot occur except within the prescribed rules. There can be no winner or loser without adherence to the rules, for the terms winning and losing mean that two or more persons have attempted the same task and the one who performs it better is the winner. In relation to other ideas of winning and losing, this meaning can be characterized as winning and losing of the sports contest. Inasmuch as the sports contest is partially constituted by the end of winning, and inasmuch as no sports contest is complete without this end, winning and losing of the sports contest is part of the normative meaning of winning and losing in the good sports contest.

***Winning and Losing as Achievement or Nonachievement of Some Goal Within the Contest.***    This meaning indicates that a participant or a group has set a personal goal within the contest other than trying to win. For instance, a participant may succeed in scoring more points than previously attained, in running or swimming faster than previous efforts, or in holding down an opponent's scoring. Such personal goals may be achieved independently of the participant's winning or losing of the sports contest. In relation to other ideas of winning and losing, this meaning can be characterized as winning or losing in the sports contest. If the personal goal is seen by the goal setter as instrumental in trying to win the contest, this meaning is consistent with, but not a necessary part of, the normative meaning of winning and losing in the good sports contest. If the goal setter sees such a personal goal as the only one he/she will pursue, and rejects the goal of trying to win, this is inconsistent with the normative meaning of winning or losing in the good sports contest. That is, if one contestant restricts the goal to scoring X number of points, while the other contestant adopts the normal goal of trying to score more points than the opponent, then no contest occurs because the two participants are not mutually attempting to outdo each other at the same task. In such instances there is no test shared by the participants—thus, no contest.[1] Accordingly, winning or losing here is not a part of the normative meaning of winning or losing in the good sports contest.

### *Winning or Losing Some External Objective Due to Winning or Losing the Sports Contest.*

This means that the objective is external to the sports contest itself, but that achieving or failing in that objective depends upon the outcome of the sports contest. Winning or losing a beer bet, a championship, a cash award, or a scholarship are such external objectives that may be won or lost. In relation to other meanings of winning and losing, this meaning is characterized as winning or losing *from* the contest. If the external objective is a direct result of the winning or losing of the sports contest, this meaning is consistent with, but not a necessary part of, the normative meaning of winning or losing in the good sports contest.

### *Winning and Losing as Trying to Win or Lose the Sports Contest.*

Trying to win means attempting to perform the constitutive motor skills, to exert the physiological and psychological effort, and to utilize the appropriate tactics and strategy better than one's opponent. In unusual circumstances, such as attempting a field goal in basketball when behind by two points with one second to go, one's best effort may include trying to tie or trying not to lose. Finally, exerting one's best effort in the contest means attempting to show the most favorable comparison of relative ability possible. Trying to lose means attempting these same actions poorer than one's opponent. As indicated in Chapter 3, the end of trying to win, or contesting, must be adopted by all sports participants as a personal intended end for the good sports contest to occur. Accordingly, the meaning of winning as trying to win, or contesting, is a necessary part of the normative meaning of winning in the good sports contest. Conversely, trying to lose is the opposite of contest and, since no contest can exist[2] if one participant is trying to do poorly while the other is trying to do better, this meaning of trying to lose is incongruent with the normative meaning of losing in the good sports contest.

From this discussion of five meanings of the terms winning and losing, we can now identify which are normative for, which are consistent with, and which are incongruent with the good sports contest. We have noted that three concepts are normative, that is, winning and losing for the contest, winning or losing of the contest, and trying to win or contesting. Winning and losing *for* the contest is essential simply because no contest exists without the idea of a terminal point of closure. By nature the contest is a bounded human event which has a beginning, an end, and a process in between. Winning and losing *of* the contest signifies which participant has performed better or worse than the other, and no contest is complete until such a determination is reached. As indicated earlier, the sports contest that is tied is incomplete and, as our experience so adequately demonstrates, a tie is not satisfactory precisely because it does not terminate the contest. Finally, winning as trying to win or contesting is essential simply because there cannot be a good contest unless all participants are trying to win and accordingly are performing somewhere near their potential.

Conceptions of winning and losing that are incongruent and contradictory to the good sports contest are trying to lose (noncontesting), and winning or losing a limited goal in the contest—a goal that contradicts the goal of trying to win. In both cases, such meanings contradict the normative meaning of winning and losing in the good sports contest because one is the negation of contesting while the other results in no contest because the participants are not engaged in the same test.

Two meanings of winning and losing are consistent with the normative meanings in the good sports contest. One is the meaning of winning or losing some end external to the contest, that end being directly dependent upon the outcome of the contest. Winning or losing from the contest, however, although consistent with the normative meaning of these terms, is not a necessary meaning in comprehending what the good sports contest is. In short, it is possible both to comprehend the idea of and to have a good sports contest without actually winning or losing *from* the contest.

Winning or losing a limited goal in the contest is consistent with the normative meaning of winning or losing when the participant who sets the limited goal sees it as instrumental to the outcome of the contest. For instance, if a tennis player sets a limited goal of completing 75% of his/her first serves successfully, and sets such a goal as one achievement that will help to win the contest, then winning or losing in the contest is consistent with normative meanings.

## THE NORMATIVE MEANINGS
## OF PLAYING WELL AND PLAYING POORLY

The normative meanings of the phrases "playing well" and "playing poorly" must be clarified to understand the good sports contest. These phrases signify the quality of the participants' performances. The meaning of these phrases must be expressed first in relevant categories of sports performance, and second, in relation to some standards that allow the use of such terms as well and poorly in appraising specific performance. Relevant categories means, what do we examine when we want to evaluate the quality of performance? Standards means, what is the basic criterion against which we compare performance in the relevant categories?

To evaluate the quality of a sports performance we examine it in three categories: (a) executing the motor skills that constitute a particular sport; (b) exerting the physiological and psychological effort demanded; and (c) using the appropriate tactics and strategy.

We could compare performance in these three categories against three very different basic criteria to evaluate whether it was well done or poorly done. One criterion could be the best performance ever in a particular sport, or some perfect standard (the world's record, or a hole in one in golf). A second criterion could be the quality of our opponent's performance during the contest. The third criterion could be the reasonable expectancy of highest quality of play for a particular athlete or team based upon their prior performances.

When the relevant categories are combined with the criteria, we find different meanings for the phrases playing well and playing poorly. In the first instance, we find that playing well means the performer executes all the motor skills of the sport at least as well as, or better than, they have ever been executed before; that the performer is able to meet all physiological demands without being hampered by fatigue; that the performer can withstand the psychological demands imposed by tension, distraction, or bad luck; and that the performer employs the best strategy and tactics for the particular sport. In contrast, playing poorly means the performer executes the motor skills at a low, or the lowest possible, level; is incapable of meeting the sustained physiological demands; is continually bothered by tension, distraction, or bad luck; and chooses the worst possible strategy and tactics for the particular sport.

For example, suppose that in the United States Golf Association Open (The National Open), one player hit almost all his shots perfectly so that on the 18th hole he could realistically equal or better the lowest number of strokes taken by a golfer in a sanctioned tournament. Suppose, also, that the weather was hot and humid, thus placing great physiological demands on the player, and that the spectator gallery completely surrounded the entire 18th tee, fairway, and green while international television transmission focused upon him. Yet these conditions did not have a negative effect on the player's performance. Finally, suppose that on the difficult 18th hole the golfer could break the low round record by scoring one less than par (a birdie), and that a tee shot left him in a position of having to hit a second shot over a deep sand trap in front of the green and land close to it to stop the ball near the hole. And suppose that by scoring a birdie he would be assured a lone first place finish in the tournament while a par would assure a tie for first. Under these conditions, the player chose to hit the second shot close to the pin and did make the birdie and establish the new record.

Playing poorly where the criterion is the best performance ever or a perfect performance would entail, using the same example and player, executing the motor skills of golf in such a way that even the logical possibility of a record low round is eliminated early in the 18 holes, that the player tires early in the round and is easily distracted by the actions of spectators or bothered psychologically by other events, and that the player attempts shots which even on better days he normally would be unable to do.

When the criterion for playing well or poorly is the quality of the opponent's performance, we find that playing well means executing the motor skills somewhat better than the opponent, displaying physiological and psychological effort slightly better than or at least equal to the opponent, and using strategy and tactics equal to or slightly better than the opponent — although none of these necessarily as good as the participant is capable. In relation to this standard, playing well means, in short, good enough to win or as well as the opponent and the situation demands, but not necessarily playing one's best.

This conception of playing well is illustrated by a tennis player who hits her forehand and backhand drives with less pace on them, slows the velocity of her first serves, and decreases the angle on her volleys at the net. She also does not try as hard to retrieve her opponent's "sure winners" because this would demand greater physiological exertion. Finally, she deliberately avoids certain strokes which, although within her ability level and for which there are opportunities, would score points easily. In all of these examples, the tennis player executes her strokes, responds to physiological and psychological demands, and chooses tactics and strategy in direct relationship to achieving and maintaining a score advantage over her opponent. Playing poorly in relation to the quality of an opponent's play means not executing skills sufficiently well, not exerting sufficient physiological and psychological effort, and not making appropriate tactical and strategic choices when these are well within a player's abilities. In short, playing poorly here means badly enough to lose or not as well as the opponent and situation demand although such demands are within the player's competency as verified by previous performance.

When the standard of play is the highest level of performance that can be reasonably expected for a particular performer or team, the meaning of playing well and playing poorly is different than in the first two cases. Playing well means performing all the requisite motor skills at or close to the participant's best previous performance, meeting the physiological and psychological demands of the contest as well as or close to previous best performance, and utilizing tactics and strategy that both exemplify the performer's strategic knowledge of the sport and employ his/her repertoire of varied skills at opportune times. Playing poorly means performing the requisite motor skills well below the participant's reasonable expected competency, meeting the physiological and psychological demands of the contest at a level below previous good performance, and choosing tactics and strategy that contradict the participant's strategic knowledge of the sport and limit the number and use of developed skills to inopportune times.

Which of these conceptions of playing well and playing poorly is normative for the good sports contest? To answer this, we will examine the three meanings of playing well and playing poorly in relation to the substantive characteristics of the moral point of view. Which of the three meanings best embodies these characteristics?

When we examine the meaning of playing well and playing poorly in relation to the standard of the best performance or of perfection, we find very quickly that such a conception cannot embody the moral point of view. Such a standard could apply only to a few world-class participants and not to all sports participants, so it cannot be meant for everybody. For in using such a standard we would find quickly that only a few participants could ever play well and that most participants, particularly amateurs, could never say that they played well in any contest. Furthermore, to hold a standard for everyone that is literally impossible for most cannot be for the good of everyone alike simply because it inevitably reduces almost all participants to playing poorly all the time. Not only is such a standard logically unrealistic but it is psychologically destructive. It makes almost all sports participants failures at the outset when they attempt to play well and contribute to the good sports contest. For these reasons, we must eliminate the meanings of playing well and playing poorly in relation to the standard of the best-ever performance or of perfection, which is nonnormative for the good sports contest.

The meanings of playing well and playing poorly in relation to the standard of the quality of the opponent's play, or the standard of the previous highest level of the participant's performance, both appear to be meant for everybody. At least logically, such standards appear to be possible for all participants. Accordingly, the amateur or the professional, the novice or the long-time devotee, the child or the adult, and the male or the female may either play well or poorly when the standard is one of these two.

The characteristic for the good of everyone alike must be carefully applied to the standard of the quality of the opponent's performance and to the standard of each participant's best previous performance. Advocates of the former standard would make several statements to support a conviction that such a standard is for the good of everyone alike. To cite three:

1.  If one participant is performing much better than the opponent, adjusting performance so as not to run up the score is appropriate. That is, reducing the velocity of the tennis serve, not

exerting oneself extremely in retrieving all the opponent's winners, and not executing difficult cross-court passing shots are appropriate adjustments because they would cause less embarrassment to the opponent and at the same time maintain the scoring superiority for the person who is performing better.

2. In such a situation, the better performing player conserves energies and conceals some of his/her abilities, which is good strategy for future matches.

3. If all performers adjusted the quality of their performances in such a manner, then no one would be seeking the wipe-out in sports contests, and unnecessary embarrassment would be avoided while relative superior performance would be rewarded by winning. Thus, if everyone performed in a reciprocal manner when in such a role, it would in the long run be for the good of everyone alike.

Advocates of the standard of quality being each participant's previous best performance would support the conviction that such a standard is for the good of everyone alike also. Three possible reasons are:

1. Only when all participants are performing to the best of their ability will consistent maximum demands be made upon each participant so that each is stimulated to achieve his/her best.

2. Deliberately circumscribing one's performance detracts from one's ability to the extent, at times, that the participant who does so in a particular contest is unable to perform well when an opponent begins to play well enough to win the contest.

3. If everyone plays close to his/her best most of the time, then all participants can know, most of the time, how well they really perform. In the long run, this is for the good of everyone alike.

How do we decide between the relative merits of these statements which support the conviction that each of these different standards for playing well and playing poorly is for the good of everyone alike? First, we need to be clear that we are comparing standards in relation to the same kind of situation in the sports contest. In this regard, it is necessary to understand that we are speaking of the sports contest wherein the contestants are, at the outset, equally competent performers. We are referring, in principle, to contests between members of the same testing family.[3] Also, we are not referring to any temporary and unusual conditions which, even when performers have been equally competent, provide a distinct advantage for one of them before the contest begins. Therefore we must eliminate temporary debilitating conditions that affect only one of the contestants and make the match unequal before the start. Examples could be serious injury or illness, personal tragedy, or unusual defects in the sports equipment used by one of the performers. The net effect of these two conditions is that we wish to determine which kind of standard for playing well is more for the good of everyone alike in sports contests which, in principle, engage participants who are equally matched.

We can determine this by seeing which standard contributes more to achieving a common purpose shared by all sports participants. The shared purpose of sports participants that will ascertain the better standard is the purpose of the sports contest, because this is what sports participants are about, in common, when they begin a sports contest. We must also remember that the sports contest's purpose differs from the concept of individual purposes of its participants. Again, the sports contest serves to provide equitable opportunity for the mutual contesting of the participants' relative abilities to move mass in space and time within the confines prescribed by an agreed-upon set of rules. That is the only purpose which, in principle, all participants share because of the nature of the sports contest.

In order for true mutual contesting of the participants' relative abilities to take place, the opponents must be as equally matched as possible; when one contestant's abilities are markedly superior to the other's, the two are really not engaging in the same contest. Kretchmar[4] illustrates this important idea.

> An advanced golfer sees his test for example, in much different terms than the beginner. A high rough, a heavy cross wind, or a 225 yard distance, which must be traversed in a single shot with the ball moving from left to right, provides testing ambiguity for the excellent golfer. These same phenomena may be seen by the beginner as impossible situations.

With contestants of equal ability at the outset, the same idea is relevant to the proper standard for playing well and playing poorly. A true mutual contesting of the relative abilities of the two presumably equal performers requires that each one perform at his/her best level of achievement. Otherwise, the true relative abilities are not determined for either contestant. If one contestant plays as well as capable and the other plays much more poorly than is reasonably expected, no true determination of relative ability is possible here because the opponent is part of the test. If one opponent cannot demand the highest possible quality of play from the other, then he/she is not providing the other the same kind of challenge that the other is providing for him/her. To illustrate, if two equally competent tennis players meet in a match and one executes his or her repertoire of developed skills very well while the other, who possesses the same skills, executes them very poorly, then one player is being challenged to the utmost while the other is not. The player who is not being challenged cannot know his or her true relative ability because the opponent, who is part of the test, is not demanding it.

With equally matched contestants, it is inappropriate for one to circumscribe his/her ability for the primary reason that he/she is not now providing the kind of test the opponent desires. Further, our experience with such contests shows that for one contestant to circumscribe his/her skill deliberately is often viewed by the other as a gratuitous insult. It is viewed as an insult either because the lower scoring contestant expects to be thoroughly tested, and in many cases is still contesting, or because the player who has so circumscribed his/her skills appears to be saying, "I can beat you with much less than my best."

It follows, then, that the normative concept of playing well and playing poorly in the good sports contest is derived from the standard of the highest quality play of which each performer is capable. Still another condition necessary for the good sports contest is that all contestants do play well by performing the requisite motor skills, exerting the physiological and psychological efforts demanded, and employing the tactics and strategy that the performers are capable of — at a level which is at, or very close to, all performers' previous best performances. This condition by itself does not guarantee the good sports contest but, along with the others, is indispensable.

## THE RELATIONSHIP
## OF THE NORMATIVE MEANING
## OF WINNING/LOSING
## AND PLAYING WELL/PLAYING POORLY

We must now ascertain what kind of relationships between these terms and phrases is normative to the good sports contest. There is a way to accomplish this task using our conventional bits of hyperbole about winning/losing and quality of play. Here the exaggerations, which are part of any bit of hyperbole, will be clarified as exaggerations that cannot be taken literally. Yet the important elements of meaning, which these exaggerations so forcefully attempt to express, will be preserved for their value in establishing the relationships.

An often-repeated piece of hyperbole is, "It is better to win while playing poorly than to lose while playing well." With this statement we will focus on determining the normative meanings of winning/losing in relation to playing well, playing poorly. It suggests that the product of the contest (winning or losing) is more important than the process of the contest (playing well or playing poorly) in establishing the correct relationship of winning/losing to quality of play.

The basic assertion of that statement is in agreement with such often-heard statements as, "Winning sure beats whatever comes in second," and "Defeat is worse than death because you have to live with defeat." The agreement in principle of such statements is that the product of the contest, winning or losing, (a) is more important than the process, the quality of play; or (b) is exclusively important, that is, the process, playing well or playing poorly, is not to be considered.

The assertion "It is better to win while playing poorly than to lose while playing well," completely contradicts "Winning isn't everything, it's nothing," in that it ascribes great importance to the product while the latter statement gives the product no importance whatsoever. The former assertion also contradicts "It matters not whether you win or lose but how you play the game" because this latter statement asserts that the process of the game (playing well or poorly) is exclusively important over the product (winning or losing).

We can see from this brief analysis of our various cliches that conceiving of winning/losing as the products and of playing well, playing poorly as the process of the sports contest is relevant to determining the normative relationships of the meanings of these terms and phrases. A useful way to begin is to examine different rankings of four logically possible relations of the product terms with the process phrases. This will clarify the logic of different rankings and show how they treat the previously established normative meanings of the product terms and the process phrases. This is not to establish the normative relationships of those terms and phrases for the good sports contest.

The four logically possible combinations are winning – playing well, winning – playing poorly, losing – playing poorly, and losing – playing well. If we exhaust the logical possibilities of various rankings of these four combinations, we find that 24 are possible. Three have been selected for analysis, chosen because they emphasize either that the product (winning-losing), or that the process (playing well and playing poorly), or that the logical relationship between product and process is of greater importance in establishing the ranking. These three sets of rankings will be labeled product emphasis, process emphasis, and logical relationship emphasis. They are:

### *Product Emphasis Ranking*

1. Winning – playing well
2. Winning – playing poorly
3. Losing – playing well
4. Losing – playing poorly

### Process Emphasis Ranking

1. Winning – playing well
2. Losing – playing well
3. Winning – playing poorly
4. Losing – playing poorly

### Logical Relationship Emphasis Ranking

1. Winning – playing well
2. Losing – playing poorly
3. Losing – playing well
4. Winning – playing poorly

The greater importance of the product (winning or losing) is illustrated in the product emphasis ranking by the fact that winning is ranked first and second while the process of playing well occupies only one of the first two ranks. In short, advocates of this type of ranking believe that winning, as a product, is more important to achieve than the process of playing well. The normative concepts of winning and losing discussed early in this chapter appear to be embodied here, that is, winning for the contest, winning of the contest, and trying to win or contesting. Inasmuch as second place combines winning and playing poorly, and third place combines losing and playing well, it appears that the normative meaning of playing well as playing at, or close to, each contestant's maximum is not embodied here. That is, the product of winning is predominant in the second-place ranking so that in the total picture it becomes more important to win than to play to one's capacity when we consider the ranking for all participants in a particular sports contest. Finally, the product emphasis ranking places winning in the highest two and losing in the lowest two ranks. This shows that the controlling elements in the logic of total ranking are the products of winning and losing.

In the process emphasis ranking, the two highest are playing well while the two lowest are playing poorly. Thus, the controlling element in this ranking's logic is the process of quality of play. Nonetheless, the normative meaning of winning and losing appears to be embodied in an undistorted manner; that is, nothing in this ranking denies the normative meanings of winning as trying to win, as an end state of affairs, or as identifying one contestant as the winner. The normative meaning of quality of play as performing at, or close to, the participants' maximum is also embodied accurately in the process emphasis ranking in that when all participants play their best, any one of them can win and the other lose, or vice versa. The same is true if all participants play poorly as determined by the normative meaning of that phrase.

The logical relationship emphasis ranking indicates that the two highest rankings are dictated not by either the product or the process alone, but by the logical relationship of the product and the process. This means that if one contestant plays well, it is logical to expect that contestant to win. It may also be said that the contestant who plays well deserves to win. This ranking means, moreover, that if one contestant plays poorly while the other plays well, it is logical to expect that the former will lose and that he/she deserves to. The normative meanings of winning and losing appear to be accurately embodied in these rankings. The normative meaning of playing well and playing poorly as playing at, or close to, one's maximum seems to be embodied; however, the positive process of playing well is less important, in the overall rankings, than the logical relationship of winning and losing to the quality of play.

This analysis of the product, process, and logical relationship emphasis rankings gives us some insight into what each means in its totality, but does not yet answer which of the three must be considered normative for the good sports contest. To arrive at the normative meaning of this relationship, the totality of each ranking must be inspected in terms of the substantive characteristics of the moral point of view—that is, meant for everybody and for the good of everyone alike. This will be done by asking a question that applies these two characteristics to the present issue: If we consider all participants (meant for everybody) in any sports contest, which ranking would best enhance achieving a good sports contest (for the good of everyone alike)?

To begin, we notice that all of these emphases place winning-playing well at the highest ranking. In doing so, each emphasis is true to its own sense of what is more important. The product emphasis places the positive product of winning as first, the process emphasis finds the positive process of playing well as first, and the logical relationship emphasis finds the positive logical relationship of playing well and winning as first. For everybody, winning and playing well is the very best combination to achieve and deserves first ranking in the normative relationships of product and process in the good sports contest. With this first ranking secure, it establishes a point of reference for the other three rankings in each emphasis. Given this reference point, and in relation to meant for everybody and for the good of everyone alike, what may now be said about the other three combinations as they are ranked in each emphasis?

In the product emphasis ranking, the second-ranked combination of winning-playing poorly cannot go with the first ranking of winning-playing well when all contestants are considered. For even if all contestants play well, only one can also win, which signifies that only one contestant can achieve the combination of winning-playing well. Given that one contestant achieves winning-playing well, what is possible for the other contestant? Or, what is the best possible combination for the second ranking? It is obvious that if the first ranking includes winning the second best cannot also include winning when everybody is being considered in a sports contest. Therefore, the combination of winning-playing poorly cannot be ranked second because it is impossible to have two winners. Accordingly, the second ranking must include the term losing, and when it does the second ranking becomes the same as either the process emphasis (losing-playing well) or the logical relationship emphasis (losing-playing poorly). Thus, we find that the product emphasis rankings are not possible when meant for everybody, and they cannot be for the good of everyone alike. The good sports contest must have a winner and a loser in the normative meaning of those words. For this logical reason, we know that "Winning isn't the most important thing, it's the only thing" is not only an exaggerated hyperbole, but it is nonsense. We know that such emphasis upon winning is nonsense for a psychological reason as well. We know from our experience — of trying to contest with opponents of equal ability by proper scheduling and by trying to make unequal contests equal by handicapping efforts — that winning itself is not of the greatest importance. Indeed, to make the case even more evident, Keating[5] says, "But victory in itself is not enough for the athlete. If this were so the schedule would be filled with inferior opponents."

When we examine the process emphasis and the logical relationship emphasis rankings with the first-ranked combination of winning-playing well, and when we consider the other possible rankings being meant for everybody, we find that these two rankings, as totalities, can be meant for everybody. In the process emphasis rankings one and two can go together; one contestant can play well and win while the other can play well and lose. Similarly, the third and fourth rankings can go together. One contestant can play poorly and win while the other can play poorly and lose. All four of these rankings make logical sense for everybody and are thus meant for everybody. In the logical relationship emphasis, one contestant can play well and win while the other can play poorly and lose. However, with equal opponents it is unlikely that one contestant can play well and lose (rank 3) while the other can play poorly and win (rank 4).

Both the process emphasis and the logical relationship emphasis ranking can be meant for everybody. Which of them is for the good of everyone alike? This question is applied to the present issue by asking, "Which pattern of relationships between winning, losing, and quality of play, if achieved, will assure a better sports contest, in the same way, for all participants?" If we reestablish that the contestants are equally competent performers and no one has any temporary, debilitating condition that would prevent maximum performance, the answer to the question becomes clear. To assure a better sports contest, in the same way, it is essential that all participants play well. For the same kinds of good are available to all only if all play well. First, not all the participants can experience meaningful personal satisfaction in the sports contest unless they all play well. Thus, in terms of satisfaction for everyone alike, playing well is necessary. Second, unless all participants play well together, the contest becomes less of a contest in that all participants do not have equal demands made upon their abilities and, consequently, the participant who plays well against an opponent who plays poorly must be less satisfied simply because of the clear knowledge that he/she has not been thoroughly tested. Also, if one participant plays poorly while the other plays well and wins, then the former has a triple dissatisfaction: losing, playing poorly, and not providing the best test for his/her opponent.

Still another approach to this problem is to examine each of the three rankings separately with three questions in mind. That is, having established the common reference point of the first ranking of winning-playing well in each of the three rankings, look at the remaining three rankings in each of the product emphasis, the process emphasis and the logical relationship emphasis. Now examine each ranking with these three questions in mind:

1. What combination would I rank in second, third, and fourth place if I considered my own self-interest only? Why?

2. What combination would I rank in second, third, and fourth place if I considered my own self-interest and the interest of my opponent with regard only to how his/her interest would affect my self-interest? Why?

3. What combination would I rank in second, third, and fourth place if I considered my own self-interest and the interest of my opponent equally? Why?

The only circumstance in any contest that makes it possible for a contestant to rank winning in the first two places is when that person is considering self-interest only. It is clear that if the contestant considers her opponent in any way, either with respect to how the opponent's welfare affects her own self-interest or with the interests of both as equal, she must include losing in the second ranking. Furthermore, it is very likely that considering the opponent in any way will encourage the contestant to place losing-playing well in the second rank. For if the contestant achieves winning-playing well (rank 1), she is likely to rank as second losing-playing well. If she wins along with playing well, her victory is more satisfying if the opponent has also played well. For if the contestant loses and her opponent achieves winning-playing well (rank 1), then the loser would prefer to play well nevertheless. If the contestant considers the interests equally, both her own and the opponent's, she will obviously include playing well in each of the first two ranks because playing well by all parties would be everyone's interest equally.

Examining the three kinds of rankings in light of these three questions shows that it is prudent (e.g., in one's self-interest) to rank winning-losing and quality of play with priority upon the quality of play. At the same time, what is prudent in such ranking is also meant for everybody and for the good of everyone alike. Accordingly, the resultant ranking is both prudent and moral, which is to say that the ranking may be supported both by self-interested reasons and moral reasons.

Even though it is correct to assert that quality of play is more important than winning or losing in establishing a necessary condition for the good sports contest, one must also reassert that winning and losing is another necessary condition for the good sports contest. The normative meanings of winning and losing—as the terms indicative of the contest termination, of superior performance by one contestant, and of trying to win—are still necessary for the good sports contest. These are logical requirements for the good sports contest, and it is correct to say that winning and losing do matter contra "It matters not whether you win or lose, but how you play the game." Beyond such logical requirements, winning and losing matter psychologically because, obviously, all sports participants prefer to win while playing well rather than to lose in spite of playing well. The reason for the psychological importance of winning and losing is an outcome of the necessary condition of playing well. For it is obvious that given equally competent opponents in a sports contest, both will have a reasonable expectancy of victory. The contestant who wins has that expectancy wholly fulfilled, whereas the contestant who loses, although certainly not crushed, feels some measure of disappointment; that is, he/she is fulfilled but not completely. It is a matter of mutual positive degree of satisfaction for all contestants. The idea is expressed in a negative fashion as follows:

> To tell a competitive athlete...not to be concerned with victory is liberal snobbery. At best, it is the remark of someone who simply does not understand the agonistic struggle which is an integral part of the competitive sports experience. It is just as wrong to say winning isn't anything as it is to say winning is the only thing.[6]

Probably the reason for our excesses in both directions with respect to the importance (or lack of it) of winning and losing is an outgrowth of our undeclared presuppositions about the nature of competition. This problem, though recognized here, will be analyzed and discussed in the chapter on relationships of opponents.

Let us now state, formally, the normative meaning of the relationships of winning/losing and the quality of play for the good sports contest. The normative meaning of the product terms (winning-losing) with the process phrases (playing well, playing poorly) is determined by that kind of relationship that is both logically possible between these terms and phrases, and that is for the good of all contestants alike. A normative meaning is preferable when derived from emphasis on the positive process of both contestants playing well and, at the same time, determining winner and loser, because when all contestants play well, it is for the good of everyone alike in that it assures (a) the best possible contest, (b) the determination of the true relative abilities of all, and (c) the maximum positive personal satisfaction of all.

## NOTES

[1] R. Scott Kretchmar, "From Test to Contest, An Analysis of Two Kinds of Counterpoint in Sport," *Journal of the Philosophy of Sport* II (September 1975), pp. 27-29.

[2] It is possible to construct a real contest that consists of opponents trying to do something more poorly than one another. However, paradoxically, if each is attempting to do something more poorly than the other, then each is really attempting to be better at doing poorly. Thus, a contest does occur and the opponents are not trying to lose but trying to win at doing poorly.

[3] Kretchmar, "From Test to Contest," pp. 28-29.

[4] Ibid., p. 28.

[5] James W. Keating, "Winning in Sport and Athletics," *Thought* 38 (Summer 1963), p. 209.

[6] Jack Scott, "Sport and the Radical Ethic," *Quest* XIX (January 1973), p. 74.

# Chapter Five

## Rules
## and Their Functions

Rules are another and obvious element in the good sports contest. How rules function can be understood by examining the constitutive rules of sports contests, the attitudes of participants toward those rules, rule violations, and the problem of intentional rule violations, constitutive rules, and the good sports contest.

### THE CONSTITUTIVE RULES
### OF SPORTS CONTESTS

Constitutive rules are those regulations which make a particular sport what it is. Typically, constitutive rules specify in advance the special area of the sports contest, its duration, the specific state of affairs to be achieved by contestants, or the prelusory goal,[1] and the means used to achieve that goal, or lusory means,[2] the allowable equipment and materials to be used, the scoring or evaluation system, and regulations which, if violated, specify a prescribed penalty. For example, golf is constituted as the sport in which:

1.  The teeing area for each hole is a determinant distance from the hole. (special area)
2.  Each participant has a specified number of holes to complete, and there are certain time limits for playing each shot. (duration of time)

3. The goal is to get the golf ball into the holes. (prelusory goal)

4. Striking the golf ball with golf clubs are the actions used in getting the golf ball into the holes. (lusory means)

5. Only so many golf clubs, of known materials, and a certain type of ball which meets certain specifications may be used. (allowable equipment and materials)

6. The participant who swings at the ball the fewest times (medal play) in getting it into the holes is deemed the better performer. (evaluation system)

7. A penalty is accessed each time a participant loses a ball during the duration of play. (prescribed penalty for a rule violation)

A set of constitutive rules is one enabling condition that allows the sports contest to exist. Without this condition, no contestants could attempt deliberately to do the same task and, thus, there could not be a contest. Given a set of constitutive rules, the contest requires yet a second enabling condition: The participants must affirm the constitutive rules by agreeing to play the sport,[3] that is, to follow the rules.[4] In the description of the good sports contest between John and Bob, the two agreed to play a game of badminton singles. In reaching that agreement, they did not say such a silly thing as: "Shall we follow the rules of badminton?" Indeed, when they agreed to play badminton, they both knew that they both were, at the same time and without explicit statement, agreeing to follow the constitutive rules of badminton. The existence of these two enabling conditions together now allows the constitutive rules to take on another function. This is the regulative function of the constitutive rules and it refers to regulating the actions of contestants after the contest starts. So, the constitutive rules specify what the sport is a contest of before any single contest begins, agreement to play a contest is needed before a contest starts, and constitutive rules regulate actions after a contest begins.

## THE ATTITUDES OF PARTICIPANTS TOWARD THE CONSTITUTIVE RULES

The attitudes of participants toward the rules are of great significance to the good sports contest. The attitude that is most significant is one of complete respect, and it grows out of several realizations by the sports participants. One is that the rules of sport are self-legislated in that the free choice of the participant signifies acceptance of the rules as laws which he/she wills to govern his/her action.[5] Further, the rules of sport "obtain their efficacy only through the athlete's free affirmation of them".[6] In these ways the rules of sport are not laws imposed upon the individual without his/her direct assent but are laws, the regulatory effect of which the sports participant directly chooses and thus legislates for himself or herself.

Another realization is that choosing to be bound by the rules of the sport is not a restriction upon the participant's freedom, but is the choice of conditions which allow the person's expression as an athlete.[7] Metheny states this paradox very well:

> Within the complex conditions of life, we are seldom, if ever, free to focus all our attention on one well defined task and bring all the energies of our being to bear on one whole hearted attempt to perform that task effectively.
>
> In contrast, the rules of sport provide us with a man-made world in which this freedom is fully guaranteed. These rules eliminate the demands of necessity by defining an unnecessary task.
>
> In this sense, the rules of sport provide each performer with a rare opportunity to concentrate all the energies of his being in one meaningful effort to perform a task of his own choosing.[8]

In choosing the sports contest with its rules, the participant is choosing a world which "is his own self-constructed 'world,' one in which he is comfortable rather than alien. And it is in entering such a world that...he literally uses externally controlling necessities such as space, time, and gravity to serve his own purposes which are, themselves, not controlled by necessities."[9] The rules of sport provide a world in which there is a "freedom from absence."[10] It is a world in which the rules provide a freedom for expression and testimony of the participants' relative abilities to move mass in space and time. Inasmuch as sports participants freely choose that rule-bound world, it follows that utter respect for the rules is to be expected and natural.

Understanding the distinction between and the functions of the letter and spirit of the rules is another foundation from which complete respect grows. The letter of a rule is what the rule states explicitly, or its legal sports substance. For example, a rule states that golf participants will execute their strokes from where the ball lies on the golf course, that they will hit the ball from where they have previously hit the ball to. The letter of this rule states, positively, to play the shots as they lie and, negatively, that improving one's lie is prohibited except under clearly specified exceptions. This is all the rule says explicitly. However, what is not explicitly stated but nonetheless is a very real dimension of this same rule is its spirit. The spirit of a sports rule is not what the rule states, explicitly; rather, it is the reason why the rules makers made that particular rule a constitutive rule. Concerning the golf rule, the spirit of that rule is to reward previous good shots (such as balls hit into the middle of a fairway) and to penalize poor shots (such as balls hit into the rough, behind trees, and so on). The spirit of the rule assures that every golfer in the contest plays under conditions that reflect, equally for all, the quality of his previous shots and provides an equally good or poor lie, in principle, from which the players hit their next shots. If participants understand only the letter of a rule, they have a limited base from which to determine how to follow the rules. Improving a golf lie may seem an innocent act to a contestant who does not comprehend the spirit of that rule. But when he knows that the spirit is absolutely essential to a fair contest, he has something more than the letter to guide appropriate action. For the good sports contest, comprehending the letter and the spirit of constitutive rules is meant for everybody and for the good of everyone alike because it helps assure that all are facing the same test and, thus, are contesting.

## RULE VIOLATIONS

Rule violations occur in most sports contests; not all the participants act in strict accord with both the letter and the spirit of the constitutive rules. Rule violations may be either intentional or unintentional, the latter occurring accidentally. For instance, a basketball player may trip an opposing player inadvertently. Unintentional violations also occur when a player violates a rule—not by accident, and not by a desire to violate the rule—but because he or she does not know the rule. For instance, a novice golfer may not know that it is illegal to improve his/her lie.

Intentional violations are of two kinds. One is a conscious violation wherein the player expects to be caught but is willing to be penalized in order to attain some tactical advantage the violation affords. A second kind occurs when a player deliberately violates a rule but hopes not to be detected in the violation and, thus, escape the penalty.

Complete respect for and observance of the rules are essential for the sports contest, and specifically for the good sports contest. What must be said regarding the unintentional and intentional violations of the rules? Except in a certain limited sense, it is obvious that unintentional violations cannot be avoided. Often a sports participant unintentionally violates rules in an eagerness to play well. Witness the basketball player who inadvertently trips an opponent while trying to retain effective defensive position, the tennis player who foot faults on a serve because she wishes to rush the net, and the volleyball spiker who hits the net while attempting to hit a spike with maximum force. These are essentially errors in skillful performance. Although such rule violations will occur even in the good sports contest, their frequency and influence upon the outcome can be reduced to an insignificant level by precontest practice. Unintentional violations that occur because participants do not know the rules can be reduced by precontest study.

Nonetheless, in a contest in which one player is consistently violating a rule that he/she is unaware of while the opponent is following the rule, the contest is destroyed because the two contestants are not now facing the same test. For instance, if one golfer in a match continually improves his/her lie while the others play the ball as it lies, then the players are not facing the same test together and, consequently, this is no true contest. However, if both golfers consistently improve their lies because they do not know the rules, or agreed that improved lies will be allowed, then they are both facing the same test. The principle is clear. Even an inadvertent rule violation, caused by lack of rules knowledge, but resulting in a different test for the participants, is contrary to the good sports contest. Yet so long as the participants face the same test, even if they both unknowingly or by agreement violate a rule, a condition for the good sports contest is retained.

Intentional rules violations are much more complex. Concerning those in which the violator hopes to gain an advantage without invoking a penalty, the principle is that all such intentional violations are absolutely contradictory to any sports contest. It is always wrong for a golfer to deliberately improve his/her lie and secretly avoid the penalty for such illegal actions. It is always wrong for a hurdler, who occupies the outside right lane on a track and who hurdles with the right leg trailing, to deliberately run on the extreme right side of the lane so that his/her trailing leg does not have to clear the hurdles. It is always wrong for a football blocker to deliberately hold his opponent to prevent the latter from getting by him to rush the passer, holding the opponent in a way the officials cannot detect. All of these actions are cheating—if we understand cheating to be deliberate violation of the rules to gain advantage while avoiding a penalty so that the opponents are not now facing the same test. When a golfer improves his/her lie secretly while the opponent does not, the contest no longer really exists because the two golfers are not taking the same test together. When the hurdler does not raise his/her trailing leg over all the hurdles, though the opponents do, that hurdler is not sharing the same test with those opponents. When the football blocker deliberately holds, while his opponents do not, the contest is destroyed. The reasons are very clear:

> The rules of a game are the definition of that game. If this is the case, a player who deliberately breaks the rules of that game is deliberately no longer playing that game.... How can it be determined which of two players (or teams) is more skillful in a game if one of the players (or teams) is not even playing that particular game?"[11]

> Competing, winning, and losing in athletics are intelligible only within the framework of rules which define a specific competitive sport. A person may cheat at a game or compete at it, but it is logically impossible for him to do both. To cheat is to cease to compete. It is for this reason that cheaters are the greatest failure of all in competitive athletics, not because of any considerations of winning or failing to do so, but because they fail even to compete.[12]

These reasons show that, logically, the cheater is not even competing (contesting). Since cheating destroys the contest it clearly prevents the good sports contest. But, there is a different kind of argument against cheating. It is that cheating is intentional violation which denies the implicit promise a sports participant makes in agreeing to contest, the promise to follow the rules. Denial of such a promise in order to enhance the possibility of victory is a moral concern because it is an "exploitation of those who competed in good faith."[13] Such exploitation is certainly contrary to the good of everyone alike.

The kind of intentional rules violation in which the participant deliberately violates the rule but expects a penalty to be assessed for the violation is much more complex. Of the several subtypes of this kind of intentional violation, three are:

1. Personal fouls such as tripping, holding, or hitting an opponent: three subcategories occur here. First is a deliberate violent action intended to injure the opponent so that either the opponent cannot continue or his/her effectiveness is reduced. Examples of this are deliberately hitting a forward passer after he has released the football, jabbing the butt end of a hockey stick into an opponent's face, or running under a basketball player who has leaped into the air so that the player will be hit in the legs and flip over in mid-air. A second subcategory includes tripping or holding an opponent deliberately to prevent him/her from scoring what appears to be a sure goal. Examples would be tackling a soccer player from behind when he/she is about to kick for a goal from within the penalty area, or tripping a lacrosse player from behind by deliberately thrusting the stick between an offensive player's legs who is shooting for a goal. A third subcategory is deliberately holding, pushing, or otherwise illegally touching an offensive player so as to incur a foul which will afford an opportunity for the defensive team to gain possession of the ball. An example would be a defensive basketball player's deliberately holding an offensive dribbler from the leading team in the final minute of a 54-53 basketball game.

2. Deliberate rules violations which do not involve personal fouls but are done intentionally to attain an otherwise unattainable tactical advantage while accepting some sort of penalty: An example of this would be a forward passer in American football deliberately throwing a forward pass out of bounds late in a game in which his team is behind and has used its time outs, so that the clock is stopped and another play may be called or a substitution made.

3. Deliberate violation of a rule, such as intentional delay of a game by the leading team in order to limit the opponent's

chances to score: An example would be stalling in basketball by the team that is ahead in the last 5 minutes of the game.

We find different interpretations of the idea of intentional rules violation which, on one hand, say an intentional rules violation is never appropriate. Pearson[14] says:

> I have argued earlier that a particular game is defined by its rules — that the rules of a game are the definition of that game. If this is the case, a player who deliberately breaks the rules of the game is deliberately no longer playing that game.... These kinds of acts are designed to interfere with the purpose of the game in which they occur.

The basic logic of Pearson's argument is that deliberate rules violation "destroys the vital frame of agreement which makes sports possible"[15] or, in the words used previously here, changes the nature of the event so that the opponents are now facing different tests but have not mutually agreed to such a change.

It would appear, on the other hand, that absolute prohibition of intentional rules violation in cases where a penalty is both expected and imposed is viewed differently by Suits. He says, after discussing constitutive rules and rules of skill:

> There is a third kind of rule in games which appears to be unlike either of these. This is the kind of rule for which there is a fixed penalty such that violating the rules is neither to fail to play the game nor [necessarily] to fail to play the game well, since it is sometimes tactically correct to incur such a penalty, [e.g., in hockey] for the sake of the advantage gained. But these rules and the lusory consequences of their violation are established by the constitutive rules, and are simply extensions of them.[16]

Delattre appears to agree with Suits in that intentional violation of rules does not necessarily constitute failure to play the game unless the violator seeks to ignore the penalty for the violation. He implies that intentional violation which expects the appropriate penalty to be imposed is justified because of the penalty and because it is advantageous to the violator.[17] The logic of both Suits' and Delattre's argument, and current conventional attitudes of sports participants, is that intentional violations — done with the expectancy of penalty and because of the advantage gained — thereby fall legitimately under the title "tactical use of the rules." In short, it is appropriate to violate rules intentionally so long as escape from the prescribed penalty is not intended and attained. The one general exception to such approval is intentional personal fouling of an opponent which intends injury. Even in the exceptionally rough sports, such as American professional football and ice hockey, intentional fouling with the intent of injury is not condoned.[18] Let us eliminate any ambiguity about the possible legitimacy of intentional personal fouling done with the intent of injuring an opponent. Such action can never be permitted in any sports contest for three reasons. First, all participants would have to agree to legitimize such actions, something they would never do because of the inevitable possibility for all of serious injury. Second, any contest which had as its primary purpose the intentional injury of the participants could not be a sports contest, but instead would be a type of war.[19] Third, a general principle of nonmaleficence which is applicable to all of life would prohibit intentional harm or injury to another except under unusual circumstances, and these do not apply to intentional injury in sport. Our analysis will proceed, then, in consideration of intentional rules violations which do not include intentional injury to an opponent.

How is this issue to be resolved? It was stated early in this chapter that playing the sport means the same thing as following the rules, which means abiding by both the letter and the spirit of the constitutive rules. Regulations stated in this chapter that prescribed a penalty for violation were included as part of a sport's constitutive rules. Accordingly, our issue is whether or not intentional violation of constitutive rules of a sport, done for tactical advantage and with the expectancy and imposition of the prescribed penalty, is appropriate action in the good sports contest. For that matter, what is intentional violation of the constitutive rules of a sport? The issue will be treated in principle now, and doing so will expose some serious practical problems for contemporary sport practice. Consideration of these practical problems later will reveal the existing gap between what is right in principle and what is current practice.

To illustrate the issue, let's focus on U.S. collegiate men's basketball under the rules of the NCAA (National Collegiate Athletic Association), whose rules and practices vividly reveal the problems. Let it be reiterated that to have the best contest, all the basketball players must be facing the same test insofar as their intended actions influence whether the test is the same for all. What consitutes and governs that test to make it the same is the rules of the sport. Therefore, actions that intentionally violate the rules, in principle, affect whether the test is the same. How so?

First, the rules state, in positive terms, what the participants must do to achieve the purpose of the particular sport. In basketball, these terms prescribe that players must use the basic means of throwing, rolling, or dribbling the ball in order to achieve the offensive prelusory goal of the game. The basketball rules clarify these terms by further stating which actions are allowable in conjunction with the necessary, prescribed means of throwing, rolling, or dribbling the ball. Basketball rules specify such allowable actions as pivoting, passing, and screening, to mention a few. Finally, the rules specify certain times when specific ways of using the basic means of throwing, rolling, or dribbling must be used. These include throw-in, jump-ball, and free throw. The common element in the basketball terms throwing, rolling, dribbling, pivoting, passing, trying for a field goal, screening, throw-in, jump-ball, and free throw, is that all participants are given these same positive injunctions to perform these actions. Because these actions are positively stated by the rules, all participants know in advance that everyone will be doing those actions in basketball. Consequently, all participants know that the kinds of actions by which they must *contest* the basketball game are specific. These kinds of positive injunctions specified in the rules will be labeled the *positively constitutive* skills and tactics of the sport.

Second, the rules state, or imply clearly, a specific achievable state of affairs that Suits terms the prelusory goal of the game. In men's intercollegiate basketball in the United States, the prelusory goal is stated as, "The purpose of each team is to throw the ball into its own basket and to prevent the other team from scoring."[20] In short, all participants know in advance what specific result they are trying to achieve by using the positively constitutive skills and tactics of basketball. Consequently, they all know that successful or unsuccessful use of the positively constitutive skills and tactics is determined by whether they do throw the ball through their own basket, and whether they prevent the other team from throwing the ball through theirs. This clearly understood purpose will be labeled the *prelusory goal* of a sport.[21]

In any sport, some actions are neither necessary, recommended, nor prohibited by the rules, and thus are potentially useable. Sports participants are continually experimenting with actions that have not been widely used. Constantly pursuing better performance, they introduce new skill techniques such as the jump shot in basketball and the Fosberry flop in high jumping, new tactics such as the forward pass introduced in American football by Gus Dorais and Knute Rockne, and new training routines such as interval training method in track and field and in swimming. Such experimentations are tested to determine whether the new action improves sports performance and whether it falls within the rules of the sport. Often, such new actions cause sports participants and officials to question their legality. Such actions are accepted or rejected primarily by ascertaining whether they are in accord with the letter and spirit of the constitutive rules of the sport.

The constitutive rules set a limited "zone of consistency" within which a new action must fall in order to be allowable. In fact, many sports rules are written precisely because some participant(s) performed a novel action, an action which was later determined to be unacceptable because it fell outside the zone of consistency of the existing rules. The NCAA Football Rules now specifically identify actions such as feigning injury and the "sucker" shift as being outside the rules. The NCAA Basketball Rules now contain a rule that addresses lack of action, to reduce the occurrence of noncontesting actions. The NCAA Track and Field Guide now has a rule on honest effort to require maximum effort from runners who enter several events in a meet but would otherwise save themselves for later events because of tactical team motivations. The zone of consistency test for new actions assures that no contestant can alter the nature of the test so drastically that he/she faces a markedly easier and different test than does his/her opponent. This zone of consistency test operates to maintain the same test for all participants, but also allows some reasonable latitude in how to legitimately meet the test.

We have found that any sport's constitutive rules clearly state which specific skills and tactics must and may be used. The constitutive rules also state, or imply clearly, which specific prelusory goal all participants must intend. Third, the constitutive rules supply a zone of consistency test for appraising new experimental actions. But the constitutive rules do still another thing to try to guarantee that all participants face the same test. The rules specifically contain proscriptions of action by identifying specific actions that are illegal and inappropriate. The basketball rules, for example, proscribe blocking (but allow screening), double dribble, goal tending, holding, pushing, charging, and tripping. The proscriptions have come about in two ways. First, certain actions were prohibited at the outset of the sport to give it its character. Thus, basketball has a proscription against running with the ball, soccer has a proscription against handling the ball, and swimming has a proscription against the use of swim fins in competition. Second, certain new actions used by participants have been judged to fall outside the zone of consistency test for that sport. Because that action represented a threat to the letter and/or spirit of the positively constitutive skills and tactics or to the prelusory goal of the sport, sports organizations, through rules committees, have written proscriptions into the rules against the questionable action. Proscriptions in sports rules are direct attempts to reduce, or better yet to eliminate, certain actions so that the participants face the same test: the contest in which known skills and tactics are used by all (the positively constitutive skills and tactics), a known goal is pursued by all (the prelusory goal), and wherein novel actions fall within the zone of consistency test. Proscriptions are not for making certain actions and their penalties fall within the letter and spirit of the constitutive rules. The spirit of these proscriptions is to help assure a contest of known skills and tactics by eliminating the use of certain inappropriate skills and tactics.

The answer to the question "What is intentional violation of the constitutive rules of sport?" is now clear. It is deliberately performing an action which is contradictory to the positively constitutive skills and tactics of the sport, to the prelusory goal of the sport and/or to the proscriptions in the constitutive rules of the sport. Because these three elements, along with the zone of consistency test, are necessary to help assure that the test facing all participants is the same and therefore that the contest exists, the rules must be obeyed. That is what following the rules really means. The possibility for a good sports contest is reduced drastically if all participants do not try to follow the rules in these ways. A fair outcome of any sports contest is basically dependent upon obedience to the rules.

> The outcome of the game will always be just, or at least not unjust, provided internal and external rules, whether formal or informal, are followed.... No one can guarantee that the best team shall win; all that can be guaranteed on any particular occasion is that the outcome shall not be unjust.... Once the rules of games are established as definite and just social aims, parties to the games are free to pursue their own good within the limits of arrangements.[22]

The rules of NCAA men's intercollegiate basketball include proscriptions against holding, blocking, tripping, and pushing and specified penalties for intentional violation of these proscriptions. These proscriptions and their penalties are in the rules so that such actions do not become skills of contesting. The spirit of such rules is that such intentional fouls are not part of the officially agreed-upon skills and tactics of basketball. Therefore, such intentional rules violations are wrong because, in principle, they are contrary to what following the rules must mean for the good sports contest. This in-principle conclusion does not consider whether the prescribed penalties for intentional fouls are the correct penalties; that is a practical problem. The problem of the correct penalty presupposes the in-principle conclusion that intentional fouls are not part of the positively constituted skills and tactics of basketball.

Advocates of intentional rules violations under certain contest circumstances might argue that all participants have equal access to intentional violations as tactical use of the rules. Such an argument fails for two reasons. First, not all participants, for instance in basketball, have the same attitude toward deliberately holding an opponent in order to force free throws as they all have toward the legitimacy of passing, dribbling, or shooting the ball. Some participants think it is alright but others do not. Yet all participants think it is alright to pass, dribble, and shoot. Second, if the participants always had the same attitude that intentional violations were alright, a basketball contest, for example, would become other than what the constitutive rules design it to be. It would become, in addition to a contest of throwing, dribbling, and rolling the ball, a contest in holding, tripping, charging, and so on. This latter change in the very nature of basketball's constitutive skills and tactics becomes basketball only when such actions become part of the positively constitutive skills and tactics of basketball—rather than part of the proscriptions of basketball. Until such a change takes place, intentional actions that are proscribed in the rules are not legitimate tactical use of the rules. These actions amount to not playing the game because they are not following the rules.

The reasoning for intentional rules violations cannot stand critical examination precisely because it only supports self-interested intended ends, that is, intentional violation of the rules which gains an advantage otherwise unattainable even though a penalty is invoked. Such reasoning cannot embody the substance of the moral point of view: meant for everybody and for the good of everyone alike.

## THE PROBLEM OF INTENTIONAL RULES VIOLATIONS, CONSTITUTIVE RULES, AND THE GOOD SPORTS CONTEST

The position taken against intentional rules violation causes some very difficult problems which must be recognized. First, it implies that intentional rules violation is always inappropriate. That is not so, for it is possible that an intentional rules violation may be performed in order to test the violated rule itself. That is, a participant may violate a rule, not to get away with it or even to gain some tactical advantage, but to challenge the justness of the rule through legal actions. Suppose, for instance, that a rule required a contestant to act in a certain circumstance to increase the possibility of injury to an opponent in a way not necessary to the sport. In such a case, intentional violation of a rule would be the right thing to do because of an overriding concern. Intentional rule violation of this sort is similar, in principle, to an act of deliberate civil disobedience done to initiate legal action and to force debate of the rule itself. Obviously, acts performed with such intended ends cannot and ought not to be prohibited. To do so would leave no recourse, other than revolution, to sports participants who have an unjust rule imposed upon them, perhaps by institutionalized sport governed by unjust agents.

The second kind of problem created by the position against intentional rules violation can be illustrated by a situation in basketball. Suppose Team A is ahead of Team B by a score of 54-53 in the last 2 minutes of a game and that Team A has possession of the ball. What is Team B to do if Team A successfully maintains possession of the ball while the clock ticks away all opportunity for Team B to gain possession and a chance to win the game? At least five basic options appear.

1. Pursue the offensive players vigorously and try to gain possession of the ball legally without fouling.
2. Pursue the offensive players vigorously and try to gain a held ball situation.

3. Stay away from the offensive players in the hope that one will make an error and turn the ball over.

4. Pursue the offensive players vigorously and try to gain possession of the ball legally, but not exercising great care against fouling although not fouling intentionally.

5. Pursue the offensive players vigorously and foul one of them intentionally by holding to create a free throw situation and the possibility of gaining possession of the ball.

Option 3 is to be rejected because it is an irrational expectancy, usually, that the other team will err easily when not being pursued and because Team B can be penalized under NCAA rules by a technical foul for lack of sufficient action. Option 5 is to be rejected because of the position against intentional fouling. Options 1, 2, and 4 appear to be acceptable because they all follow the letter and spirit of the rules and have some rational expectancy of success without penalty.

The situation described above illustrates a practical problem in basketball and its rules. Under certain circumstances a team may promote its interest by acting in a way that legally violates the spirit of the game. If the rules make it possible and practical to violate them intentionally, then they reduce the possibility of keeping the contest one of the positively prescribed skills and tactics. The rules in U.S. men's intercollegiate basketball allow a team, ahead in the closing minutes, to maintain possession of the ball without really making serious effort to score field goals. It is one rational way for the ahead team to try to maintain or to increase its lead, by forcing the defensive team to foul them intentionally and thus score by means of free throws. NCAA rules attempt to reduce this by requiring certain actions of the offensive team when pursued by the defensive team. To date it appears that these rules are not effective because the offensive teams still find it possible and practical to stall. That practical, rational stalling by the offensive team makes it practical and rational for the behind defensive team to foul intentionally. The practical problem for basketball, and all sports, is to so constitute the rules that the sport becomes clearly a contest in the positively constituted skills and tactics of the game. Doing that becomes the practical outcome of the principle that intentional rules violations done to attain an advantage but with the expectancy and imposition of a penalty are contrary to the good sports contest.

Whether all sports can eliminate, or at least reduce to a minimum, intentional rules violations that are rational and practical cannot yet be answered. It may be that some sports are inherently imperfect in this way. However, it is also possible that the right combination of prescriptions, proscriptions, and penalties can be congruent with the principle of keeping the contest one of the positively constituted skills and tactics of the sport. It may be that if rules makers focus on that principle, rather than upon what kind of basketball will attract more paying spectators, they would encourage more good sports contests. It may also be that this kind of good sports contest could be more appealing to spectators.

## NOTES

[1] Bernard Suits, "The Elements of Sport," in *The Philosophy of Sport*, ed. Robert G. Osterhoudt (Springfield, IL: C.C. Thomas, 1973), p. 50.

[2] Ibid., pp. 51-52.

[3] William J. Morgan, "An Analysis of the Sartrean Ethic of Ambiguity as the Moral Ground for the Conduct of Sport," *Journal of the Philosophy of Sport* II (September 1976), p. 90.

[4] Anthony Ralls, "The Game of Life," *The Philosophical Quarterly* 16 (January 1966), p. 26.

[5] Robert G. Osterhoudt, "In Praise of Harmony: The Kantian Imperative and Hegelian Sittlichkeit as the Principle and Substance of Moral Conduct in Sport," *Journal of the Philosophy of Sport* III (September 1976), pp. 67-68.

[6] Morgan, "Analysis of the Sartrean Ethic," p. 90.

[7] Ibid., p. 90.

[8] Eleanor Metheny, *Movement and Meaning* (New York: McGraw-Hill, 1968), p. 63.

[9] Warren P. Fraleigh, "The Moving-'I' " in *The Philosophy of Sport*, ed. Robert G. Osterhoudt (Springfield, IL: C.C. Thomas, 1973), p. 114.

[10] Scott Kretchmar, "Ontological Possibilities: Sport as Play," in *The Philosophy of Sport*, ed. Robert G. Osterhoudt (Springfield, IL: C.C. Thomas, 1973), p. 69.

[11] Kathleen M. Pearson, "Deception, Sportsmanship, and Ethics," *Quest* XIX (January 1973) p. 117.

[12] Edwin J. Delattre, "Some Reflections on Success and Failure in Competitive Athletics," *Journal of the Philosophy of Sport* II (September 1975), p. 136.

[13] Ibid., p. 136.

[14] Pearson, "Deception, Sportsmanship, and Ethics," p. 117.

[15] Ibid., p. 118.

[16] Suits, "Elements of Sport," p. 52.

[17] Delattre, "Reflections on Success and Failure," p. 137.

[18] Recent court cases in the United States and Canada appear to be moving toward the distinction that intentional injury is not permissible but that, in such rough sports, intimidation is to be expected.

[19] For several relevant distinctions between sport and war, see Paul Weiss, *Sport: A Philosophic Inquiry* (Carbondale, IL: Southern Illinois University Press, 1969), pp. 177-183.

[20]Edward S. Steitz, ed., *The Official National Collegiate Athletic Association Basketball Rules 1978* (Shawnee Mission, KS: National Collegiate Athletic Association, 1974), p. BR-9.

[21]The prelusory goal of a sport must not be confused with the purpose of the sports contest. If any confusion exists, the reader is referred to the section on the purpose of the sports contest in Chapter 3.

[22]Francis W. Keenan, "Justice and Sport," *Journal of the Philosophy of Sport* II (September 1975), p. 116.

# Chapter Six

# Relationships
# of Opponents

The fourth element of the good sports contest that needs discussion is the kind and quality of relationships between opponents. As with the elements discussed so far, a certain kind of relationship is normative and provides another enabling condition from which the good sports contest may grow. But its existence does not guarantee the good sports contest.

The understanding of the normative relationships between opponents requires the clarification and comparison of alternatives, two of which will be explained here. One alternative is labeled "opponent as obstacle" and the other is "opponent as facilitator."

## OPPONENT AS OBSTACLE

Opponent as obstacle is a phrase that expresses a rather common view of the relationships of opponents. Consistent with this view are certain conceptions of competition and of excellence.

*Competition.* Competition here is understood as "an attempt (according to agreed upon rules) to get or to keep any valuable thing either to the exclusion of others or in greater measure than others."[1] This understanding of competition is compatible with a view of the opponent as the agent who stands between me and my goal and is, thus, an obstacle. The opponent as obstacle hinders me from my goal, in basketball for example, of scoring points.[2] Seen in this way, the opponent as the hindrance from my goal, "is at once feared and needed." The hindrance is needed because scoring points requires opposition while shooting baskets does not. Yet hindrance is feared because it threatens my success in scoring points.[3] The view of the opponent as the obstacle in the way of my competitive desire "to get or to keep any valuable thing either to the exclusion of others or in greater measure than others" requires me to eliminate the obstacle by defeating my opponent. If only one agent can have that which two agents are pursuing, then one must eliminate the other by conquest.

*Excellence.*    Excellence here is understood as "excellence in an ever-expanding field until 'to excel' truly means to stand alone—at the top. Such a spirit craves a recognizable and recognized superiority over all."[4] This idea applies to the individual or to a team. It signifies that very few individuals or teams can participate in excellence and that it is logically impossible for more than a few to be excellent. Excellence in sport, then, is an inherently and numerically exclusive concept.

In sport, the measure of excellence is the winning of contests. Thus, only those individuals or teams who win all or most of their contests can be called excellent. Accordingly, an excellent performance is identified by comparing the difference between the winning score and the losing score. An excellent performance means vanquishing or "annihilating" the opponent, a "wipe-out," or "winning big."

This idea of excellence is essentially a quantitative concept. Only a few can be excellent, the measure being the number of wins and amount of difference in scores. In accord with the concept of competition described, the opponent is viewed as the obstacle in the path of the person who would be excellent. Indeed, the opponent is an obstacle to be dominated, overwhelmed, conquered. Finally, since the ideas of competition and excellence here both embrace a quantitative distinction and exclusivity, then victory in the sports contest means defeating the opponent—as differentiated from winning the contest.

## OPPONENT AS FACILITATOR

Opponent as facilitator expresses a less obvious view of the relationships of opponents. This view of the opponent is consistent with different conceptions of competition and of excellence.

*Competition.*    Competition here is understood as an attempt to perform the same skillful actions better than opponents in order to express and develop competence. Such a concept of competition views the opponents as the mutually necessary condition for expression and development. Competition is viewed by such opponents "as an activity *with* another rather than against him."[5] The hindrance provided by opponents is a hindrance for mutual expression,[6] which allows them to express and develop competence, is valued for itself, and must be preserved because it is essential to continued expression.[7] This view of competition binds opponents together as mutual facilitators and enablers.[8] If one agent can have what he/she is pursuing only by pursuing it with another agent, then each must sustain the other.

*Excellence.* Excellence here is a qualitative concept concerned primarily with how well the contest is played. Well played contests are seen and felt qualitatively as an aesthetic event. As Kaelin[9] observes,

> The game itself considered as an aesthetic object is perceived as a tense experience in which pressure is built up from moment to moment sustained through continuous opposition, until the climax of victory or defeat. The closer this climax occurs to the end of the game, the stronger is our feeling of its qualitative uniqueness. Sudden death play-offs and perhaps extra-inning games, are as close as a sport may come to achieving this aesthetic ideal.

As a qualitative concept, excellence in the sports contest can result only from the quality of play of all opponents — excellence is not good play by only one opponent. Sports participants who would produce the qualitative excellence of the well played game are dependent upon each other and are, again, one anothers' facilitators. The measure of excellence here is the experience of the well played game by those who perceive it, both participants and spectators. The sports contest as an aesthetic event is known intuitively and qualitatively because it happens — not because of some preexistent quantitative measure.

This conception of excellence does not impose any restriction upon how many participants may achieve it. Each contest begins with the potential of being a well played contest by all participants and, thus, the potential of producing the aesthetic object for the participants. Excellence is available in principle to all participants even though excellent, well played contests do not always, or often, occur. Since such excellence is produced by all participants, the meaning of winning reflects the mutuality of opponents as facilitators. Winning means winning the contest — that produced by all — not defeating an opponent.

## THE NORMATIVE CONCEPT
## OF THE RELATIONSHIPS OF OPPONENTS

The normative concept of the relationships of opponents results from examining the concepts of the opponent as obstacle and as facilitator in terms of their probable consequences and the subsequent evaluation of those consequences. Following are three probable consequences of the view of opponent as obstacle.

The atmosphere between opponents is more likely to be hostile because each views the other as a negative barrier (hindrance from) in achieving an immediate goal (scoring points) or achieving a long-range goal (excellence). The barrier here is primarily that which prevents each from achieving his/her desires.

Opponents are more likely to be viewed as means only to the achievement of goals. The participants view one another as necessary obstacles; they do not view the sports contest as a means of mutual satisfaction but in terms of the goals of the individual alone. Each opponent does not care about the satisfaction of the other and will therefore more likely see that other as only a means to his/her own satisfaction.

Excellence in sport will necessarily be discriminatory, as it can be achieved only by a very few participants. Further, excellence can be achieved only by those who win most of the time and by a large point margin in any one contest. Accordingly, excellence in sport is available only to those who perform at a very high level of skill, which means the great mass of lower-skilled performers are eliminated from excellence.

Of the probable consequences of the view of opponent as facilitator, the first is that the atmosphere between opponents is more likely to be one of mutual respect because of the recognition of mutual interdependence.

A second consequence is that opponents are more likely to be viewed as both means and ends. Each recognizes that the opponent is a necessary hindrance for his/her own satisfaction and vice versa. Each views the other as a positive barrier (hindrance for) in achieving an immediate goal (scoring points) or in achieving a long-range goal that can be consummated only by the opponents together (excellence). The barrier here is what allows both to achieve their desires together.

A third is that excellence in sport will occur infrequently but not in a necessarily quantitatively limited manner. Because well played games are infrequent, excellence will still be a discriminatory term, useful in describing only a few of many contests. Furthermore, well played contests would be available in principle to all who possess some reasonable modicum of the constitutive skills and tactics of the sport.[10] Accordingly, the possibility of excellence in sport would be available to a larger number of participants.

The views of opponent as obstacle and as facilitator each have positive value when seen from the framework of a particular cultural context. There is neither a single, worldwide definition of competition nor one conception of its cultural function and value. Sadler[11] has examined competition cross-culturally by using the constants of "views of time, space, normative activity, interpersonal and social relations, and life goals or aspired final states." Using these constants, Sadler characterizes the cultural constellation he labels the "doing" culture. The important time is in the future, while space is to be mastered. Valued activity achieves results. The self is conceived as individualistic while good relationships between humans are viewed as enhancing greater efficiency. The goal of life is success and the culture is practical, active, and productive. In the doing culture as characterized, "one competes to accomplish results which may be extrinsic to the actual competitive process. The aim of competition in this context is logically to excel."[12]

Thus, in the context of the doing culture, competing effectively is valuable in achieving success. Also, the view of opponent as obstacle in the doing culture carries the idea of competition as possessing some valuable thing to the exclusion of or in greater amount than the other. This is praised as a strong motivation. Such strong motivation toward a singular excellence, in Keating's words, "supplies us with splendid demonstrations of human excellence."[13]

Using the same constants, Sadler characterizes the "becoming" culture. The present is the important time, space is an area to develop potentialities, and the proper relation to nature is cooperative. Time and space both present opportunity for achievement and failure. Reality is driven by the realization of potential while humans are the highest expression of that reality and self-development is the proper standard of personal life. In interpersonal and social relations equality is stressed over hierarchy. Cooperative activity is valued over obedience to authority. The goal of life is fullest actualization, human and nature; accordingly, individuals and social groups should strive to achieve excellence.[14]

The view of opponent as facilitator seems compatible with this characterization of the becoming culture. For as Sadler indicates, "In a becoming orientation, one normally competes with another to develop human potential and make it manifest. Competition is thus an intrinsic part of the actualization of self and the other person. It is governed by those goals."[15] The value of mutual expression and development is congruent with the value of the excellence of the well played contest, that which reaches the aesthetic ideal through the mutual efforts of the opponents.

In opponent as obstacle and opponent as facilitator we have different, and in some respects contradictory, conceptions of excellence and competition within differing cultural contexts. How do we determine which conceptions are better? How do we decide whether seeing the opponent as obstacle or as facilitator is normative for the good sports contest? Let us now examine these conceptions in the light of the substance of the moral point of view, that is, meant for everybody and for the good of everyone alike.

We can use the analogy of a human activity in which two different ideas of oppositional relationship (e.g., roughly speaking, competition) and excellence are evident. The human activity used will be sexual intercourse because it can exemplify vividly the differences in relationships of human participants. Though the sports contest and human sexual intercourse are certainly not identical, the important point is that they can be reasonably similar in their views of the opponent (partner) as obstacle and the opponent (partner) as facilitator.

The act of sexual intercourse is sometimes viewed as a conquest of one person by another person. In this case the aggressive seeker of intercourse roams about looking for a sex object to seduce. The partner in such seduction is viewed as an object, a something, to be used for the seeker's sexual satisfaction. In such intercourse, there is opposition between the partners in the friction between the sexual organs. A person who succeeds in seducing a partner into such intercourse is said, interestingly, to have "scored." The person who succeeds in scoring is sometimes called a "stud," or whatever the female version is of the same, and excellence is the quantity of "scores." Although the partner is needed to score, the aggressive stud views the partner as a something to be overcome by seduction, an obstacle. The sexual activity is a conquest by subjugating the partner for the pleasure of the aggressor. Inasmuch as the aggressor will find other sex objects to seduce, there is little regard for the welfare of the any one seduced person.

Sexual intercourse is also viewed as a mutual activity that partners engage in with mutual regard for one another, each concerned for the mutual satisfaction of the act. The partners stimulate each other intentionally so that the actions and reactions of stimulation develop a "sweet tension." This sweet tension is experienced as ambivalent in that the partners enjoy the tension as tension (the continuously mounting stimulation), yet move continually and eagerly toward its release through orgasm. Both want it, simultaneously, to continue to increase and to be resolved by orgasm. The partners oppose each other through the actions and reactions of lovemaking and the hindrance for satisfaction created by friction of the sexual organs. The partners, who are now lovers, are coupled together and view each other as positive facilitators who must be sustained. Sexual intercourse is viewed as a mutual activity wherein the expression and development of regard, affection, and tenderness occur. Excellence in sexual intercourse occurs when the partners, through mutual and continuous stimulation, both arrive at orgasm close to the same time and the success of the act is incomplete without mutual satisfaction.

These rough analogues on the relationships of "opponents" in the sports contest and in sexual intercourse provide the relevant contrast required. Choosing between such views on the relationships of opponents is made by a judgment regarding the better normative relationships of persons.

What we have here as well, then, it seems, is the term of too radically discrete manners of conceiving man, the social substance, and the common good — two combinations which are so clearly and distinctly different as to be incompatible. That is, the principles supporting these two codes of moral conduct are so incongruent as to oppose one another. It is not a mere difference in degree, but one of a substantial sort.[16]

Such a judgment regarding normative relationships of opponents in the sports contest is a judgment about two different kinds of worlds in terms of meant for everybody and for the good of everyone alike.

The concepts of the opponent as obstacle and as facilitator can each be meant for everybody, because it is logically possible that everybody can regard the opponent as an obstacle or as a facilitator. There is no logical reason to negate either possibility. Now, which way is for the good of everyone alike?

Regarding the opponent as facilitator appears to be more for the good of everyone alike for several reasons. First, the idea of hindrance is fully retained in the concept of opponent as facilitator. The opponent is viewed as a necessary hindrance, but the negative idea of hindrance *from* the goal becomes hindrance for mutual pursuit of the goal. Positive regard for the opponent as the cooperative agent fully recognizes the opposition necessary but transforms that opposition into a recognized and necessary condition to sustain.

Second, quantitative excellence will occur within a qualitative framework. This means very few individuals or teams in each sport will win all or most of their contests even though all participants try to win as a necessary end in achieving the well played contest. Paradoxically, the participants will intend the end of trying to win primarily because it is essential to producing the well played contest and it will produce, secondarily, those few individuals and teams who win all or most of their contests. Thus, both the qualitative excellence of the well played contest and the quantitative excellence of the singularly outstanding individual or team can come from the mutual, positive endeavor of all participants. In short, the excellence sought is constructive for all without eliminating, in principle, all from the possibility of excellence of one kind. At the same time, this constructive structure "becomes a means by which humans extend the boundaries of achievement by thrusting a *superman* into history. This *superman* (the record achiever) is the best produced by many humans striving mutually for the fulfillment of the well-played game."[17] All is available, potentially, while nothing is lost except a quantitative overemphasis which reduces the qualitative emphasis to an incidental concern.

Third, nothing in the concept of opponent as facilitator prevents each participant from attempting and achieving at his/her qualitative best.

> The ingredients of such a well-played and well-contested game are; (1) contestants who are well-matched in terms of performance, skills and physical condition, (2) interesting and demanding strategic situations in conjunction with comparable strategic abilities among the participants, and (3) an outcome which is in doubt until the final moments of the event. In combination, these elements show that a well-played, well-contested event is the product of the process of mutual facilitation by the participants. In their immediate pursuit of scoring or winning of the event, the participants are actually engaging in the cooperative achievement of the well-played and well-contested event. Each point in the event is a mini-achievement to which all the participants contribute. The participants each utilize the very best of their abilities, conditioning, and strategy. In so doing, they mutually aid each other in the cooperative achievement.

> If one party in the athletic event increases the quality of his performance, his startegy [sic], and his conditioning, he provides a basic condition for the completion and fulfillment of the other. That is, each qualitative increase is the condition whereby a corresponding qualitative increase is evoked in order for the participants to achieve the well-played, well-contested event. *Intrinsic in the structure of the well-played event is this back-and-forth facilitation of fulfillment.*[18]

The well contested sports contest develops a sweet tension in a way similar to an act of sexual intercourse in which the lovers stimulate one another into a tension state which seeks its own continuation simultaneously with seeking its own resolution in orgasm. The badminton contest between John and Bob described earlier can illustrate this idea. In it, most of the points played may be characterized as a back-and-forth mutual stimulation. Each contestant hits the shuttle each time in such a way that he stimulates the other to move to a distant position on the court so that he must exercise his skills fully and perform a shot which will then stimulate his opponent to move to a distant position and use all of his powers. Each shot demands an effective response and a reciprocal demand. In the process of playing a point, the continuous action and demand increases the tension with each shot. This tension seeks its own resolution by each player trying to win the point, yet at the same time each player relishes the challenge of each shot in a way where there is positive appreciation of the continuation of the actions. Thus, a sweet tension occurs which seeks both continuation by further action and resolution by winning a point. In the badminton contest, this sweet tension occurred also when, at the final stages, a "set" game going beyond the normal winning point total was played. If John and Bob had played a complete match of three full games, with John winning the first game and Bob winning the second game in a set game, and if the third game was completed as a set game also, then the sweet tension would be magnified and its resolution delayed until the last point of the whole match.

This is the kind of contest that nearly all sports participants prefer, and the completion of such contests becomes, to participants and spectators alike, a very special and long-remembered event. Such events are special precisely because they are qualitatively unique, achieved by the mutual "artistry" of all participants contributing to the production of the aesthetic ideal. Tense contests which create such sweet tension occur in all sports. Recent examples include the sixth game of the baseball World Series between Boston & Cincinnatti, the British Open Golf Tournament final round between Jack Nicklaus and Tom Watson in 1977, and several recent final men's matches in the Wimbledon.

Finally, regarding the opponent as facilitator helps to make the sports contest a human event wherein the mutal respect and regard of opponents is evident. Opponents fully appreciate the good plays of one another, both because they are good plays and because such good plays are what they want to test their own abilities. A participant dislikes his/her own poor plays both because they do not reflect his/her true ability and do not present the challenge an opponent desires.

In summary, regarding the opponent as facilitator is normative for the good sports contest because it provides the maximum positive achievements for everyone in conjunction with an atmosphere of mutual respect and regard by all participants.[19] This is for the good of everyone alike and stands in sharp contrast to an atmosphere in which successful achievement is attained at the expense of others and the opponent is regarded with suspicion and sometimes even with hate.

## NOTES

[1] James W. Keating, "The Ethics of Competition and its Relation to Some Moral Problems in Athletics," in *The Philosophy of Sport*, ed. Robert G. Osterhoudt (Springfield, IL: C.C. Thomas, 1973), p. 159.

[2] Scott Kretchmar, "Ontological Possibilities: Sport as Play," in *The Philosophy of Sport*, ed. Robert G. Osterhoudt (Springfield, IL: C.C. Thomas, 1973), p. 73.

[3] Ibid., p. 74

[4] James W. Keating, "Winning in Sport and Athletics," *Thought* 38 (Summer 1963), p. 209.

[5] William A. Sadler, Jr. "A Contextual Approach to an Understanding of Competition: A Response to Keating's Philosophy of Athletics," in *The Philosophy of Sport*, ed. Robert G. Osterhoudt (Springfield, IL: C.C. Thomas, 1973), p. 184.

[6] Kretchmar, "Ontological Possibilities," pp. 74-75.

[7] Ibid., p. 74.

[8] Warren P. Fraleigh "The Moving 'I'," in *The Philosophy of Sport*, ed. Robert G. Osterhoudt (Springfield, IL: C.C. Thomas, 1973), p. 126.

[9] E. F. Kaelin, "The Well-Played Game: Notes Toward an Aesthetics of Sport," *Quest* X (May 1968), p. 25.

[10]Setting a clear level of skill essential for the well played contest is difficult. Obviously, some level of skill is necessary just to have the contest! It is clear that skill of the world-class level is not required and that some level of skill proficiency beyond that of a novice is required.

[11]Sadler, "Contextual Approach," p. 181

[12]Ibid., pp. 184-185.

[13]Keating, "Winning in Sport and Athletics," p. 207.

[14]Sadler, "Contextual Approach," pp. 182-183.

[15]Ibid., p. 185.

[16]Robert G. Osterhoudt, "On Keating on the Competitive Motif in Athletics and Playful Activity," in *The Philosophy of Sport*, ed. Robert G. Osterhoudt (Springfield, IL: C.C. Thomas, 1973), pp. 196-197.

[17]Warren P. Fraleigh, "On Weiss on Records and on the Significance of Athletic Records," in *The Philosophy of Sport*, ed. Robert G. Osterhoudt (Springfield, IL: C.C. Thomas, 1973), p. 38.

[18]Ibid., p. 37.

[19]Since this chapter was written, Professor Drew Hyland has published an illuminating analysis, to which the reader is referred: Drew A. Hyland, "Competition and Friendship," *Journal of the Philosophy of Sport* V (Fall 1978), pp. 27-37.

# Chapter Seven

# Values
# and the Sports Contest

The function of this chapter is to characterize what the good sports contest is in terms of value(s). To do this it is necessary (a) to briefly explore possible values and (b) to identify which value fulfills the substantive characteristics of meant for everybody and for the good of everyone alike. Thus we will isolate the value that should have priority for sports contestants. Knowing the priority among diverse values allows sports participants to intend personal ends that are more likely to achieve the priority value.

The sports contest is valued in a variety of ways. For instance, it has been said that the battle of Waterloo was won on the playing fields of Eton. This statement asserts that the sports contest is valued in terms of preparation for war, evaluated from the military point of view. Or it is said that the sports contest is valued in developing physical fitness; thus, it is evaluated from the point of view of health. As one more example, the sports contest is valued for producing monetary profit and therefore is evaluated from the economic point of view. Specified ways of looking at something supply the appropriate standards against which the features of that thing are evaluated to ascertain if it is a good thing.[1]

Accordingly, if we look at the sports contest from an economic point of view and find that it is a marketable commodity, then we may evaluate the sports contest as being good because it possesses a feature that is necessary for economic profit. If we look at the sports contest from a health point of view and find that it has the feature of physiological demand, we may evaluate it as a good contest because it possesses a feature relevant to physical fitness which is, in turn, a facet of positive health status. If we look at the sports contest from a military point of view, and it contains the qualities of aggressiveness, perseverance, and tactical and strategic decision making, we may evaluate the sports contest as being good because it possesses features important in military success.

These examples indicate that valuing something is the outcome of our positive attitude toward that thing which properly comes from a process of evaluating it according to appropriate standards. *"Evaluating, then, constitutes the rational ground for valuing."*[2] To complete an evaluation we must adopt a point of view so that we know what kinds of standards must be used. As our examples here show, the sports contest can be called the good sports contest from the point of view of health, of economics, of military, and other points of view as well.

## VALUES OF THE SPORTS CONTEST – OBJECTIVELY RELATIVE

The values of the sports contest are objectively relative; they are relational properties that emerge in the sports contest, in Beck's words "that is judged to be valuable, in its relationship to the person who has an interest in it or appreciates it."[3] Thus, the sports contest has values that "have objective bases and conditions independent of the person."[4] But "human need or interest is a necessary condition for anything to have value."[5] To say that the sports contest is good, from any point of view, means it has specifiable conditions that become values as experienced by persons. So, the value of the sports contest emerges both from the objective pole of experience, the conditions in the sports contest by its nature, and the subjective pole of experience, the person(s) engaging in the sports contest.

This theory of value helps us to understand why different persons see the value of the sports contest differently, since they may have different interests and, accordingly, be appreciative of differing values of the contest. Also, we can understand that if two or more persons use the same point of view it is more likely they can mutually evaluate the contest as good, bad, or neutral since the objective conditions are likely to be similar under the same point of view. For instance, if several persons evaluate the relative economic good of sports in the United States, they would likely agree that football or baseball is better from the economic standpoint than rugby or cricket. This economic evaluation would be influenced markedly by such objective conditions as availability of appropriate facilities and size, sophistication, and background of potential audience. These conditions would become value properties of football and baseball when examined with economic interests in mind in the United States. The same objective conditions would become value properties of rugby and cricket in England.

## OBJECTIVE FEATURES
## OF THE MORAL POINT OF VIEW

The moral point of view establishes specifiable objective features that operate as standards for evaluating the sports contest from the moral point of view. In ways similar to the evaluations from the economic, military, or health points of view, evaluations may also be made from the moral point of view. What are those values? Again, they are those which are meant for everybody and are for the good of everyone alike.

We must isolate a kind of value which has guaranteed accessibility to those who participate in the sports contest. We are seeking to identify here the kind of value that is necessarily available because of the nature of the sports contest rather than a value that results, primarily, from the different kind of interests that various participants bring to the contest. Different individuals may evaluate the quality of a sports contest from different points of view; one may say it is a good contest from the economic point of view, another may say it is poor from the health point of view, and a third may say it is neutral from the military point of view. Yet each of these evaluations of the same contest can be accurate from these different points of view. We need to identify here the kind of value that is a *necessary* consequence of participation in the sports contest. This kind of value is an objective value property of the sports contest, regardless of each participant's point of view, and thus is necessarily for everybody. Also, this value must be good in the same way and therefore necessarily for the good of everyone alike.

## INHERENT VALUE
## AND THE GOOD SPORTS CONTEST

The inherent value of something "is the capacity of an object, event, situation, process, or any kind of thing *other than* a quality of our own experience to produce in us when we respond to it...a quality of experience which has intrinsic value."[6] What is this capacity of the sports contest? If the inherent value of the sports contest can be identified, we will have found that value which is necessarily available to all who participate. Identifying this value will separate the value of the sports contest as contest from other values for which the sports contest may be used by different participants. The inherent value of the sports contest is that shared by participants, in common, because of what the sports contest itself is.

The inherent value of the sports contest is its capacity, its objective value property, to produce in the participants a quality of experience that they evaluate as good in itself. Inherent value and intrinsic value are related but different. Inherent value is the objective property of the sports contest; intrinsic value is the contest's quality of experience which participants evaluate as good in itself. The intrinsic value of anything, says Taylor, "is nonderivative."[7] According to Rescher, "The benefit of realizing a value designated in this manner is seen to reside primarily in this realization of itself and for itself."[8] What, then, is the sports contest's capacity to produce a quality of experience for the participants which is intrinsically good? To answer this we must identify a value that is inherent in the sports contest as sports contest, differentiate this inherent value in good, bad, and neutral sports contests, and indicate how this inherent value produces in the participants a quality of experience which is intrinsically good.

The value inherent in the nature of the sports contest as contest may be identified by examining, briefly, what the sports contest is, as stated in Chapter 3:

> A sports contest is a voluntary, agreed upon, human event in which one or more human participants opposes at least one human other to seek the mutual appraisal of the relative abilities of all participants to move mass in space and time by utilizing bodily moves which exhibit developed motor skills, physiological and psychological endurance and socially approved tactics and strategy.

From this definition it is inferred, as also stated in Chapter 3, that:

> The purpose of the sports contest is to provide equal opportunity for mutual contesting of the relative abilities of the participants to move mass in space and time within the confines prescribed by an agreed-upon set of rules.

If we examine these statements together, we find a clear value outcome that is necessarily accessible to all participants. The necessitated value consequence for participants in the sports contest is knowledge of relative abilities to move mass in space and time as prescribed by the rules. Knowledge of a participant's relative ability to move mass in space and time is guaranteed in the sports contest because it is the objective nature of the sports contest to produce such result. Further, this guaranteed result is encapsulated in the contest score—the summary statement of the participants' relative abilities. To state that the inherent value of the sports contest as sports contest is knowledge of relative ability does not of itself mean that all participants will evaluate that inherent value as the most important one to each of them. It means that the inherent value is guaranteed, necessarily, to all participants regardless of each one's personal value priorities. When compared to other values, the priority of the inherent value of the sports contest is a matter for evaluation according to the appropriate standards of a point of view. Accordingly, the relative priority of knowledge of relative ability to move mass in space and time will be evaluated, later, in relation to the appropriate standards of the moral point of view.

To differentiate this inherent value as it is realized in the good sports contest, in contrast to the bad and the neutral sports contests, we must contrast the differences in the knowledge of relative abilities to move mass in space and time in these three categories of contests. We can do this by clarifying the characteristics of good, bad, and neutral sports contests and by then examining their impact on the completeness and the accuracy of the knowledge of relative ability to move mass in space and time.

The characteristics of the good sports contest are that the opponents are of relatively equal ability as determined by previous performance, that the opponents play well in the contest as detailed in Chapter 4, that the contest is completed and designates a winner and a loser in the sense previously discussed, that the rules are adhered to by all participants, that the personal ends intended by all participants are congruent with or consistent with the purpose of the sports contest, and that opponents relate to one another as facilitators.

When we view all these characteristics together and examine their impact upon the completeness and accuracy of knowledge of relative ability to move mass in space and time, we find that they assure, together, the most comprehensive and nonequivocal knowledge possible of such relative ability. For if opponents of equal ability both play well, they demand from one another the very best performance of which each is capable and, thus, assure that knowledge of the relative ability of each at his/her best is manifest. If the personal intended ends of all participants are congruent or consistent with the purpose of the sports contest (which is to provide equal opportunity) and if all participants adhere to the rules (which assures that they are taking the same test together), then knowledge of relative ability in the same test is guaranteed because each is assured the equal opportunity to do his/her best in the same test. If a winner is determined from among participants who have had equal opportunity to do their best on the same shared test, and all have done so, then the winner and loser designations most accurately and most completely encapsulate nonequivocal knowledge of relative abilities to move mass in space and time.

In asserting that the good sports contest as characterized assures the most accurate and complete knowledge, the claim applies only to those conditions that are under the control of participants. No such claim of assurance can be made for sports contests in which uncontrollable contingencies markedly influence the true evaluation of relative abilities. Examples would be markedly different weather conditions in the same day for early and late golf players, differences in ski slope conditions for early and late contestants, or crucial equipment misfunction such as a broken baseball bat which stifles an important rally or a racquetball which breaks just before a contestant has an easy point winning shot.

The characteristics of the bad sports contest are such that, for one or more reasons, the contest provides either incomplete or inaccurate knowledge of the participants' relative abilities. Like the good sports contest, the bad contest designates a winner and a loser in the sense discussed in Chapter 4. Therefore it provides some summary knowledge of the relative ability to move mass in space and time.

Such knowledge is flawed, however, either in its completeness or accuracy or both because of one or more of the following weaknesses: If any or all participants do not adhere to the rules, then the shared test is not the same and consequently the knowledge of relative ability to perform the same task cannot be accurate. If all participants play well but are not of equal ability, then the knowledge of relative ability is accurate only in terms of whom among unequal opponents is better in that contest—it does not show the relative ability of the winner at his/her best since the loser, being an unequal opponent, is unable to supply the test which demands the best of the winner. If all participants are of equal ability but only one plays well, then the knowledge of relative ability is accurate, again, only in terms of who is better in that particular contest—not in terms of the relative ability of the winner at his/her best since the opponent does not supply the best test. If any or all participants pursue personal intended ends that are inconsistent or incongruent with the purpose of the sports contest, as discussed in Chapter 3, then knowledge of relative abilities is both inaccurate and incomplete. Such personal intended ends involve actions in which a person attempts skills beyond his or her ability or shows greater concern with an external end, such as entertainment, than the end of contesting. Knowledge of relative ability under such a circumstance can be neither accurate nor complete for any of the participants, whether of equal ability or not.

Personal intended ends that are incongruent with the purpose of the sports contest involve actions in which a person is not trying to win but rather is trying to tie the contest because he/she is more concerned with an external end (such as maintaining a national ranking). Again, knowledge of relative ability under such a circumstance can be neither accurate nor complete for any participants, whether of equal ability or not.

Many more possible combinations of these characteristics of the bad sports contest could be examined. But suffice it to say here that the value of knowledge of relative ability is diminished, either in accuracy, completeness, or both, if the participants are of unequal ability, do not play well, do not adhere to the rules, or if they pursue personal intended ends that are inconsistent or incongruent with the purpose of the sports contest. This does not mean that the bad sports contest has no value whatsoever in knowledge of the relative abilities of the participants. Any sports contest has some degree of value in providing such knowledge. Because such knowledge is inherent in the sports contest, the differences in its realization are differences in degree but not in kind.

The neutral sports contest contains all the characteristics of the good sports contest except that it is incomplete because no winner and loser have been determined, as noted in Chapter 4. Although knowledge of the relative abilities of the participants is accurate in that they perform with equal ability, it is incomplete in the sense that the neutral contest does not differentiate between the participants' relative ability and does not arrive at closure. Such tie games, although supplying accurate knowledge, are unsatisfactory precisely because they have not supplied the complete knowledge of relative ability that the participants have set out to gain when they entered the contest. Because they are unsatisfactory, tie games are resolved through such conventions as tie breakers and overtimes so that the contest may be completed.

In accord with its characteristics, the good sports contest provides both the most complete (quantity) and the most accurate (quality) knowledge of the participants' relative abilities to move mass in space and time. The neutral sports contest provides the most accurate but less complete knowledge, whereas the bad sports contest provides either the least accurate and/or the least complete knowledge. All sport contests have the capacity, the inherent value, to provide some such knowledge.

Finally, how does the inherent value of the sports contest produce a quality of experience that is intrinsically good? How does knowledge of the relative ability to move mass in space and time produce a quality of experience for the participants which is valued for itself? The answer is that acquiring the knowledge of such relative ability is what inherently satisfies the free choice all participants make when they engage in the sports contest. Completing the sports contest in itself is satisfying, and this satisfaction is valued for itself. This is because concluding the sports contest closes the knowledge gap inherent in the choice to enter; the contestant has no prior knowledge of his/her relative ability in this particular contest.

To say that knowledge of relative ability to move mass in space and time is satisfying is not to say that the satisfaction is always pleasant. After all, a sports participant may find unpleasant the knowledge that his/her relative ability is poorer than someone else's. Despite the satisfaction of the knowledge gap, a sports participant may find it very unpleasant, for instance, to know that he/she is less able than some despised opponent. This does not deny the intrinsic good of satisfying the knowledge gap. It does indicate that the loser can be satisfied in attaining the knowledge sought without being pleased with the content of the knowledge. Such experience is similar, in principle, to the intrinsically good satisfaction of viewing a well performed tragic drama, yet not finding that experience as pleasant. In short, knowledge does not have to be pleasant to be satisfying in its acquisition.

Saying that knowledge of relative ability to move mass in space and time is deemed intrinsically good does not mean that each participant values such satisfaction over all other values. Certainly each participant will have his/her own value priorities for the sports contest. For instance, if a participant views the sports contest primarily from an economic point of view and it produces little monetary gain, then the sports contest would be evaluated as bad. Nonetheless, the same participant in the same contest can experience the intrinsic good of satisfaction with knowledge of relative ability. The questions of what kinds of values do take priority for each participant, and what values ought to take precedence, cannot be answered without reference to a point of view.

## THE INHERENT VALUE
## OF THE GOOD SPORTS CONTEST
## AND THE MORAL POINT OF VIEW

The inherent value of the good sports contest is that it provides the greatest accuracy in and the most complete knowledge of the relative abilities of all participants to move mass in space and time. But how is this inherent value meant for everybody and for the good of everyone alike?

Accurate and complete knowledge of relative ability is meant for everybody, first, because it is both objectively *there* in the good sports contest and because it is subjectively *in* the intention of all participants by their choice to enter. To say it is objectively there means that the good sports contest has objective properties guaranteeing that the participant(s) who performs the task better will be designated the winner precisely because of better performance. To say that it is subjectively in the intention of all participants by their choosing to enter the sports contest means the choice to enter necessarily signifies the desire, on each person's part, to ascertain relative ability. Further, this desire to ascertain relative ability must be shared by all participants since each one's choice to engage in a contest necessarily entails that desire. No one can engage in a contest without desiring to ascertain relative ability because contesting means seeking knowledge of ability in the same task. The necessary conditions for the realization of the value of accurate and complete knowledge are in the good sports contest necessarily.

That the choice to contest must entail the desire to ascertain relative ability is not to say that is the only desire with which a sports participant may enter the contest. Anyone may enter the contest with a desire to engage in vigorous physical activity, achieve prestige, make money, enjoy oneself, and so on. However, none of these particular desires need be present for all participants although any one of them might be present for all.

Because accurate and complete knowledge is both objectively and subjectively in the good sports contest, it becomes, second, a *realized* value for all who participate. A realized value is meant for everybody in the sense that it becomes actual, rather than potential. Whatever other values may be realized by individual participants, be they economic, military, or health values, the value of accurate and complete knowledge of relative ability must be realized by all participants.

How is this accurate and complete knowledge of relative ability to move mass in space and time for the good of everyone alike? First, it meets the test of reversibility. It is a value which, in desiring it for myself, I can also will it for all other sports participants; and if others would desire it, they can also will it for me. If I ask, "What effect does my desire for such knowledge have on the welfare of my opponent?", the answer is that my desire for such knowledge has positive benefits of the same kind for my opponent. Since complete and accurate knowledge cannot be achieved, either by myself or by my opponent, without effective contesting by us together, my pursuit of this value is essential to the realization of the same value by my opponent. If I ask, "What effect will my opponent's desire for such knowledge have on me?", I find the answer is that his/her desire for complete and accurate knowledge has a positive benefit of the same kind for me.

However, although my desire and my opponent's desire for such knowledge are each supported by our own self-interested reasons,[9] independently, the realization of such knowledge is dependent upon our both desiring it. So each of us can pursue such a value with a self-interested reason, independently. But if we wish to have accurate and complete knowledge of relative ability in a sports contest, we must each pursue it because such knowledge necessarily depends upon the best performance of all participants. This allows us to see when self-interested reason in support of value coalesces with moral reason. If I pursue the value of accurate and complete knowledge for my own benefit, my pursuit is for a self-interested reason. If I pursue this same value for the benefit of my opponent and myself, my pursuit is for a moral reason. For, as Baier said, "doing good is doing for another person what, if he was following (self-interested) reason, he would do for himself."[10] Accordingly, pursuit of the value of accurate and complete knowledge of all participants' relative ability to move mass in space and time is supported by moral reason when all participants independently pursue the value—because it is for the good of everyone alike.

This value is also for the good of everyone alike in the sense that everyone is better off with the realization of such knowledge. This is because the knowledge supplies, for everyone, something that was lacking before the completion of the contest, something that is mutually desired by all when they enter the contest, and something that is intrinsically good, to the maximum degree, for all participants together. As indicated earlier in this chapter, completion of the sports contest closes the knowledge gap that exists for everyone alike and fulfills the common desire of all participants in entering the sports contest. Also, the good sports contest has the inherent value of supplying for all participants the greatest satisfaction, which is experienced as good in itself by the maximum number of participants. This maximal satisfaction results from the knowledge obtained from the good sports contest if it is ranked in comparison with the bad sports contest and the neutral sports contest.

> To rank an object as inherently good on the whole, is to claim two things—that the object has a greater capacity than most objects in the class of comparison to produce intrinsic value...and that the object has the capacity to produce, in a greater number of experiences of a greater number of people, an overbalance of intrinsic goodness.[11]

Because the good sports contest provides accurate and complete knowledge, it ranks the highest in achieving this inherent good of knowledge. Everyone is better off, at the completion of the good sports contest, than he/she would be upon completion of either the neutral or the bad sports contest in terms of the quality of the experience as intrinsically good.


## THE INHERENT VALUE
## OF THE GOOD SPORTS CONTEST
## AS SUPERIOR TO OTHER VALUES

The superiority, from the moral point of view, of accurate and complete knowledge of relative ability to move mass in space and time results from the evaluation that this particular value is guaranteed, in principle, to be meant for everybody and for the good of everyone alike. This assertion needs to be explained.

First, everyone who chooses to participate in the sports contest must desire knowledge of relative ability. For it is the nature of contest to attempt to perform the same test better than someone else.[12] This attempt, when the test is constituted by moving mass in space and time, means the same thing as seeking knowledge of relative abilities to do so.

Although opponents may also seek other values mutually in the sports contest, the inherent value of knowledge of relative ability is the unique value that is guaranteed for all participants, in principle, by the nature of sports contesting itself. For example, two opponents may each choose, independently, to pursue the economic value of monetary profit. They may also choose that value together rather than independently. Nonetheless, this economic value of monetary profit is not guaranteed, in principle, by the nature of contest itself. For while a sports contest cannot help but provide knowledge of relative ability to move mass in space and time, it can occur without providing monetary profit.

This illustrates how the choice to contest necessarily entails pursuit and realization of the sports contest's inherent value, whereas the choice to pursue another type of value cannot, of itself, assure the realization of that other value. Referring again to the economic value of monetary profit, it is possible that one participant may gain this value at the expense of the opponent. If two opponents bet on their own sports contest against one another, like a beer bet on a golf match, the economic value for one is gained at the expense of the other.

Second, the inherent value of knowledge of opponents' relative abilities is probably the only value to be realized solely by the sports contest itself, whereas another value of the sports contest, which seems guaranteed to all participants to some degree, may be available from other activities. For example, consider the health value of physical fitness that is provided in principle and to some degree by the sports contest. This same health value is available from activities other than the sports contest itself. These include activities such as jogging, cultivating a garden, shoveling snow, walking, dancing, or exercising. In contrast, no human activity other than the sports contest provides knowledge of the relative abilities of the participants to move mass in space and time.

Third, individuals may find the sports contest more important for economic, health, or other values, but because these are not inherent values of the sports contest, individuals cannot guarantee either that these values will be realized or that they will be realized for all who participate. So it is quite possible, and appears to happen frequently, that an individual may rank the economic value of monetary profit or the social value of personal prestige higher than the inherent value of knowledge of relative ability. In ranking such values higher in his/her value priorities, the individual is viewing the sports contest from an economic or a social point of view. But in viewing the contest from such points of view, the elements of the sports contest that become values differ from those appropriate to the moral point of view. Because these other points of view do not evaluate the relative goodness of the sports contest by looking for properties which assure that the desired values are meant for everybody and for the good of everyone alike, the resulting evaluation cannot guarantee, in principle, that the desired values are realized for all participants. As a result, an individual may value monetary profit more than the knowledge of relative ability but cannot guarantee that such profit value will be realized for all participants. So such economic value cannot be evaluated to be guaranteed for all participants, and is inferior to the inherent value of the sports contest when it is evaluated from the moral point of view.

Of course, the economic value of monetary profit can be realized for the benefit of all participants in a particular sports contest, such as the profits they gain from some commercialized sports contests. The point is that the sports contest in itself cannot assure the realization of such value precisely because such realization is also dependent upon elements external to the sports contest itself.

We can conclude that the inherent value of the good sports contest is superior to other possible values when the contest is evaluated from the moral point of view. This is true because accurate and complete knowledge of all participants' relative abilities is guaranteed to be realized for all, and solely in the sports contest at that. No other value can be guaranteed to be realized for all participants within the good sports contest itself.

## THE GOOD SPORTS CONTEST
## AND EXTRINSIC VALUE

The good sports contest may be instrumentally effective, also, in leading to extrinsic value. While it has been argued earlier in this chapter that the good sports contest provides a quality of experience that participants feel is intrinsically good, this does not exhaust the value possibilities of the good sports contest. Something that has intrinsic value may also have extrinsic value.[13] That is, the good sports contest may be deemed good for something other than the satisfying quality of the experience itself; being good for something beyond itself is to say that it is instrumental to an extrinsic value.[14] Two examples will illustrate this.

As described in Chapter 4, the good sports contest requires that all participants play well, part of which means using maximal physiological and psychological effort. If we evaluate the sports contest from the health point of view, we can see that it is physiologically demanding, which is useful in achieving the health value of physical fitness. Further, when we look at the relative possibility for physiological demand in the good, the bad, and the neutral sports contests, it is evident that the good and the neutral contests are more useful than the bad sports contest in providing physiological demand. Although in some sports such as golf and bowling an individual's playing well will involve less physiological demand because of fewer strokes or fewer bowled balls, what we are referring to here is the total physiological demand placed upon all participants together in the sports contest. It follows that the good and the neutral sports contests are more effective in achieving the extrinsic health value of physical fitness.

The good sports contest also engages equally competent participants who play well and, in doing so, the game becomes, in Kaelin's words, "a unique context of dramatically significant wholes."[15] It is this dramatic characteristic, or more accurately the promise of it, that invests some prospective sports contest, partially, with greater profit-making economic value. Frequently, sports contests predicted to be tense struggles between participants of great ability attract more ticket buyers. Thus, in general the potential good sports contest has greater economic value than the potential bad sports contest. Consider championship events that attract ticket buyers not only in greater numbers but also who are willing to pay higher prices for the event.

From these two illustrations it can be seen that the good sports contest, so described and evaluated from the moral point of view, can have relatively greater value from the economic and health points of view. Although it is too early to make such a claim here, it is possible that the kind of sports contest deemed good from the moral point of view may have at least some objective characteristics that make it good from other points of view. For instance, the dramatic characteristic of the good sports contest gives it greater economic value. Yet this dramatic characteristic alone cannot guarantee that even a good sports contest will be financially profitable. Indeed, such economic value can be realized only if some external characteristics are present, such as potentially high ticket sales, a large spectating facility, and good advance publicity by the media.

Again, although no universal claim can be made this early, it may be that some characteristics that make the sports contest good from the moral point of view may also make it good from other points of view. There seems no reason to believe that the characteristics are contradictory. That is, the morally good sports contest does not seem to interfere with the sports contest that is good economically, healthwise, socially, politically, or educationally.

## CONCLUSION

Still another characteristic of the good sports contest is that the participants realize that the value of complete and accurate knowledge of relative abilities to move mass in space and time ought to be the most important value. Such a realization, along with the other characteristics of the good sports contest, will help achieve more good sports contests.

## NOTES

[1]Paul W. Taylor, *Normative Discourse* (Englewood Cliffs, NJ: Prentice-Hall, 1961), pp. 6-8.

[2]Ibid., p. 21.

[3]Lewis White Beck, *Philosophic Inquiry* (New York: Prentice-Hall, 1952), p. 213.

[4]Ibid., pp. 213-214.

[5]Ibid., p. 213.

[6]Taylor, *Normative Discourse*, p. 26.

[7]Ibid., pp. 23-24.

[8]Nicholas Rescher, *Introduction to Value Theory* (Englewood Cliffs, NJ: Prentice-Hall, 1969), p. 19.

[9]Kurt Baier, *The Moral Point of View: A Rational Basis for Ethics* (Ithaca & London: Cornell University Press, 1958), p. 202.

[10]Ibid., p. 202.

[11]Taylor, *Normative Discourse*, p. 27.

[12]R. Scott Kretchmar, "From Test to Contest: An Analysis of Two Kinds of Counterpoint in Sport," *Journal of the Philosophy of Sport* II (September 1975), pp. 27-29.

[13]Beck, *Philosophic Inquiry*, p. 192; Taylor, *Normative Discourse*, p. 24.

[14]Beck, *Philosophic Inquiry*, p. 191; Taylor, *Normative Discourse*, p. 28.

[15]E.F. Kaelin, "The Well-Played Game: Notes Toward an Aesthetics of Sport," *Quest* X (May 1968), p. 26.

# PART THREE

# INTRODUCTION
# TO THE GUIDES AND ENDS
# OF RIGHT ACTION
# FOR THE GOOD SPORTS CONTEST

## THE TASK OF SPORTS PARTICIPANTS
## AS RATIONAL CONTRACTORS

Part II has described and explained the good sports contest from the moral point of view and from the point of view of the nature of contest. It is now time to complete the second and third elements in the structure for establishing guides to right action. The second element develops the guides for action that are drawn from the characterization of the good sports contest, while the third element specifies the appropriate general ends of sports actions. As indicated in Chapter 2, this task will employ the concept of rational contractors.

The rational contractors in this study are those who participate directly in the sports contest — primarily athletes, coaches, and athletic trainers, and secondarily contest officials and sports organization officials. The basic task of these rational contractors is to identify, state, and explain the guides for action which, if adhered to, and the general ends of action which, if intended by all sports participants, will realize the conditions necessary for the good sports contest. How the task will be completed needs explanation.

First, the sports participants/rational contractors know and agree that there are five necessary and sufficient conditions for the good sports contest.

1.  The ends intended by the participants are congruent with or consistent with the purpose of the sports contest, namely, providing equitable opportunity for mutual contesting of their relative abilities to move mass in space and time within the confines determined by an agreed-upon set of rules, as discussed in Chapter 3.

2.  The opponents in the contest are members of the same testing family who all play well, and the contest is completed by its determination of a winner and a loser, as discussed in Chapter 4.

3.  All participants attempt to adhere strictly to the letter and the spirit of the constitutive rules, as Chapter 5 states.

4.  Opponents regard one another both as facilitators who strive together to produce excellence in the quality of the good sports contest and as competitors who hinder one another for the purpose of developing and expressing competence, as detailed in Chapter 6.

5.  The inherent value of accurate and complete knowledge of the participants' relative ability to move mass in space and time is the sports contest's most important value when evaluated from the moral point of view, as explained in Chapter 7.

Second, the sports participants/rational contractors want to agree upon the guides for action and the general ends of action that will realize the above five conditions. To reach such agreement, they assume a hypothetical stance in their deliberations, and this stance presumes that all sports participants are free, equal, rational, and wish to pursue general human self-interests. This hypothetical stance is called the original position; to reach agreement from that position the sports participants/ rational contractors must also assume the veil of ignorance. Behind this veil of ignorance, each sports participant/rational contractor operates as if he/she does not know his/her own particular desires, abilities, status, and circumstances. In principle, before agreement on the guides and ends of action, no sports participant knows whether he/she is old or young, amateur or professional, male or female, athlete or coach, or athletic trainer or contest official, or exhibits any other individual characteristics.

We may now see why the sports participants/rational contractors must state and explain the guides and ends of action so that they will create those conditions that are meant for everybody and for the good of everyone alike. For they must devise guides and ends that apply to everybody, in the widely diverse circumstances of different sports contests at different times and in different nations — guides and ends which, if observed, mean that all participants are better off. They must devise these deliberately so that they will not favor any particular sports agents in advance because, operating behind the veil of ignorance, none of the rational contractors knows what particular abilities, desires, status, or circumstances he/she will have. Not knowing how the adopted guides and ends would relate to each agent's individual status makes it rational for each agent to seek guides and ends that will be just for everyone, including that agent. No rational contractor can risk accepting guides and ends that are unjust because they could also be unjust to him/her personally.

## THE FORM AND CONTENT
## FOR THE GUIDES AND ENDS OF ACTION

The guides for action will have a consistent form and content, the knowledge of which will help in understanding how they function to guide actions. These aspects of form and content, enumerated here, are that:

1. Each statement of a guide for action will identify what must be done or be avoided.
2. Each statement of a guide will identify the sport agent(s) to whom it applies.
3. Each statement of a guide will specify, either in general terms or in restricted circumstances, the situations to which it applies.
4. Each statement of a guide that identifies required actions will use language of mandatory action, that is, the required action will be preceded by "shall."
5. Each statement of a guide that identifies a recommended, but not required, action will be preceded by "should."
6. The title of each guide will include the general end of action toward which the statement is aimed. The general intended ends consistent with the good sports contest are stated in the titles.

The identification of each guide and end of action by title and actual statement will be followed by a more detailed description and explanation. This material will include what actions are covered in the guide, how they relate to the conditions necessary to the good sports contest, the circumstances to which they apply, how they may be performed and, also, some discussion of priorities among the different guides.

## THE CONCEPT OF THE MORAL EQUILIBRIUM
## IN THE SPORTS CONTEST

The guides and the ends of right action will be organized around the concept of moral equilibrium, which here means achieving a state of balance within the sports contest in which the conditions are meant for everybody and are for the good of everyone alike. Five conditions describe the good sports contest from the moral point of view and from the view of the nature of contest and, when achieved together and to their fullest extent, illustrate the concept of moral equilibrium in the sports contest. This state of moral balance is an "ideal in terms of which all games could be evaluated."[1] To identify something as an ideal "is to think of some kind of thing as pre-eminently good within some larger class."[2] It is this pre-eminent good of the condition of moral balance within the sports contest toward which the guides and intended ends of right action are to be directed.

## THREE KINDS OF GUIDES AND ENDS OF ACTION
## AND THEIR FUNCTIONS

How do the guides and intended ends of right action direct conditions in the sports contest toward the ideal good of moral balance? It was stated previously that the statements of guides function by declaring the substance of rule-like generalizations. Also, they help sports participants select the appropriate general ends to pursue, as noted in Chapter 2. Further, establishing appropriate general ends provides reference criteria by which many specific ends of sports actions may be evaluated. Having already clarified how the form and content of the guides and ends of action contribute to these functions, our concern here is somewhat different. We are interested in how the guides and ends of action will influence the practical state of affairs in the action area so that it becomes congruent with the moral point of view, as stated in Chapter 2. In short, our question here is "In terms of their practical consequences in relation to the ideal good of the condition of moral equilibrium, how do actions performed in accord with the guides and ends affect the moral balance?" The answer is obtained by briefly identifying three kinds of guides and ends of action and how each affects the practical state of affairs with respect to the moral equilibrium.

### Primary Guides and Ends

Chapter 8 will discuss primary guides and ends for the good sports contest. These statements will establish the primary rules and ends, the adherence to and the pursuit of which are the duties of sports participants. The performance of the duties stated by these primary guides and ends of action affects the moral equilibrium in two ways. First, the actions prescribed and/or proscribed by the primary guides and ends establish the five conditions of the state of moral balance. That is, if all sports participants always acted in the ways required by these statements, the ideal of the moral equilibrium in the sports contest would be achieved. Second, actions prescribed and/or proscribed by these guides and ends maintain the ideal of the moral equilibrium once achieved. Thus, the primary guides and ends of action construct, establish, and/or maintain the moral equilibrium.

### Guides and Ends of Supererogation

Chapter 9 will discuss supererogatory guides and ends for the good sports contest. These statements will establish rules and ends that are good to adhere to and to pursue, but such is not required of all participants; that is, participants are free to do or not to do the kinds of actions specified.

Actions that adhere to these guides and pursue these ends affect the moral equilibrium by encouraging its maintenance.[3] Adherence to supererogatory guides and pursuit of supererogatory ends affects the moral equilibrium by encouraging the maintenance of what is constructed, established, and maintained by actions in accord with the primary guides and ends.

### Secondary Guides and Ends

Actions that adhere to these secondary guides and pursue these secondary ends affect the moral equilibrium in a different way than do those subsumed under primary and/or supererogatory guides and ends. Obviously, if a state of moral equilibrium can be constructed, established, and maintained, it can also become unbalanced. For instance, sports participants perform actions that sometimes violate the primary guides and ends and, by so doing, contribute to a state of moral imbalance. It is during this state of unbalance that the secondary guides and ends become applicable and perform their unique function—to restore, insofar as possible, the moral equilibrium.[4] When the moral equilibrium becomes unbalanced someone is obliged to try and restore it (Chapter 10 will discuss this). Secondary guides and ends, then, are concerned with actions for which someone has the responsibility of obligation and is, thus, required to perform.

### NOTES

[1]Paul Weiss, *Sport: A Philosophic Inquiry* (Carbondale and Edwardsville, IL: Southern Illinois University Press, 1969) , p. 91.

[2]R. M. Hare, *Freedom and Reason* (Oxford: Oxford University Press, 1963), p. 159.

[3]Kurt Baier, *The Moral Point of View* (Ithaca and London: Cornell University Press, 1958), p. 205.

[4]Ibid., pp. 204-205.

# Chapter Eight

# The Primary
# Guides and Ends
# of Right Action

Included as primary guides will be those injunctions which, if adhered to consistently by all participants, will construct, establish, and maintain the five basic conditions for the good sports contest, that is, the moral equilibrium. The major source for these guides is the characterized good sports contest with its quasi-contractual agreement of opponents, but moral principles that apply to all of life also affect these sports guides. The major moral principle here is that of nonmaleficence, which means it is morally wrong to harm another person intentionally.

These guides are understood to be guides of duty in which the features of duty are:

> (a) An individual occupies an office or a station in an organization or some kind of system. (b) A certain job is deemed of some value for the welfare of the organization. (c) This job is associated, somehow or other, with the office occupied by the individual. (d) Performance is expected and 'required' of him.[1]

In interpreting these features of duty for the sports contest, we refer to those agents who contribute directly to the contest itself: the athletes, the coaches, and the athletic trainers. Each contributes some value to the sports contest by doing a certain kind of function, which is associated with being an athlete, a coach, or an athletic trainer. Because that function is required, an athlete, coach, or athletic trainer each have certain duties.

Each of the guides to be stated will be identified by a number and a title. The titles will each state a general end of action that is consistent with the moral point of view in sport. Here let's examine the title of Guide I: The Guide of Equal Opportunity for Optimal Performance. We can see that the general end of action consistent with the moral point of view in sport is "equal opportunity for optimal performance." Thus, the kinds of specific actions required under this guide all enhance, as their intended end, this equal opportunity for optimal performance. It is now time to state and explain the primary guides and ends of right action.

## GUIDE I: THE GUIDE OF EQUAL
## OPPORTUNITY FOR OPTIMAL PERFORMANCE

*Athletes, coaches, and athletic trainers shall seek and sustain, by their acts, like equal opportunity for themselves and for opponents to achieve oppositional superiority within sports contests.*

This guide has the highest priority. It guarantees all participants equal access to the goods of the sports contest and fulfills the purpose of the sports contest, which all participants share by their choice to compete.

This guide means that all participants shall actively seek and sustain the same kind of liberty to perform well in the sports contest. Such equal liberty includes, prior to a contest, access to effective coaching, adequate facilities and equipment, effective sports medicine services, and sufficient practice time. Equal access to such essentials prior to the sports contest is necessary for maximum preparation by all so that they can perform to their capacity. The guide also means that all sports participants must seek and sustain rules or rule changes that will provide equal opportunity for all participants to perform well.

During the sports contest itself, this guide means that all participants abide strictly by the letter and spirit of the rules. As illustrated in Chapter 5, conformity to the letter and spirit of the rules is intimately related to the guide of equal opportunity because the rules operate to define the test to be taken together by the contestants. In short, there cannot by any real evaluation of how well participants perform unless they are all attempting the same thing, and unless the rules of sport guarantee that same task and an equal opportunity to perform it well. On the other hand, if participants do not conform to the letter and spirit of the rules then they cannot be performing the same task. Because they are not performing the same task there can be no contest between them and, thus, there can be no equal opportunity to do the same thing well.

This guide is basic to the good sports contest because adherence to it is essential in providing equal opportunity for both the development and demonstration of one's relative ability to move mass in space and time. If sports participants are denied the possibility of performing to capacity, accurate and complete knowledge of their relative abilities is not possible. Accordingly, access to the good of highest priority from the moral point of view is denied to all.

This guide prescribes only equal opportunity for optimal performance and not that optimal performance will occur. Optimal performance depends upon acts by the participants, acts other than those that provide equal opportunity to perform well. This guide seeks to provide only equal opportunity as a precondition for optimal performance. Following are other guides, adherence to which is necessary for optimal performance once the opportunity for it is present.

## GUIDE II:
## THE GUIDE OF NONINJURIOUS ACTION

*Athletes, coaches, and athletic trainers shall avoid acts or the encouragement of acts that intend physical injury to another person, are known to increase the possibility of physical injury unnecessarily, or are known to be detrimental to the health (or are known to increase, unnecessarily, the possibility of detriment to the health) of another person.*

This guide is of the highest priority for two reasons. Intentional and/or unnecessary physical injury and bad health conditions establish an avoidable inequality for some participants to perform optimally or, in severe cases, even to perform at all. Accordingly, the harmful avoidable actions of other persons are impositions upon the affected participants' equal opportunity to perform optimally. Such avoidable harmful actions do not meet the condition of reversibility, that is, "that the behavior in question must be acceptable to a person whether he is at the giving or receiving end of it."[2] In addition to being nonreversible, such avoidable, harmful acts would cause sports participants to lose respect for one another as mutual facilitators who pursue the good sports contest together and who aid one another by offering the necessary opposition for the development and expression of competence.

Considering avoidable, harmful acts in general, Baier says, "Doing evil is doing to another person what it would be contrary to reason for him to do to himself. Harming another, hurting another, doing to another what he dislikes having done to him are the specific forms this takes."[3] In general, nonmaleficence may be considered a principle of individual duty, a principle of action required of individuals independently of their relations within institutions. As Richards[4] informs us in the development of ultimate standards of conduct by the rational contractors:

> In considering what ultimate standards to agree to as principles of individual duty, the contractors will be aware of circumstances which bear on the general satisfaction of human interests, no matter what one's particular interests are. One set of facts...is that forms of injury, cruelty, and killing by persons, whose pursuit of their substantial interests does not indispensably require such acts, typically, frustrates the fundamental human interest of others.

If we apply a general principle of nonmaleficence to the sports contest we find, first, that in no instance do the particular interests of sports participants require them to injure or harm opponents intentionally. Nothing required by the nature of the sports contest necessitates intentional or knowing injury or harm by one participant to another. Second, we find that avoidable injurious acts that negate or diminish equal opportunity for one participant may also backfire on the agent who has caused the injury by frustrating an interest in seeking appraisal of his/her own relative ability. For if one participant performs better than an opponent because an injury or harmful health condition eliminates the opponent's opportunity to perform optimally, then, the former has eliminated the possibility of attaining complete and accurate knowledge of his/her own relative ability. Accordingly, intentional injurious action frustrates the realization of the only good that is pursued in common by all participants, namely, accurate and complete knowledge of relative abilities to move mass in space and time.

For these reasons, we may generalize that it is never appropriate, intentionally or knowingly, to perform or encourage acts that injure, are detrimental to health, or unnecessarily increase the danger of injury or detriment to the health of another person. Thus, this guide of duty requires that all sports participants avoid encouraging or performing acts with such negative consequences. This is why it is always wrong to attempt injury to an opponent in order to get him/her out of the game and increase the participant's chances of victory.[5] But a distinction must be made here before describing the kinds of acts to be avoided. The guide of noninjurious action does not apply to performing well the positively constitutive skills and tactics of sports. For instance, tackling and blocking are constitutive skills of American football and performing them well includes violent bodily contact — that is part of what is being contested and as such, it is necessary. However, what increases the possibility of injury unnecessarily are such acts as tackling around the head in American football, poking a field hockey stick between an opponent's legs to attempt retrieving a ball, or swinging an elbow violently to the chin of a basketball defender. Such acts are unnecessary either because they are not a positively constituted skill of the sport (swinging the elbow in basketball) or because they perform a constitutive skill in an unnecessary way (tackling around the head in American football).

Intentional injurious acts can be classified as follows: First, there is a class of acts inherently dangerous to others such as tackling a soccer opponent from behind, stepping under and in front of a basketball player who is already in midair in executing a shot at the basket, and tackling a football opponent by the head.

Second, there is a class of acts either inherently detrimental or possibly detrimental to the health status of others. Some instances are administering pain killers to injured areas so that a player may continue playing while the pain is masked, or giving drugs with known harmful side effects to a player in order to increase performance rather than to restore health. Whether or not such actions are prohibited when an individual takes a pain killer or an additive drug himself/herself is to be determined by referring to the guide of equal opportunity. The action of self-administered drugs, taken for additive rather than restorative purposes, cannot be analyzed completely here.

However, a few general observations are in order. If, for instance, a certain drug would enhance the performance of an athlete who takes it and if such a drug is prohibited by the rules, then taking the drug clearly violates the guide of equal opportunity. A certain drug that enhances performance might also cause serious deleterious side effects, and taking such a drug then becomes a matter for discussion under the general morality of intentional self-harm. Or, if a certain drug enhances performance and has no known deleterious side effects, then its use needs to be considered as part of the permissable training methods in sport. Needless to say, we do not yet have a comprehensive, well informed study of the ethics of drug use in sport.

Third, there is a class of acts that unnecessarily increase the possibility of injury by physical intimidation or other interference of a kind not prescribed by the constitutive rules. Some examples are the "brush back" pitch in baseball, "sacking" the American football quarterback after he has released a forward pass, and going out of one's way to slide into the pivot man in a baseball double-play effort. Such acts are performed solely for either intimidation or interference, are not skills prescribed by the constitutive rules, and increase the possibility of injury to another. By contrast, avoiding such acts helps to make the contest a true contest wherein the allowable skills are known to all participants. Unless we wish to promote intimidation and interference, avoiding such acts keeps the contest focused upon known skills.

In addition to avoiding the performance of acts intended to harm another person, the guide of noninjurious action also addresses the encouragement of such acts. This half of the guide is intended to cover these avoidable negative acts from the standpoint of recommending them to another person, or recommending against them.

Positive recommendation of such acts can occur in at least three different ways: teaching, directing, and prescribing. Teaching would involve demonstrating, describing, and explaining such acts as spearing in American football or hooking in ice hockey. It could also involve commending the technique of such acts through one's writings. Directing would involve such acts as signaling for a brush back pitch in baseball or telling a subordinate to perform avoidable harmful acts. Prescribing would involve directly or indirectly supplying harmful or potentially harmful drugs for additive rather than restorative purposes.

Recommending against these avoidable negative acts means specifically identifying the acts and clearly indicating they are not acceptable. This can take the form of direct teaching before they occur or reacting negatively after they have happened. A coach, for example, can identify the nonapproved act beforehand and then clearly indicate that it is not condoned. Negative reaction after such an act is performed can be verbal, nonverbal (shaking one's head in negation), and can involve removing the offending player from the game immediately.

## GUIDE III: THE GUIDE OF NONHARASSMENT

*Athletes, coaches, and athletic trainers shall avoid acts, or their encouragement, that are intended to insult or derogate the character, intelligence, physical appearance, ancestry, or the motor abilities of others in the sports contest.*

This guide is of the highest priority for two reasons. First, insulting or derogatory acts can create an avoidable inequality by making it difficult for some participants to perform optimally because of their emotional sensitivity to such acts. Condoning such actions, then, violates the equal opportunity to perform well because it allows the participant who intentionally insults another to introduce skills in the contest that have not been agreed upon as the skills to be contested.[6] Such acts are also to be avoided because they do not meet the condition of reversibility.[7] In addition, insulting and derogatory harassment is to be avoided because it would cause sports participants to lose respect for one another. Accordingly, one condition necessary for the good sports contest — the relationship of opponents as facilitators — would be negatively influenced.

Second, harassment, as well as avoidable injurious or harmful acts, is to be avoided because of the general principle of nonmaleficence that applies to all individuals independently of their relationships within institutions. This is a principle of individual duty, which prescribes that actions intentionally injurious or cruel to another person are prohibited.[8] Again, in applying the general principle of nonmaleficence to the sport contest, there is nothing that necessitates intentional insulting or derogatory harassment of another person. This means that such acts of harassment are not needed for the good sports contest and must therefore be avoided. Furthermore, just as with intentional injurious acts, intentional harassment of an opponent may affect his/her ability to perform optimally and, at the same time, may frustrate the realization of what sports participants pursue in common: accurate and complete knowledge of their relative abilities.

Harassment, of course, takes many different forms. One of the most obvious and frequent acts of harassment is name-calling and taunting of opponents or officials, for instance, in "bench jockeying" in baseball. Insults to oppontents also occur in gestures of disrespect which sometimes carry sexual innuendo. Cheering or ridiculing the mistakes or poor plays of others is yet another form of insult. Refusing to enter sports contests with others because of their race, religion, or nationality is also a derogatory act.

Nor should acts of harassment be encouraged, such as by teaching players to abuse their opponents verbally or commending such acts by a smile, a nod, or words of approval.

Acts of harassment may be avoided by specifically identifying such acts and clearly indicating disapproval of them. For instance, a coach can specifically identify insulting and derogatory language that is not acceptable. After the fact, coaches, athletes, and athletic trainers can discourage further acts of harassment by stating that they are wrong or by reprimanding the offending participant.

To further clarify the avoidable negative acts of harassment which are prohibited, we must contrast them with another kind of act that has the superficial appearance of harassment. Reference here is to acts performed with the intention of and the desired consequence of good humor and developing and/or maintaining an atmosphere of fun and camaraderie in the contest. For instance, a golfer in the spirit of good-natured kidding may refer to an opponent's poorly hit drive from the tee as a career best or as the best drive he/she has ever observed that person hit. Or a basketball player may refer to another basketball player as a "gunner" after the latter has had an unusually successful scoring record in a contest. Or a racquetball player who is behind in a contest by 18-6 may jokingly implore his/her opponent not to give up. These kinds of acts, not unusual in sports contests, are intended to increase the mutual enjoyment of the contest. They do not detract whatsoever from the quality of the contesting. On the contrary, they help to keep the contesting a more mutually enjoyable event and, in doing so, help to develop the positive attitude of opponents' viewing one another as mutual facilitators.

## GUIDE IV:
## THE GUIDE OF EFFECTIVE PREPARATION

*Athletes, coaches, and athletic trainers, while observing the letter and spirit of relevant rules and with due regard for time demands consistent with their level of sports involvement, shall prepare as fully as possible for scheduled sports contests without contradicting the guides of equal opportunity, noninjurious action, or nonharassment.*

The relative priority of this guide must be expressed in two ways. First, to be able to play at or near previous higher levels of performance, all participants must be as fully prepared as reasonable given their level of sports involvement (i.e., professionals, amateurs, experts, novices, etc.). Second, the acts preparatory to the sports contest must not contradict or negate the guides of equal opportunity, of noninjurious action, or of nonharassment. Effective preparation is as necessary and important as equal opportunity, noninjurious action, and nonharassment because the good sports contest is unlikely to occur if, for instance, some participants have better developed skills, more physiological and psychological effectiveness, or more knowledge of the rules than their counterparts do (for their level of involvement). Such differences would preclude all participants from playing their best and thus provide the mutual facilitation needed to realize accurate and complete knowledge of their relative abilities.

On the other hand, preparatory acts can contradict or negate equal opportunity, noninjurious action, or nonharassment and decrease the possibility of the good sports contest. Suppose, for instance, that the rules in a league or conference specify dates when participants may begin organized practice prior to the scheduled season but some participants begin weeks before that date. Inasmuch as equal opportunity to perform well is strongly influenced by the duration of preparation, the equal opportunity guide would be partially negated. Or suppose that a player is coerced by coaches to practice when such is contraindicated because of injury. Because such practice can lead to further injury now or may be detrimental to future health status, the noninjurious action guide would be contradicted. Or suppose that a participant is ridiculed for not practicing when the participant is ill, injured, or faces a family emergency. Such ridicule would be insulting or derogating and would contradict the guide of nonharassment.

Several categories of acts fall under the guide of effective preparation: teaching, learning, practicing, training, rehabilitating and advising, dieting, and rehearsing (warming up). Coaches, for example, are responsible for effectively teaching athletes about skills, tactics and strategy, rules and interpretations, courtesies, prohibited and non-acceptable acts, and training routines. Coaches are also responsible for updating their own knowledge in these areas. Athletes are responsible for learning and practicing skills, strategy and tactics, for training and rehearsing routines, and for following an appropriate diet. Athletes are to learn the rules and their interpretations, courtesies, and be aware of prohibited and nonacceptable acts. Athletes have this responsibility regardless of whether there are coaches to relate to.

Athletic trainers are responsible for advising coaches and athletes on appropriate diets and training routines as well as using effective rehabilitation procedures for injury. All of these are to be accomplished under the supervision of qualified physicians.

This guide of effective preparation guides sports participants so that they are able to provide mutual facilitation by playing well. The guide, as stated, recognizes that sports participants differ in their commitment to sport and, accordingly, the amount and complexity of the preparation required will differ markedly. The preparation needed for an informal picnic volleyball game would be considerably less than for participation in interscholastic varsity volleyball. And the preparation required for professional volleyball would be considerably more than for interscholastic volleyball. No static list of expectancies can identify these differences, due to the continuing changes and development in this or any sport. But the general directions can be illustrated here by differentiating between preparation for volleyball at the informal picnic, high school varsity, and professional contests.

All of these levels of participation would require, at the least, eligibility to participate, knowledge of rudimentary rules of volleyball (such as three hit rule), ability to perform some type of serve, pass, and set, and physiological condition to persevere through the contest. Preparation for an informal picnic contest may require only eligibility to play by reason of being at the picnic, ability to serve the ball in any legal way, and to volley the ball rather than catch and throw it, knowledge of the three hit rule, and minimal level of physical stamina. Preparation for a high school varsity contest may require, in addition to being eligible, ability to serve the ball legally with at least one type of overhand serve, to receive serve with the forearm pass, to set with conventional front and back sets, to spike with one hand, to attempt to block spikes, knowledge of the most relevant rules for high school volleyball, and physical ability to play two matches per week.

Preparation for professional volleyball contests obviously requires the requisite skill for selection to a professional team and the time to devote to professional volleyball. It may require ability to serve the ball, legally, with two or more overhead serves, to receive all kinds of serves with variations of the forearm pass, to execute several types of sets, to spike with either hand, to block effectively alone and with teammates, knowledge of all rules and their current interpretations, and the physical stamina to play in four matches per week with games involving frequent long rallies. Again, although it is not possible to list all the kinds of preparation required for different levels of sport commitment, the fact remains that the amount and complexity of effective preparation differ markedly. This guide of effective preparation simply requires all contestants to prepare adequately for sports contests at their own level of commitment.

## GUIDE IVa:
## THE GUIDE OF EFFECTIVE SCHEDULING

*Those agents responsible for scheduling sports contests shall, to the best of their ability and barring unusual circumstances, schedule contests between opponents whose experience and preparation promise to provide an equal contest.*

This guide supplements the guide of effective preparation and warrants explicit, separate statement because it is essential to the conditions for the good sports contest. Even if the specifications of effective preparation are adhered to, the good sports contest will not occur, in principle, unless the contestants are of equal ability. Along with effective preparation, this guide is of high priority in realizing the basic conditions for the good sports contest. It is contingent upon not contradicting or negating the guides of equal opportunity, noninjurious action, and nonharassment.

Matching the contestants according to their ability is a prime condition for the good sports contest because it assures, in principle, that opponents will be able to demand the best performance from one another and thus enhance the development and expression of competence. This does not guarantee, of course, that equally matched opponents will always play well and demand the best performance of one another. It only establishes a basic condition essential for maximizing this possibility. Participants who are equally competent may play poorly, while unequally matched opponents may reverse skill levels and have a closely contested game; but this does not affect the principle involved.

Persons who schedule sports contests usually emphasize equal competition by trying to schedule equal oponents. Those seeking informal nonleague or nontournament contests normally attempt to contest with persons of equal ability. Tournament schedules, by seeding and placement in tournament brackets, attempt to assure more equal matches in the later rounds of the tournament. Professional sports groups attempt to facilitate effective scheduling by such things as the reverse draft. College athletic conferences seek to affiliate institutions that will provide, in principle, equally competent opponents. Standards for participation are prescribed for events such as the Boston Marathon and for certain Olympic and pre-Olympic events. As these efforts illustrate, when the good sports contest is sought schedule makers will attempt to schedule contests between equally competent participants.

## GUIDE V:
## THE GUIDE OF EFFECTIVE CONTESTING

*Athletes, coaches, and athletic trainers shall seek oppositional superiority in the sports contest continuously by acting according to the letter and spirit of relevant rules and in ways that do not contradict or negate the guides of equal opportunity, noninjurious action, or nonharassment.*

This guide, similar to the guide of effective preparation, is of high priority in its positive sense, but effective contesting does not include acts that contradict or negate the guides of equal opportunity, noninjurious action, or nonharassment. In a general way, effective contesting completes the primary guides for sports participants in selecting ends to pursue. Equal opportunity is an overarching guide, which assures all participants equal possibility to effective performance and thus to the inherent value of the sports contest. The guides of noninjurious actions and nonharassment identify acts that either deny equal opportunity or that derogate or insult others, and thus detract from the good sports contest. Effective preparation, as stated, guides sports participants to prepare adequately for playing well and to contribute to the good sports contest. The guide of effective contesting guides sports participants in their positive acts during the sports contest. It maximizes the mutual facilitation that sports participants provide in developing and expressing their competence and is essential for the realization of the inherent value of the good sports contest. Shared by all participants, that inherent value is accurate and complete knowledge of relative ability to move mass in space and time.

By way of comparison, then, adherence to the guide of equal opportunity *assures the possibility* that this inherent value will be realized; the guides of noninjurious action and nonharassment *eliminate interference* with the realization of that value; and the guide of effective preparation *prepares for contribution* to the realization of that value. For its part, the guide of effective contesting is the *realization* of that same inherent value of the good sports contest.

This guide specifies that participants shall seek oppositional superiority. It has two dimensions, one being to perform sport in the normative sense of playing well as discussed in Chapter 4. This includes executing the constitutive skills of the sport, exerting the required effort, and choosing tactics and strategy at, or close to, each participant's best. The other dimension is to abide by the rules of the sport as discussed in Chapter 5. This includes adhering to the positive prescriptions in the constitutive rules, avoiding what the rules proscribe, pursuing the prelusory goal of the sport, and passing the zone of consistency test provided by these three elements of the constitutive rules. Taken together, these two dimensions of seeking oppositional superiority assure that all participants perform well in a contest of known and agreed-upon elements.

The guide of effective contesting means that all participants can seek oppositional superiority without contradicting the guides of equal opportunity, noninjurious action, or nonharassment. Effective contesting is further defined by a supplemental guide.

## GUIDE Va: THE GUIDE
## OF NONREVERSIBLE EARNED ADVANTAGE

*Athletes, coaches, and athletic trainers shall avoid acts that are proscribed by the rules and that attempt to negate an opponent's oppositional advantage gained legally through performance of the positively constitutive skills of the sport.*

Positive effective contesting includes performance of offensive and defensive acts within the letter and spirit of the rules. Participants perform acts within the letter and spirit of the rules which, because of their positive effectiveness, attain oppositional advantage over opponents. For example, suppose that offensive basketball player A, by skillful feinting and dribbling with the ball, gets completely around defensive player B and has an unimpeded route to the basket to shoot a lay-up shot. And suppose that defensive player B prevents the shot by intentionally tripping player A and forcing player A to shoot for the basket instead with two foul shots to score two points. The guide of nonreversible earned advantage discourages such acts so that legitimate skilled performance is not negated by the use of illegal skills.

Avoiding acts that are not within the letter and spirit of the rules — acts that intentionally negate an opponent's earned and deserved advantage — is important for maintaining a contest of known and agreed-upon skills.[9] This guide attempts to distinguish between legal acts intended to neutralize an opponent's skillful performance and illegal acts that do likewise. In the basketball example above, if defensive player B had negated offensive player A's earned advantage by blocking the shot or attempting to do so, player B would have been performing a positive act of effective contesting. Such a positive act is prescribed by the guide of effective contesting and could be labeled as an act of reversible earned advantage.

Effective contesting, then, is performing positive acts in order to attain earned advantage, performing positive acts to reverse earned advantage, and avoiding proscribed acts that would negate earned advantage.

## NOTES

[1]David A. J. Richards, *A Theory of Reasons for Action* (Oxford: Oxford University Press), 1971, p. 102.

[2]Kurt Baier, *The Moral Point of View* (Ithaca and London: Cornell University Press, 1958), p. 202.

[3]Ibid., p. 202.

[4]Richards, *Theory of Reasons*, pp. 176-177.

[5]This principle obviously raises a very serious problem: The rules in sports such as boxing allow a participant to win a contest by intentionally injuring an opponent. Boxing is

one of the few sports permitting intentional injury and rewarding it with victory. In most other sports, victory as a sure consequence of intentional injury is impossible either because there is no direct bodily contact or the rules rigorously prohibit certain kinds of injurious action. Put another way, intentional injury to an opponent cannot guarantee victory but only indirectly influence the outcome, such as in soccer, football, or basketball. In boxing, however, such intentional injury is sanctioned by rules and becomes an integral part of the contest to which all participants agree by their choice to enter. Boxers also engage in a form of reversible action. That is, by their choice to enter a boxing match and with knowledge of its rules, boxers choose to be able to injure an opponent intentionally and vice versa; the action is willed as reversible. Boxers are fully aware of the potentional for injury and freely choose that possibility. The guide of noninjurious action indicates that any sport which allows and encourages reversible intentional injury to another is morally suspect. So boxing itself is morally suspect, regardless of whether boxers unnecessarily increase the possibility of injury. Boxing encourages the pursuit of intentional injury to an opponent as a necessary skill. *That is the point:* Any sport practiced on balance so that intentional injury to another becomes a necessary skill is morally wrong. Some commendable efforts to reduce injury have been made (such as thumbless gloves and quicker termination of contests by technical knockout), but the fact still remains that the rules allow someone to win as a direct result of injuring the opponent.

[6]Some sociological literature describes a contest called "playing the dozens," wherein the participants engage in insult and counter insult in an attempt to top one another for the sake of entertainment. Such contests differ from sports contests in that their purpose is to contest the ability to insult whereas sports contests are to provide equal opportunity for contesting the ability to move mass in space and time.

[7]Baier, *Moral Point of View*, p. 202.

[8]Richards, *Theory of Reasons*, p. 177.

[9]For the rationale that clarifies why skills proscribed by the rules are not "within the rules," see Chapter 5.

# Chapter Nine

# The Supererogatory
# Guides and Ends
# of Right Action

While the primary guides and ends discussed in Chapter 8 construct, establish, and maintain the moral equilibrium of the good sports contest, supererogatory guides and ends encourage the maintenance of that equilibrium.[1] In general, the acts that adhere to supererogatory guides and pursue supererogatory ends establish a quality of relationships among participants that makes it unlikely the primary guides and ends will be violated.

Supererogatory acts are those of which it can be said, as Rawls did, "It is good to do...but it is not one's duty or obligation."[2] That broad statement contains two ideas of the supererogatory: One is extraordinary acts that "are acts of benevolence and mercy, of heroism and self sacrifice;"[3] the other refers to "many perfectly ordinary and typical acts, e.g., 'ordinary politeness.'"[4] Neither idea entails the notion that agents are required to perform supererogatory acts. Concerning extraordinary acts, agents are not required to do such things because to do so would necessarily entail risks or losses to themselves. Requiring risks or losses to self is not appropriate because it is not, in principle, for the good of everyone alike; it does not consider the good of the acting agent. Ordinary acts such as politeness are not required of agents because such compulsion would falsify the nature of the act itself. After all, forced politeness is not really politeness.

Finally, compulsion to perform supererogatory acts would remove from them a constitutive feature that encourages the maintenance of the moral equilibrium. This feature is that supererogatory acts are performed freely by an agent who, at the least, equates the good of other agents to his/her own and, at the most, considers it paramount. Agents who benefit from such freely performed acts recognize them as the acts of a considerate person since they are not required by duty or obligation. The development of guides for nonrequired actions in the sports contest demonstrates two things: (a) a complete morality will include nonrequired actions which nonetheless are important to an effective morality; (b) the guides developed here will illustrate clearly that certain aspects of a morality are applicable to all of life, including sports contests. We do not abandon ordinary morality when we engage in sports contests.

Supererogatory acts clearly help maintain the moral equilibrium because they help establish a quality of relationships among participants in which the primary guides are less likely to be violated. To illustrate, if my opponent freely performs nonrequired acts indicating that my good is being equated to his/her own, it is unlikely I would reciprocate by violating the guides of equal opportunity, noninjurious action, nonharassment, effective preparation, effective scheduling, effective contesting, or of nonreversible earned advantage. On the contrary, considerate acts freely performed encourage considerate acts in response, thus reinforcing the maintainance of the moral equilibrium.

This discussion of supererogatory guides and ends will not include extraordinary acts such as heroism or self-sacrifice, even though these kinds of acts are more commonly termed supererogatory. Because we are talking about guides and ends appropriate within the sports contest, and because the good sports contest is an oppositional event in which opponents try to outdo each other at the same task, it would be inappropriate for a contestant to consider the opponent's good as more important than his/her own. The nature of the good sports contest requires that all contestants' good be considered as equal, in principle. However, the second and less common meaning of supererogatory will be retained. This idea focuses upon many perfectly ordinary acts such as courtesy. Though ordinary, these acts are nonetheless important aspects of a morality and include the sense of going beyond what is required, which is a common understanding of the supererogatory.[5] The contrast of these nonrequired ordinary acts with those acts that are required for the good sports contest will enrich our comprehension of an operative morality.

The statement and discussion of the supererogatory guides and ends will reveal that sometimes the interpretation of such guides and ends could result in situations that contradict the primary guides and ends. For instance, an athlete could spend so much time giving gratuitous instruction to a future opponent that the athlete neglects his/her own effective preparation for the contest. Doing so would violate his or her duty under the primary guide of effective preparation, which is necessary for the good, equally, of both opponent and self.

Encouraging the maintenance of the moral equilibrium in the good sports contest is of high priority for the good sports contest. But it must be clearly stated that encouraging the maintenance of the moral equilibrium can only come after its construction and establishment. Thus, the supererogatory guides and ends are of the highest priority in their particular function of encouraging maintenance of the moral equilibrium — no other set of guides and ends of right action can perform that particular function as well. That is because the positive quality of human relationships resulting from freely chosen, noncoercive supererogatory acts cannot be achieved through acts of duty or obligation. The combination of the primary and the supererogatory guides and ends mutually reinforces the construction, establishment, and maintenance of the moral equilibrium.

Each of the supererogatory guides and ends will be identified by a number and a title. The titles will state the general ends of action consistent with the moral point of view in sport. The title of Guide VI, the Guide of Positive Recognition, indicates that positive recognition is one general end of action that is consistent with the moral point of view in sport. Then we may discern that many specific actions all have the general end of positive recognition as their goal.

## GUIDE VI:
## THE GUIDE OF POSITIVE RECOGNITION

*Athletes, coaches, and athletic trainers should recognize, voluntarily and in a positive manner through acts that do not contradict the primary guides, the skilled and effective actions of other participants including opponents and officials in the sports contest.*

In the good sports contest, as described in Part II, all participants perform well in a contest of known skills and mutually facilitate the attainment of complete and accurate knowledge of relative athletic ability. To support such performance, therefore, all participants must recognize and appreciate the skilled and effective acts of others in the contest. Such open appreciation reinforces other participants in their efforts to perform well because positive recognition for good performance tends to encourage the effort to repeat it. This in turn increases the possibility of future effectiveness and enhances the likelihood of more good sports contests. Also, positive recognition of good performance tends to develop an atmosphere of mutual positive regard and facilitates the bond of mutual participation and contribution to the common enterprise of the good sports contest. Since the good sports contest cannot be achieved without the effective performance of all participants, it is for the good of everyone alike that positive recognition be given to all other deserving participants, including opponents and officials, and not in a partisan manner to teammates only.

Many acts of positive recognition can illustrate this guide. A coach can say "good for you" when a player voluntarily acknowledges he/she touched an out-of-bounds ball last, a badminton player can say "nice shot" to an opponent, a tennis player can call "yes" when an opponent executes a difficult passing shot, a basketball player can compliment a teammate by the words "good hustle," or a coach can recognize a good official by shouting "fair call," for example. Nonverbal acts of recognition could include a soccer goalie's affirmative nod when an opposing player's skillful shot eludes the goalie's effort to stop a goal, a football player's patting a teammate on the shoulder following an excellent tackle, a baseball player's or coach's applauding the spectacular defensive play of an opponent, or a gymnast's raising one hand with the thumb and forefinger zero of perfection sign in response to a superb performance by an opponent.

When a contest ends, opponents can shake hands or seek each other out in the locker room, commend others' quality performance to the media, and write or telephone other participants to state appreciation of their effectiveness. Or, a coach can ask an opposing coach for information on some unusual and effective strategy used in the contest, or an athletic trainer can compliment another trainer on the superior physiological conditioning of the athletes under his/her supervision.

These illustrations have several things in common: First, they are overt acts that show approval of others' effective actions. Second, these acts are not necessarily partisan. Third, they do not intrude unnecessarily in the ongoing contest. Fourth, they do not contradict any primary guide such as the guide of effective contesting by commending actions that are not skillful. Fifth, they recognize and applaud good skill performance, appropriate physiological and psychological efforts, intelligent tactics and strategy, and actions in accord with the letter and spirit of rules. These common elements show how positive recognition encourages adherence to the primary guides and, in so doing, encourages maintenance of the moral equilibrium in the good sports contest.


## GUIDE VII:
## THE GUIDE OF POSITIVE INSTRUCTION

*Athletes, coaches, and athletic trainers should instruct other sports participants, voluntarily and in a positive manner through acts that do not contradict the primary guides, in sports actions that improve performance.*

This guide does not refer to the duties of instruction described earlier under the primary guides—a coach's duty to instruct his/her own team. It refers, rather, to voluntary instruction of sports participants one is *not* required to instruct, either for a fee or otherwise. Such voluntary and free instruction can be provided, for example, by athletes to other athletes, by coaches to other coaches, by coaches to members of other teams, and by athletic trainers to other athletic trainers, coaches, and athletes of other teams.

Instructional acts covered by this guide are gratuitously provided by an agent to a recipient for the recipient's own benefit. The immediate end of such instruction is improving the performance of another participant. If all participants adhere to this guide of positive instruction without contradicting, for instance, the duties they all have under the guide of effective preparation, the general result would be an overall, cumulative improvement in performance. Such general improvement would also enhance the mutual facilitation that sports participants provide by increasing their general ability to give and meet challenges for one another. Accordingly, such positive instruction enhances competence and the attainment of complete and accurate knowledge of relative ability. Also, recipients of the free instruction are more likely to perceive the instructors as considerate persons, and are less likely to interfere inappropriately with their benefactors' opportunity to perform well.

Of the several different acts of positive instructions, one type is informal, direct teaching. Golf professionals often help one another on practice tees and practice greens by diagnosing one another's strokes. Track athletes share new techniques and innovations with one another during practice sessions or during warm-ups for contests. Coaches explain new strategies and tactics to one another during a social event at a coaches' conference. Athletic trainers may offer technical assistance to one another in attending to an injured athlete at a contest.

A second, more formal type of positive instruction occurs when athletes, coaches, or athletic trainers share expertise with other sports participants by lecturing or demonstrating at sports clinics. A third type of positive instruction is exemplified when sports participants instruct others by participating in television, radio, or motion picture presentations or by writing instructional materials for newspapers, journals, or books.

These acts of positive instruction share certain characteristics: First, they are all instructional acts not required of the performers. Second, they intend the improvement of another's performance. Third, this improvement in performance is intended regardless of partisanship. Fourth, they are performed gratuitously. Fifth, they are performed at a cost of time and energy that does not interfere with a participant's own necessary preparation for the sports contest. Taken together, these five common elements illustrate how positive instruction encourages maintenance of the moral equilibrium.

## GUIDE VIII: THE GUIDE OF MUTUAL RESPECT

*Athletes, coaches, contest officials, and athletic trainers should act toward other sports participants with respect for their competence to discharge the duties and obligations of their roles in the sports contest.*

Exhibiting trust and confidence in others helps to develop an atmosphere of mutual respect among sports participants. Such mutual respect encourages maintenance of the moral equilibrium by making it less likely that participants, because of their mutual respect, will violate the primary guides. For example, athletes who are opponents in a contest but have mutual respect for one another are much less likely to violate the guides of noninjurious action or of nonharassment.

Showing trust and confidence in the competence of other sports participants is one way by which participants gain mutual respect for one another. Agents demonstrate trust and confidence, sometimes by doing certain things and sometimes by refraining.

Coaches display trust and confidence by teaching their athletes to assume responsibility for tactical decisions in sports contests. Athletes in turn seek advice from other team members in order to make tactical decisions. For instance, a football quarterback may ask linemen about defensive positioning and tactics prior to calling an offensive play. Athletes also seek the advice of coaches regarding tactical decisions and, by so doing, display trust and confidence in the coaches' competence.

Athletes in many sports contests display trust and confidence in their opponents by accepting, without any negative verbal or nonverbal action, certain calls as accurate. For example, a handball or racquetball player who has just had a hinder called on him/her by an opponent exhibits trust and confidence both by commission and omission. That is, the player walks immediately to the appropriate position and does not indicate any displeasure, either verbally or nonverbally, with the opponent and the hinder call. Tennis and badminton players show their trust and confidence mutually by calling their opponents' shots "in" or "out" of court and by not questioning the accuracy of such calls from their opponents.

Coaches display confidence in officials by remaining on the bench and by not demonstrating disgust at certain calls that go against their teams. At times, this also requires that coaches calm down their own players or coaches who are demonstrating negatively against officials' calls. For their part, officials show trust and confidence by asking, for instance, a basketball or volleyball player if they touched an out-of-bounds ball and by using the answer in their decision.

All of these examples illustrate the major facet of the guide of mutual respect, namely, that sports participants invest confidence in one another to make competent decisions and that they will honor such decisions. Such demonstrations of mutual respect definitely encourage the maintenance of moral equilibrium in the sports contest.

Although the guide of mutual respect rightfully guides most actions of sports participants, it must not be interpreted to mean that sports participants must never disagree with certain calls. Exceptions to this general guide will be dealt with under secondary guides.

## GUIDE IX: THE GUIDE OF COURTESY

*Athletes, coaches, contest officials, and athletic trainers should exhibit ordinary politeness and courtesy to other participants in the sports contest.*

This guide acts as a supplement in three ways. First, it recommends some actions that are the opposite of those prohibited by the guide of nonharassment. Second, it recommends some acts that support the guides of equal opportunity, effective contesting, and effective preparation. Third, along with the other guides of supererogation, it recommends actions that develop the quality of relationships which encourage maintenance of the moral equilibrium.

Ordinary courtesy and politeness is exhibited in several ways, one being the normal conventions of courtesy that are expected, generally, in most sports. For instance, golfers generally observe a convention of silence while other golfers are preparing for and executing shots. Such a convention is the opposite of acts prohibited by the guide of nonharassment. Also, it supports the guides of equal opportunity and of effective contesting by providing one equal condition, silence, for all golfers to perform at their best. In tournament tennis, when the server is given new tennis balls to replace used ones, it is conventional for the server to hold the new tennis balls up as a signal to his/her opponent. This courtesy lets the service receiver know that new tennis balls are now in play and may be livelier than the ones just removed. This courtesy supports equal opportunity and effective contesting.

In bowling it is conventional to wait for persons on adjacent alleys to complete their throws before crossing their lane to get a ball from the ball return. It is also conventional in tennis to wait for action on adjacent courts to cease before pursuing one's own tennis balls there. Such courtesies uphold the guide of effective contesting and of equal opportunity. In most sports it is conventional that both space and time are provided by the home team or individual to visiting contestants for the purpose of precontest warm-up. Such a courtesy supports the guides of equal opportunity and effective preparation.

In addition to acts of conventional courtesy specific to various sports are acts that are conventional in human relationships, whether in sports or elsewhere. For instance, introduction of and exhange of greetings to opponents in a sports contest is similar to introducing strangers to one another at any social event or meeting. In sports, treating visiting contestants and officials like guests in one's home is similar. Also, visiting contestants and officials should observe the kind of politeness and civility exhibited by guests in someone else's home. Sports hosts often provide clean locker and shower areas and sometimes clean towels for visiting participants. Visiting teams treat facilities, equipment, and supplies with care.

All participants should use ordinary politeness in addressing one another, such as by using proper names or titles as appropriate. Of course, the use of proper names or titles of respect entails using them in respectful ways.

The kinds of acts recommended by the guide of courtesy help develop friendly, supportive, and positive human relationships among participants and, by doing so, make it less likely that primary guides will be violated.

## GUIDE X:
## THE GUIDE OF SYMPATHETIC REGARD

*Athletes, coaches, and other sports participants should act toward other participants in ways that exhibit sympathy for their unwarranted misfortunes.*

This guide applies to a limited number of negative events that adversely affect either a participant's opportunity to play or his/her ability to play well in the sports contest. The guide of sympathetic regard applies only to negative events that do not result from effective play by an opponent or do not result from poor play on the part of the negatively affected participant. This guide applies to unfortunate events that are difficult or impossible to foresee and thus to prevent.

There are four categories of these unfortunate events: injury, environment, equipment, and interference. Injury or illness either prevents a participant from playing in the contest, continuing in the contest, or playing to capacity. Depending on the circumstances, this kind of event negates one or more of the guides of equal opportunity, of effective preparation, or of effective contesting, and such negation does not result from the responsible acts of the participants themselves.

A second category of unfortunate events occurs when some factor of the environment imposes an undeserved penalty or a difficulty on a sports participant. Suppose, for instance, that a basketball player slips badly on an unnoticed wet spot on the floor and this slip prevents him/her from scoring a basket or from defending an opponent effectively. Or suppose a golfer's otherwise well directed and played shot hits a sprinkler head on the course and rebounds wildly off its course and drops out of bounds, resulting in a stroke and distance penalty. This kind of unfortunate event negates the guide of effective contesting.

A third category of unfortunate events is that of equipment failure, which detracts from a participant's ability to play up to capacity. Imagine a racquetball racket breaking during a contest, or a previously inspected ski binding breaking loose during a downhill run, or a crewsman's oarlock malfunctioning during a race. This category also negates the guide of effective contesting.

The fourth category of unfortunate events is that of spectator interference with effective performance or perhaps the inadvertent and unintentional acts of other sports contest participants. Suppose a baseball fan, eager to catch a batted ball for a souvenir, deflects what would have been a home run into the stands back onto the playing field where it is ruled a groundrule double. Or suppose a tennis player does not return an opponent's lob because some spectator shouts "out" as the lob drops in the court and, accordingly, draws no call from the linesman. Or suppose a golfer, immediately after hitting an errant tee shot, shouts "fore" loudly while another golfer on an adjacent green is in his/her putting backswing. Or suppose a tennis player hits a ball on an adjoining court in such a way that it distracts a player engaging in another match who is about to hit his/her own shot. This category of unfortunate events negates the guides of equal opportunity or of effective contesting.

These four categories of negative events undermine participants' performances by means not within the positively prescribed constitutive skills of the contest. Inasmuch as such events affect the quality of performance, they sometimes are major factors in determining a winner and a loser. Such events cannot really be prevented. However, since their negative effects are undeserved by those affected it is appropriate for other participants to show sympathy.

To be sincere, sympathy for such unwarranted misfortunes must be spontaneous, not calculated. It can be verbal such as in saying "tough luck" or "that's a shame" when another player's effectiveness is negated by an environmental condition such as the slippery spot on the basketball court or the sprinkler head in golf. Such verbal expressions of sympathy are appropriate reactions to any of the four categories of unfortunate events. It can also be nonverbal such as quietly shaking the hand of an injured player, or shaking one's head in negative disapproval of a bad environmental condition, or glaring in disapproval of spectator interference. A third type of appropriate act is writing condolences to other participants who have been beset by illness, injury, or personal tragedy. Finally, sports participants may be in a good position to perform spontaneous acts of recompense. For instance, a racquetball, tennis, or badminton player may lend one of his/her rackets to another participant whose racket is broken. Acts of recompense not only express sympathy but, insofar as is possible, attempt to alleviate the misfortune. The kinds of acts recommended by the principle of sympathetic regard enhance a desirable quality of human relations.

The kinds of acts recommended by the supererogatory guides are neither required nor obligatory for sports participants but are good acts to do. Taken together, they influence a quality of relationships among sports contestants that encourages them to maintain the moral equilibrium. The "should" used in the statement of the five supererogatory guides is the should of recommendation and not the should of imperative requirement. We must reiterate that acts of supererogation should not be contradictory to the primary guides. In general, we can state that acts in accord with these guides of supererogation may be performed so that they benefit all participants but yet are not so costly that they interfere with duties required by the primary guides.

## NOTES

[1] Kurt Baier, *The Moral Point of View* (Ithaca and London: Cornell University Press, 1958), p. 205.

[2] John Rawls, *A Theory of Justice* (Cambridge, MA: The Belknap Press of Harvard University Press, 1971), p. 117.

[3] Ibid., p. 117.

[4] David A. J. Richards, *A Theory of Reasons for Action* (Oxford: Oxford University Press, 1971), p. 197.

[5] Ibid., p. 197.

# Chapter Ten

## Secondary Guides
## and Ends of Right Action

Secondary guides and ends perform yet another function with respect to the moral equilibrium of the sports contest. They guide actions that attempt to restore the moral equilibrium after it has been upset.[1] When this occurs, the imbalance is normally a result of an agent's action, and some agent is placed in an inappropriately disadvantaged position. Accordingly, secondary guides and ends of right action, in Baier's words, "are determined by the concept of desert....They state what a person deserves, that is, ought to get or have done to him as a result of the upset of the moral balance."[2]

The moral equilibrium of the sports contest becomes unbalanced when sports agents violate the primary guides. The two basic kinds of moral imbalance are (a) the negating of equal opportunity for optimal performance and (b) inappropriate interference with effective preparation or with effective contesting. Both kinds of imbalance can result from acts that intend such results or that have the inadvertent result of same. That is, sports agents sometimes intend to negate equal opportunity, or they inappropriately interfere with effective preparation or contesting. Or the consequences of negating equal opportunity or of inappropriate interference may occur inadvertently.

When the guide of equal opportunity is negated or the guides of effective preparation or of effective contesting are interfered with, an obligation to restore the moral equilibrium exists.

The paradigm features of obligation are: (a) A roughly specifiable service is 'required' of one person. (b) Two parties are involved: the one who is required to perform a service, and the one for whom, or at the bidding of whom, the service is to be performed. (c) A prior transaction, the promise or benefaction is the source of the relationship.[3]

Participants choose to enter the sports contest and promise to fulfill a tacit social contract.[4] This promise is the source of the obligation which exists when the moral equilibrium has been broken. Both duty and obligation deal with required actions. Duty comes with a particular role such as that of athlete, coach, or athletic trainer; obligation comes from the source of a prior transaction, such as the tacit promise made by sports participants. In this normative ethic, *duty*, as described in Chapter 8, adheres to primary guides and ends to construct, establish, or maintain the necessary conditions for the good sports contest, whereas *obligation* requires certain actions to restore those conditions. Accordingly, these secondary guides will be labeled guides of obligation by which "To discharge one's obligations *is* to restore the moral equilibrium."[5]

When people engage in the sports contest they are a generally obligated to restore the moral equilibrium if it is broken. The question is, who has that obligation, and when? Of the factors that determine this, one is the consideration of who broke the moral equilibrium and to what extent that person is responsible. A second is consideration of the kind of benefaction assumed by each participant and how this common benefaction affects obligation under particular circumstances.

Moreover, whatever will restore the moral equilibrium depends upon how much the equilibrium has been affected. This may range from very serious to moderate, a very serious imbalance perhaps requiring stronger action to restore the equilibrium. Another consideration is whether compensation to the negatively affected agent(s) alone restores the equilibrium or whether retribution against the offending agent(s) is also needed.

The idea of retributive sanctions has two aspects which must be clarified. First is the problem of retribution that goes beyond the constitutive rules of sport and its relationship to moral judgments in sport. Second, one must clarify the basis for morally correct use of retributive sanctions.

McIntosh[6] recognizes the problem of retribution beyond the constitutive rules of sport as follows:

The governing body must therefore devise other rules to ensure that penalties both on and off the field of play discourage and prevent deliberate fouls and misconduct, and guarantee that victory can be won only if rules are observed and conduct is of a certain kind. It could be argued that this policy leads to the abandonment of moral judgment in sport and that any "ought" statement that is made about behavior is a

> prudential statement only and not a moral judgment. I "ought" to play fair means
> that I "ought" to keep the rules and behave in a certain way, merely in order to be
> allowed to play at all and to make victory, if I win, indisputable. No moral judgment
> is being made. If, however, we distinguish between psychological causes of behavior
> and logical reasons for it...it becomes clear that an ethical question or argument still
> remains.

McIntosh argues that it is impossible to include within the constitutive rules of sport absolute disincentives to undesirable actions because of the great amount of "money and prestige which came from victory in top-class competition."[7] Thus, he continues, sports agents may need to apply retributive sanctions outside the constitutive rules to discourage athletes from cheating, being violent, and breaking rules. Sanctions outside the constitutive rules do not simply establish the imprudence of certain kinds of actions such as violence and cheating, but also reflect a positive view of life that such actions negate. In short, such sanctions indicate that violence and cheating, in principle, are morally unacceptable — beyond the fact that they must be avoided for prudent reasons.

This analysis by McIntosh is important to this task. Here, the secondary guides are concerned with moral obligations for restoring the moral equilibrium of the sports contest when it is broken. Accordingly, these secondary guides will sometimes include statements of obligation beyond what is required by sports rules, that is, moral requirements and not solely requirements of obeying the constitutive rules of sport. As we shall see, sports officials have some moral obligations that only they can discharge because of their functions in the sports contest. Also, the secondary guides may state moral obligations, for example, for an official to expel participants from a contest when the rules of that sport do not provide for such retribution. The point is not whether the retribution is legal under the rules of a sport but whether such retribution is necessary to restore the moral equilibrium of the sports contest. So, if some of these secondary guides contradict the rules or deal with retribution outside of the rules, it means that the existing rules either cannot deal with a kind of moral disequilibrium or that the rules are morally deficient.

Let us examine briefly the idea of responsibility for retribution. After all, if secondary guides include retributive action, one must establish the bases upon which such actions are morally correct. It was stated earlier that the moral equilibrium is broken when agents violate the primary guides. What determines the moral correctness of retributive actions against those agents? First, an agent does something in a situation in which he/she could have done otherwise. Since an agent performing any action can always "do otherwise," it is clear that an agent is always responsible for those acts in the sense that he/she authors them;

the agent's acts are not things that just happen and over which he/she has no control.

Second, to say that an agent is responsible as the author of his/her acts does not automatically make him/her accountable. So, a person is responsible — accountable — for his/her actions when, as Baier states, in "possession of all those psychological powers which are necessary and sufficient for the ability to be guided by promulgated social rules."[8] This means the person is rational and thus can, at will, follow obligatory social rules.[9] Excused from such accountability are those who may have reduced psychological powers, such as minors or madmen.[10] Therefore we are concerned here with applying retribution to rational sports agents who have the psychological power to follow, at will, obligatory social rules.

Finally, a sports agent who is accountable for violating one of the primary guides becomes responsible as answerable. To be answerable means a sports agent must "answer the question, why one failed to conform to the obligatory social rule or directive in question."[11] An agent answerable to such a question may have either an inculpatory or exculpatory explanation for his/her failure to conform to the primary guides. An inculpatory explanation does not excuse the agent from responsibility, whereas an exculpatory explanation indicates that the agent's failure "was not due to an inadequacy of his will, but occurred or would have occurred despite its inadequacy."[12] An exculpatory explanation excuses the agent from responsibility for his/her action which, according to Baier, is due to inability, compulsion, or ignorance. Baier further states, "When a person has been found culpable then he becomes liable to one or more of the three types of unwanted treatment (punishment, condemnation, payment of compensation)."[13]

We may conclude that the secondary guides to be stated will, in some cases, include retributive sanctions against sports agents who are culpable. It is assumed these secondary guides will apply only to those sports agents who are culpable for breaking the moral equilibrium by violating the primary guides.

The form of the secondary guides will include several necessary elements: which sports agents are obliged to restore the moral equilibrium, how they must do so, and identification of the wrongful action and its consequences. Each guide's title will identify the general end toward which the actions subsumed under the guide are aimed.

The statements of secondary guides will be made in three classes — very serious, serious, and moderate moral imbalance. The seriousness of the moral imbalance will depend on whether it was performed intentionally and whether the resulting imbalance negated equal opportunity or inappropriately reduced or increased the effectiveness of preparation or of contesting. Not all particular instances of moral imbalance can be described here. Nonetheless, the three classes cited above should be able to subsume all particular instances on the dual basis of their intentionality or inadvertence and their negation of equal opportunity or inappropriate reduction or increase in effectiveness. Finally, each guide will be followed by a description and explanation of its meaning and its applicability.

## THE CLASS
## OF VERY SERIOUS MORAL IMBALANCE

This class will subsume secondary guides and ends designed to restore the moral equilibrium when it has been broken intentionally to negate the primary guide of equal opportunity for optimal performance by violating the guide of noninjurious action. The greatest moral imbalance occurs here, first, because the acting agent intends to harm another participant and violates the general principle of nonmaleficence which applies to all of life. Second, the acting agent intends to negate another person's equal opportunity for optimal performance. In short, the intended consequence of the agent's acts is to prevent some other person from performing whatsoever, by:

1. Preventing a person from equal opportunity for optimal performance in any future sports contest;
2. Preventing a person from equal opportunity for optimal performance in a particular sports contest just before it begins;
3. Eliminating the possibility that a person can effectively prepare for a future contest;
4. Reducing a person's ability to perform optimally in the particular sports contest now in progress.

Intentional acts that negate equal opportunity for optimal performance are reprehensible because they seek to deny the benefits of sports contesting by removing that possibility whatsoever. Such acts are more serious than acts that simply interfere with effective performance because they attempt to remove the very opportunity to perform, and that opportunity is an essential precondition to both effective preparation and effective contesting.

The paradigm case here is a sports agent's attempting to and succeeding in injuring another sports agent. Examples would be clear after-the-whistle attacks on the opponent quarterback by defensive football players, butting the opponent's eyes with one's head in boxing, undercutting the legs of a basketball player jumping for a basket, kneeing an opponent's groin or "punch ups" in rugby, and deliberately striking the head of an opponent with a hockey stick. All these examples (a) intend to incapacitate another agent, (b) they succeed, and (c) they break the moral equilibrium by negating the primary guide of equal opportunity for optimal performance.

The secondary guides needed to restore the moral equilibrium in this class must in some cases include compensation to those denied their equal opportunity, and must in all cases include retribution against those guilty of doing so. Intentional acts of this class are so serious as to require drastic action to restore the equilibrium; thus, both compensation and retribution may be necessary. Inasmuch as our concern here is only with acts that intentionally violate the primary guides and for which the acting agents are culpable, excuseless rule breaking must be penalized. Beyond the attempt to restore the moral equilibrium immediately, such penalties serve "two distinct purposes: deterring those who would otherwise be tempted to break the rules, and persuading those who have obeyed the rules that their behavior was wise, that crime does not pay."[14]

The responsibility for restoring the moral equilibrium in the class of very serious moral imbalance will be assigned to sports agents other than the violators themselves. After all, since the offending agents intended to negate equal opportunity, one cannot reasonably expect them to assume the responsibility of restoring the moral equilibrium that they have upset intentionally. Of course, it would be good if they did assume responsibility for restoring the moral equilibrium they have broken, particularly if they did so for moral reasons. Certainly, the offending agents have primary moral responsibility and if they assume it, so much the better. Desirable as such may be, however, it is unlikely that this will occur. Also, only certain sports agents can impose the necessary retributive sanctions.

## GUIDE XI: THE GUIDE OF CONDEMNATION

*Athletes, coaches, contest officials, and athletic trainers shall demonstrate disapproval of acts performed in order to injure another participant intentionally in the sports contest.*

This guide applies to all acts that intend the injury of another person — whether the acts succeed or fail. Because it applies to all such acts and because it involves condemnation by several agents,[15] it imposes a common penalty upon offending agents. Such condemnation acts to restore the moral equilibrium, partially by its clear message to the offender that acts intending injury are not condoned by any other sports agent. The condemnation also serves as a deterrent to such acts. It is impossible to enumerate all appropriate acts that demonstrate disapproval of intentional injury, be they formal written notes or less formal verbal expressions.

This guide of condemnation is intended to restore the moral equilibrium, at least partially, in all instances of a very serious moral imbalance. It guides actions that impose only one kind of penalty upon the offending agent, namely, social disapproval. Other guides are still needed to impose additional penalties on the offender and to compensate the affected agent for the loss of equal opportunity.

## GUIDE XII: THE GUIDE OF EXPULSION

*Contest officials shall expel from the contest any participant who, in the judgment of officials, attempts to injure another and is unsuccessful in such attempt. If contest officials fail to expel the offending agent then the coach of the offending agent shall do so.*

This guide applies only to acts that are intended to injure another and fail. Other guides will deal with intentional injurious acts that succeed. This guide adds to the retribution of condemnation by indicating that intending injury is so serious, even if unsuccessful, that participants who perform such acts will not be allowed to continue. It is assumed that an expelled contestant cannot win or place. The guides of condemnation and of expulsion together complete, with one exception, the necessary retribution against the offending agent whose acts of intentional injury are unsuccessful.

As noted earlier in this chapter, expulsion from a sports contest may not be within an official's power according to the rules of a particular sport, although in most cases it is. Again, because the basic function of these guides is to inform actions that are morally correct in the sports contest, the guides may specify kinds of action that are not in the constitutive rules of a particular sport.

Another problem needs to be recognized here: judging an agent's actual intention by observing his/her actions. Specifically, it is difficult to make the judgment that a sports participant actually intended to injure another person rather than, say, only to reduce the effectiveness of that other person's performance. Such judgments are difficult because one cannot get into someone else's mind to know that person's intention simply by observing an action. Nonetheless, there are cases in which injury appears to be the motive. Consider, for example, a basketball player's crouching stance when undercutting an opponent driving for the basket, a football player's forearm blow to the head of the quarterback who has just released a forward pass, and the high spikes of a baseball player sliding into an opposing player on a double play when the latter has already thrown to first base and is now some considerable distance from second base. The acting agent in each case could have performed otherwise. The basketball player could have stood erect in the defensive position, the defensive football player could have tackled or avoided the quarterback, and the baseball player could have slid to second base without high spikes. These options for doing otherwise help to inform the judgments of intention by contest officials and coaches.

## GUIDE XIII:
## THE GUIDE OF PRUDENT WITHDRAWAL

*In sports contests not governed by contest officials, a participant shall withdraw from the contest if that person perceives him/herself to be the recipient of acts that intend injury or unnecessary physical danger. In such instances, the withdrawing agent shall accompany the withdrawal with a brief, courteous, and dignified statement of his/her reason(s) to the offending agent.*

This guide serves to cover instances likely to result in bodily injury either because injury is intended or because the sport is being played in an unnecessarily dangerous manner. Withdrawal under such circumstances is prudent, considering that reckless endangerment of one agent by another cannot be corrected by officials since there are none. Therefore, the agent responsible for restoring moral equilibrium is the recipient against whom such dangerous acts are directed. In these kinds of cases, the threatened agent's withdrawal serves to protect him/her and, at the same time, acts as retribution against the offending agent by suspending the contest.

This type of act is illustrated by racquetball players who regularly take a full swing at the ball when an opponent is clearly endangered by the swing or its follow through, baseball pitchers who throw pitches directly at opposing batters frequently, or touch football players who trip opposing team pass receivers when they are running to receive a forward pass.

The stipulation that the withdrawing agent is to state his/her reason(s) for withdrawal serves to inform the offending agent that the withdrawal is a retributive sanction. This must be made clear so that offenders recognize that their actions are judged to be reprehensible and, as such, will not be condoned.

The guides of condemnation, of expulsion, and of prudent withdrawal cover unsuccessful acts that intend injury or acts of reckless endangerment. Together, they establish clearly negative sanctions against offenders. The guide of condemnation applies also to acts that intend injury and are successful. But condemnation alone is neither sufficient as retribution for injury nor does it compensate agents who are injured. Stronger guides are needed to restore the moral equilibrium when sports agents injure others.

# GUIDE XIV:
## THE GUIDE OF SUSPENSION OF CONTEST

*Contests in which successful intentional injury would clearly influence the eventual winners shall be suspended by the contest officials if, in their judgment, one or more of the contestants intentionally injured one or more of the opponents. No winner will be determined. An exception shall occur if the contest officials judge that the offending agent's performance in this contest is so poor that it is unlikely a complete contest would even the score. Such contest shall be suspended by the officials while declaring the now-ahead offended agent(s) as winner or as finishing ahead of the offending agent(s).*

The guide of suspension of contest applies to contests wherein the offended and/or the offending agent's performance will be significant in determining winners and losers. This suspension does not apply where neither the offended nor the offending agent's performance would significantly affect the determination of winners and losers. The basic intent is to compensate those intentionally injured contestants whose performance puts them in the thick of the contest so that their performance is not completely negated by such injury. Also, this guide imposes negative sanctions on the offending contestants so they cannot win or finish higher in a contest as a result of intentional injury to opponents. So long as the judgment of intentional injury is accurate, the clear sanction against it is stronger then the temptation to profit by such intentional injury. Suspension of the contest both compensates the offended agents and imposes retributive sanctions on the offending agents.

When the intentional injury is not significant in determining winners and losers, the contest officials shall simply expel the offending agent from that contest.


## GUIDE XV: THE GUIDE OF EXCLUSION

*Officials of appropriate sports organizations shall exclude from a significant number of future contests any agent(s) who has performed, in the judgment of the contest officials in two or more contests, actions intended to injure another participant.*

Retributive sanctions imposed upon an offending agent for one instance of intentional injury are intended to prevent the agent from profiting from such action in a particular contest. Stronger sanctions are needed if any agent performs such actions intentionally in more than one contest. Responsible officials must protect future opponents by not allowing the offending agent to contest. This guide is a strong deterrent; it informs offending sports participants that their actions are so reprehensible as to negate their very opportunity perform. Although this guide goes beyond one sports contest, it indicates how these secondary guides can operate to restore the moral equilibrium over an extended period of time.

This guide has two elements which provide enough latitude to operate in diverse circumstances. An element that allows necessary latitude is "exclude from a significant number of future contests." The exact number of future contests depends on the particular circumstances. For instance, is this the first time that exclusion from future contests applies to that agent? Or the second? Or the third? How will the moral equilibrium be affected by exclusion from one contest? From a full season? For the life of the offending agent? How many contests in the various sports represent a significant number? Is the number the same? A proportion of a full season for a particular sport?

The second element of latitude is "officials of appropriate sports organizations." Which organizations are appropriate may differ according to circumstances. First, only certain organizations can have powers of exclusion over certain participants. For example, the National Collegiate Athletic Association in the United States could exclude a collegiate soccer player from national collegiate tournaments, but could not exclude any player from contests in Association Football in England or from contests in the North American Soccer League. Second, exclusion by certain organizations would be significant while exclusion by other organizations would not, depending on the circumstances. For instance, exclusion from a local marathon race by the sponsoring organization would not be significant to a world-class runner but exclusion from the Boston Marathon or the marathon in the Olympic Games would be.

The secondary guides, the circumstances to which they apply, and how they restore the moral equilibrium in the class of very serious moral imbalance are summarized in Table 10-1.

**Table 10-1.　SUMMARY OF SECONDARY GUIDES**
**FOR CLASS OF VERY SERIOUS MORAL IMBALANCE**

| *Circumstances* | *Type of Action Necessary for Restoration* | *Secondary Guides Applicable* |
|---|---|---|
| Injury to another intended but action is unsuccessful | Retribution | XII – Expulsion<br>XIII – Prudent withdrawal |
| Injury to another intended and action inflicts injury | Compensation and retribution | XIV – Suspension of contest |
| Injury to another intended and action is either successful or unsuccessful | Retribution (all cases); compensation (when injury occurs) | XI – Condemnation (all cases)<br>XV – Exclusion (two or more contests) |

## THE CLASS OF SERIOUS MORAL IMBALANCE

This class will include those secondary guides and ends needed to restore the moral equilibrium when it has been broken (a) intentionally by sports agents and (b) the intended consequence of these acts is either wrongful reduction of an opponent's performance effectiveness or wrongful increase of the acting agent's performance effectiveness. Wrongful reduction or increase in performance effectiveness refers to intentional acts that violate the guides of effective contesting, or of nonreversible earned advantage, or of effective preparation, or of effective scheduling.

Several acts intentionally violate these primary guides. One kind is the intentional performance of acts proscribed in the rules of sports, acts that inappropriately reduce the performance effectiveness of another participant. Examples are illegally holding an opponent in basketball or football, screening opposing volleyball players receiving service from seeing the ball, hooking an opposing player in ice hockey, or spinning a service toss in table tennis. A second kind is intentional performance of acts either proscribed by the rules, or contradictory to prescriptions of the rules, or contradictory to the spirit of the contest but not proscribed explicitly in the rules—and which inappropriately increase the acting agent's performance effectiveness. Examples would include a hurdler running in the outside track lane and taking his/her trailing leg outside the hurdle rather then over it, illegal modification of fencing equipment to record touches unfairly (as happened in the 1976 Olympic Games), a golfer improving his lie illegally, or a baseball pitcher deliberately wetting or marring the cover of a baseball in order to change its flight. A third kind is intentional acts that increase or decrease performance effectiveness by providing more or less possibility of preparation. Related examples are teams or individuals beginning their season practice prior to an agreed-upon starting date for members of their sport organization, and home teams not providing equivalent warm-up space and time to visiting teams prior to the contest.

Serious moral imbalance occurs when agents act to increase or decrease performance in, or preparation for, the sports contest in inappropriate ways. Although the moral equilibrium is less disturbed here than in the class of very serious moral imbalance, it is still serious enough to require both compensation to the offended agent and retributive sanctions against the offending agent. For in many instances, an intentional act that inappropriately decreases an opponent's performance effectiveness would have a corresponding and inappropriate positive influence on the acting agent's performance. This is true because opponents in the sports contest are elements in a test; consequently, the test itself is made easier by decreasing an opponent's effectiveness or harder by increasing the opponent's effectiveness. Accordingly, in most cases, some measure of compensation and retribution is needed.

The agents who are responsible for restoring the moral equilibrium in the class of serious moral imbalance are persons other than the offending agent(s). Again, since the acts that disturb the moral equilibrium are intended, it would be unrealistic to expect the offending agents to correct what they have done intentionally.

## GUIDE XVI:
## THE GUIDE OF APPROPRIATE COMPENSATION

*Contest officials or sports organization officials, when appropriate to their proper jurisdiction, shall provide appropriate compensation for participants who are negatively affected by the intentional acts of opponents that decrease the participant's performance effectiveness or preparaton, or acts that inappropriately increase the offending agent's performance effectiveness or preparation.*

This guide of compensation must be general to allow application to diverse instances. First, the statement includes both contest officials and sports organization officials because neither type of agent can provide appropriate compensation in all cases. Contest officials can provide appropriate compensation in most instances of inappropriate increase or decrease of performance in the sports contest itself, but they cannot provide compensation for inappropriate increase in effectiveness of *preparation* for the sports contest. It is up to the officials of the relevant sports organization to provide compensation to participants negatively affected in effectiveness of preparation by the intentional actions of opponents who begin their practices, say, two weeks prior to the agreed starting date. Sports organization officials could, for example, reschedule the contest to allow the negatively affected participants more time for preparation.

Second, the statement is general because it is impossible to specify exact appropriate compensation in the diverse circumstances subsumed in this class. For instance, what would be appropriate compensation to the negatively affected fencer whose opponent modified her equipment in order to control her touches registered in a bout? If the offending agent was ahead in the bout, appropriate compensation might be to erase the existing score and begin the bout over with no score, or it might be to eliminate all touches scored by the offending agent while retaining those scored by the negatively affected agent. If the offending agent was behind in the bout, then appropriate compensation might be to award the number of touches now recorded by the offending agent to the negatively affected agent. In soccer the appropriate compensation to the offended agent for being tackled from behind illegally might be different if he is unmarked inside the penalty area of the opposing team or if he is unmarked while at midfield. In the first case a penalty kick may be appropriate compensation, while in the latter case a free kick might be appropriate. The point of these examples is that specific appropriate compensation will differ between sports and in relation to situational factors both between and within sports. These examples only illustrate different possibilities in different circumstances and are already in sport rules — at least in some cases.

The exact compensation appropriate for such diversity cannot be specified, but responsible officials can determine appropriate compensation through operative standards. Therefore, three standards, which supplement the guide of appropriate compensation, will be explained here.

### The Standard of Adjustment of Score

When intentional acts inappropriately cause a decrease of a participant's score or an increase in the offending agent's score, responsible officials shall adjust the score by adding or subtracting as needed so that the score relationship between the opponents will revert to what it was prior to the offending act. This standard is applicable in two types of inappropriate decrease in the negatively affected participant's score. For instance,

1. A base runner occupying third base in baseball is tripped or held by the opponent third baseman so that he cannot score when the next batter hits a 400-foot sacrifice fly to the outfield.
2. A badminton or tennis player who is in the proper position at the net to execute a point-scoring stroke cannot hit the shuttle or ball effectively because an opponent from the other side of the net thrusts her racket directly in front of the offended player's eyes or swing.

This same standard is applicable to cases involving inappropriate increase in the offending agent's score. For instance,

1. A contestant in a golf tournament does not count all the strokes he takes.
2. A runner in a cross-country race runs a shorter course than the one that is laid out.

### The Standard of Earned Advantage

When intentional acts inappropriately neutralize or reverse a participant's advantage previously earned, responsible officials shall stop the contest and restart it with the advantage restored to the negatively affected participant. If the contest cannot be halted, officials shall determine the final place in the contest for the negatively affected participant in the position of relative advantage previously gained over the offending agent but shall not, by so doing, decrease unfairly the finishing position of other participants.

This standard applies when the guide of nonreversible earned advantage has been violated intentionally. In some cases the moral equilibrium may be restored immediately when officials stop and restart the contest, as example 1 will show. In other cases, the appropriate compensation to the negatively affected participant cannot occur until after the contest is over, as illustrated by example 2.

1. A basketball player or soccer player has an earned advantage over defensive players by a clear breakaway for an unhindered shot on goal and is tripped intentionally from behind so that she is unable to take a shot. In such cases, officials shall return the advantage to the negatively affected participant.

2. A runner in a mile race is pushed or tripped by a runner who is behind him. In such cases, officials shall place the negatively affected participant ahead of the offending agent in the race.

## The Standard of No Advantage

When intentional acts inappropriately cause a participant's position to decrease from no advantage to disadvantage vis-a-vis the offending agent, responsible officials shall stop the contest and restart it, restoring the situation of no advantage. If the contest cannot be halted, officials shall award the negatively affected participant a finishing place equal to that of the offending agent without, however, making that finishing place poorer than that actually achieved. Also, if such an adjustment in finishing place is made it must not impact negatively on the finishing places of participants other than the offending agent.

This standard applies when the advantage-disadvantage relationship between opponents is neutral and, as a result of an intended act, a participant is placed in a disadvantageous position inappropriately. In some instances, the compensation may be immediate as illustrated in example 1. In other instances, the compensation can occur only after the contest, as shown in example 2.

1. A defensive waterpolo player occupying a position between an offensive player and the goal prevents the offensive player from rising in the water by wrapping his legs around those of the offensive player. A golfer steps on an opponent's golf ball intentionally. In such instances, officials shall halt the contest and

restore the position of no advantage to the negatively affected participant.

2. A runner in a race intentionally elbows a participant at her side and, by doing so, causes that participant to finish behind her in the race. In such instances, officials shall place the negatively affected participant in a finishing position equal to that of the offending agent.

Remember that these standards apply where breaking of the moral equilibrium requires compensation to negatively affected participants because they have had their status lowered inappropriately as a direct result of wrongful acts by opponents. The basic standard of such compensation is removing the inappropriate decrease on the advantage-disadvantage balance. Of course, participants may fail in their attempt to place opponents in a lower status. For example, a defensive basketball player could fail in his/her attempt to trip an offensive player who has a clear earned breakaway. Or, a runner who has been elbowed or tripped intentionally by an opponent could still finish the race ahead of the offending agent. Compensation is not needed in such cases because the negatively affected agent has overcome the temporary decrease of his/her status. The guide of appropriate compensation addresses restorative actions when the advantage-disadvantage relationship is inappropriately changed, not when it is merely threatened.

## GUIDE XVIb:
## THE GUIDE OF APPEAL TO PARTISANS

*Athletes and coaches whose fans inappropriately intend to disrupt the performance of opponents shall act clearly to attempt to halt such disruption.*

This supplements the guide of appropriate compensation. It applies to acts performed, usually by spectators, with the clear intention of negatively affecting the performance of players on visiting teams. For instance, basketball spectators at times have tried, by loud yelling, whistling, and stamping of feet, to disrupt the concentration of an opponent who is shooting free throws. Spectators at badminton matches have removed dark jackets covering white shirts and blouses when an opponent had to see the shuttle against a white background while playing a home player. Spectators at American football games sometimes make so much noise, intentionally, as to make it impossible for members of the visiting team to hear the signals called by their quarterback.

Responsible agents who can compensate the negatively affected participants, even if the rules specify this function for officials, are the athletes and the coaches of the home team. Since these athletes and coaches can best effect the needed compensation, and since they have not themselves been the offenders they must attempt such compensation. They can indicate clearly but respectfully that the disruptive acts are inappropriate and that they are now asking the fans to stop being disruptive.

In the class of serious moral imbalance restoration of the equilibrium requires retribution as well as compensation; such guides follow.

## GUIDE XIa: THE GUIDE OF CONDEMNATION

*Athletes, coaches, contest officials, and athletic trainers shall demonstrate disapproval of any acts that inappropriately intend to decrease the performance effectiveness of another or to increase one's own performance effectiveness.*

This second formulation of the guide of condemnation applies to all acts covered in the class of serious moral imbalance. It specifies social disapproval by all other sports agents in all instances of the specified wrongful acts whether or not they are successful. The retribution covered by this guide is the same as for all acts that intend the injury to another participant and are subsumed under the class of very serious moral imbalance. Thus, the guide of condemnation means that all sports agents must clearly show their disapproval of acts performed either to injure another, decrease inappropriately the other's performance effectiveness, or increase inappropriately the performance effectiveness of the acting agent. They can show their disapproval either formally or informally, either verbally or nonverbally, as discussed earlier in this chapter.

## GUIDE XVII: THE GUIDE OF WARNING

*Contest officials shall officially and publicly threaten to expel from the contest any participant who, in their judgment, inappropriately attempts to decrease an opponent's performance effectiveness or to increase his/her own. If contest officials fail to do this, then the offending agent's own coach shall inform said agent that he/she will be taken out of the contest if another offense occurs.*

This guide applies to all first acts, successful or not, covered in the class of serious moral imbalance. Beyond the social disapproval contained under the guide of condemnation, the formal warning in this guide reinforces such disapproval and notifies the offending agent that further such acts will invoke additional retribution. The formal and public nature of such warnings also informs spectators and other contest participants that a serious violation has occurred and that it will not be tolerated further.

The provision that requires the offending agent's own coach to warn the agent is intended to involve coaches, in responsible ways, in restoring the moral equilibrium. It also establishes the possibility of formal recognition of such offensive acts by an agent who can do something about it if the contest officials do not perceive the offensive action.

The particular method of formal warning may differ depending on the sport and the circumstance. Regardless, the formal method used must be understood clearly as a warning of further retribution if the offender performs another offensive act. Therefore, the necessary characteristics of the particular method used are (a) the sign, the signal, or the words used must be delivered so that everyone may perceive it clearly, (b) the method used should be codified as part of the official signals in the particular sport, and (c) where feasible, the contest action should be halted temporarily in order to highlight the warning.

## GUIDE XIIa: THE GUIDE OF EXPULSION

*Contest officials shall expel from the remainder of the contest any participant who, in their judgment, inappropriately attempts to decrease an opponent's performance effectiveness or to increase his/her own more than once in a contest. If they fail to expel the offending agent, then the agent's own coach shall do so.*

This second formulation of the guide of expulsion applies to any detected second act, successful or not, in a particular sports contest, which is subsumable under the class of serious moral imbalance. It covers the additional sanction forecast by the formal warning issued previously under the guide of warning. This guide applies to any combination of acts, characterized as intentional, which would inappropriately decrease another's performance effectiveness and/or increase one's own. It is the combination of two or more acts in the same contest which constitutes the basis for expulsion. It doesn't matter whether the two intentional acts both intend to decrease another's performance effectiveness or both intend to increase one's own.

The two formulations of the guide of expulsion together indicate that two kinds of intentional acts are so reprehensible that offending agents will not be allowed to continue. Yet there is a distinction in the two applications which shows that an act intending injury, *even when unsuccessful*, is more serious than is an act intending inappropriate increase or decrease of performance effectiveness, even when successful.

## GUIDE XIIIa:
## THE GUIDE OF PRUDENT WITHDRAWAL

*In a sports contest not governed by contest officials, a participant who feels certain that an opponent has performed two or more acts intended to inappropriately decrease the participant's effectiveness or increase the offending agent's effectiveness shall withdraw from the contest. In such instances the withdrawing agent shall accompany withdrawal with a brief, courteous, and dignified statement of his/her reason(s) to the offending agent.*

Like its predecessor, this second formulation of the guide of prudent withdrawal is intended to invoke retributive sanctions against offending agents in the absence of officials. Absence of officials means there are no effective agents to compensate the negatively affected participant, so compensation is not possible. Consequently, the only action that can restore the moral equilibrium is one which carries sanction against the offending agent and is carried out by the negatively affected participant. As with the first formulation of this guide, the withdrawing agent must state his/her reason for withdrawal so that there is no mistake that a sanction is being imposed and why.

In its immediate result, such withdrawal imposes a temporary penalty upon the contestant who withdraws. However, the long-range benefits to all when all sports participants act in accord with this guide are that the negative intentional acts leading to such withdrawal will become rare. In the long run, then, prudent withdrawal is for the good of everyone alike.

## GUIDE XVa: THE GUIDE OF EXCLUSION

*Officials of appropriate sports organizations shall exclude from a significant number of future contests any agent(s) who, in their judgment, inappropriately acted in two or more contests to decrease another's performance effectivness or to increase their own.*

This second formulation of the guide of expulsion applies to all the types of actions specified, successful or not, that have been dealt with by contest officials through the guide of warning and the guide of expulsion. Exclusion is necessary here because the offending agent has already, in two separate contests, received warnings and expulsions but apparently was not deterred by these sanctions.

Which organizations can impose such a sanction and how many future contests are included is to be determined within the context of each case, by applying the considerations already discussed earlier in this chapter under the first formulation of this guide.

Both formulations of this guide of exclusion are intended to indicate—in progressive stages of retributive sanction—that not only are certain types of intentional acts reprehensible but that their recurrence has increasingly significant punishment imposed on repeat offenders.

# GUIDE XVIII:
# THE GUIDE OF DISQUALIFICATION

*Contest officials shall disqualify agents from winning, from tying for the win, or from scoring points through wrongful acts which intend the inappropriate decrease of another's performance effectiveness or the inappropriate increase of the offender's own performance effectiveness.*

The final guide that deals with retribution in the class of serious moral imbalance covers some circumstances not necessarily dealt with by the previously stated guides. Specifically, in some cases a wrongful act intended to decrease another's effectiveness or to increase one's own would result in the offender's winning, tying, or placing in a scoring position. The guide of disqualification is intended to prevent this by disqualifying the acting agent from such unmerited consequences. This guide must be viewed in relation to the guide of appropriate compensation and its standards, as discussed earlier in this chapter.

Suppose a runner in a cross-country race intentionally runs a shorter course. Here the guide of appropriate compensation and its supplemental standards would yield the following unfortunate results.

1. If the offending agent led the race at the time he/she ran a shorter course, then the applicable standard would be the standard of adjustment of score. This standard says the adjustment would be to revert to the relative positions held before the violation. Since the violating agent was first, applying this standard would not change the position or, worse yet, if another runner finished first (ahead of the violating agent) the adjustment would make the now second place, but violating agent, the winner.

2. If the offending agent, at the time of the violation, was tied with another runner who then finished second to the violating agent, then the applicable standard would be the standard of no advantage. But this standard alone would only compensate the second place finisher with a tie for the win and, obviously, would allow the violating agent to be the other half of that tie.

Such results would be most inappropriate. Yet they would occur without the guide of disqualification because the functions of compensation and of retribution in restoring the moral equilibrium are different. The guide of appropriate compensation and its three supplemental standards are intended only to restore moral equilibrium by returning to a negatively affected participant something that was taken from him/her inappropriately: either the earned relationship of his/her score to an opponent's, an earned advantage, or a position of earned no advantage. Such restoration by compensation does not itself punish the offending agent. It only returns the situation to its former equilibrium *as if nothing untoward had occurred.* However, something untoward has occurred and, because it has an inappropriate consequence intended by the acting agent, the moral balance is not restored completely without appropriate punishment. The guide of disqualification completes the restoration of the moral balance; it punishes the offending agent by removing the possibility that he/she can profit by winning, tying, or scoring placing points.

The secondary guides, the circumstances to which they apply, and how they restore the moral equilibrium in the class of serious moral imbalance are summarized below in Table 10-2.

**Table 10-2. SUMMARY OF SECONDARY GUIDES FOR CLASS OF SERIOUS MORAL IMBALANCE**

| *Circumstances* | *Type of Action Necessary for Restoration* | *Secondary Guides Applicable* |
|---|---|---|
| Inappropriate decrease in opponent's effectiveness or inappropriate increase in acting agent's effectiveness intended but action is unsuccessful | Retribution | XIa – Condemnation<br>XVII – Warning<br>XIIa – Expulsion<br>XIIIa – Withdrawal<br>XVa – Exclusion |
| Inappropriate decrease in opponent's effectiveness or inappropriate increase in acting agent's effectiveness intended and action is successful | Compensation and retribution | XVI – Appropriate compensation<br>XVIb – Appeal to partisans<br>XIa – Condemnation<br>XVII – Warning<br>XIIa – Expulsion<br>XIIIa – Withdrawal<br>XVa – Exclusion<br>XVIII – Disqualification |

## THE CLASS OF MODERATE MORAL IMBALANCE

The class of moderate moral imbalance will include those secondary guides needed to restore moral equilibrium broken (a) by the acts of sports agents and (b) the inadvertent consequence of these acts is either denial of equal opportunity for optimal performance, or inappropriate reduction in another's performance effectiveness, or inappropriate increase one's own performance effectiveness. Denial of equal opportunity here is preventing an opponent from participating whatsoever or forestalling continued participation after the contest has started. Such acts, then, inadvertently violate the guide of equal opportunity for optimal performance and the guide of noninjurious action. Inappropriate reduction in another's effectiveness or inappropriate increase of one's own effectiveness covers acts that, by their inadvertent consequences, violate the guides of effective contesting, nonreversible earned advantage, effective preparation, or of effective scheduling.

The class of moderate moral imbalance covers situations in which the consequences of acts are essentially the same as they are in the classes of very serious moral imbalance and of serious moral imbalance. However, in the class of moderate moral imbalance, these same consequences were not intended. In general, inadvertent denial of equal opportunity for optimal performance includes acts that injure an opponent unintentionally and prevent him/her from further play. For instance, a football player might tackle an opposing runner from the side when his weight is on one leg, resulting in an incapacitating knee injury. Or a racquetball player might hit an opponent in the head with her racket on the follow-through of her swing. Or a defensive basketball player might run into a player from the other team, whom he did not see, resulting in an injury. Even though such injuries are not intentional, they still create a reparable unbalance in the contest since an injury destroys a necessary condition for the good sports contest. Injury, intentional or otherwise, denies the necessary condition of equally matched opponents who play well. Insofar as this condition can be restored, compensation is needed.

Inappropriate reduction of an opponent's effectiveness includes acts proscribed by the rules that have the unintentional consequence of preventing the opponent from scoring, removing an earned advantage, or dropping his/her position from no advantage to disadvantage. For instance, a defensive basketball player could unintentionally "hack" an offensive player who is shooting a lay-up shot when the former is trying to block the shot. Or a defensive halfback in American football may trip and fall, unintentionally, on the heels of a pass receiver who has earned a one-step advantage. Or a racquetball or handball player may unintentionally hinder an opponent who consequently cannot play the ball effectively.

Inappropriate increase in the acting agent's effectiveness includes acts proscribed by the rules, contradictory to the prescriptions of the rules or contradictory to the spirit of the rules, which have the unintended consequence of increasing the acting agent's score, providing the agent an unearned advantage, or raising his/her position from disadvantage to no advantage. For example a volleyball spiker could unintentionally reach over the net on the opponent's second hit to spike the volleyball. Or a server in handball might think his opponent is ready when he is not. Or a badminton player might stretch out to return an opponent's shot which is almost on the floor and "sling" it with her racket.

The responsibility for restoring the moral equilibrium differs here. In the classes of very serious moral imbalance and of serious moral imbalance, the responsibility fell on agents other than those who broke the moral equilibrium because the offending agents intended the consequence that would break the balance. In the class of moderate moral imbalance, by contrast, the agents who perform the acts with the inappropriate results do not intend such results. In such cases, it is reasonable to expect that they would be able and willing to take responsibility for restoring the moral equilibrium. Responsible agents in this class, first, are those whose acts break the moral equilibrium. Secondarily responsible are either the teammates or the coaches of the offending agent (athlete or coach), or the fellow officials of an offending official.

Specifying this priority of responsibility occurs on two grounds: (a) It is reasonable to assume that agents whose acts have such inadvertent and inappropriate consequences would wish to restore the moral equilibrium; (b) since we are talking about guides of moral action, we can see that agents who take responsibility for restoring the moral equilibrium, voluntarily and intentionally, would be performing a morally good act. For in order to merit praise for a good act, the agent must perform the act intentionally, foresee the good consequences of this intentional act, and intend the good consequences for their own sake.[16] A sports agent who performs an act that meets these three conditions will have performed a good act that is praiseworthy.

Restoration of the moral equilibrium in this class requires compensation for the negatively affected agent(s), but punishment is not needed. Inasmuch as the agents did not intend the negative consequences of their act, compensation to the negatively affected participant(s) is sufficient. Also, since the offending agent(s) assumes the responsibility to restore the equilibrium voluntarily, such voluntary compensation restores the equilibrium fully.

## GUIDE XIX:
## THE GUIDE OF VOLUNTARY ASSESSMENT

*Athletes, coaches, or contest officials whose acts inadvertently result in denial of equal opportunity of optimal performance by a contestant, or inappropriately decrease the performance effectiveness of a contestant or inappropriately increase their own performance effectiveness, shall volunteer the correct assessment of the situation to allow the necessary compensation for the negatively affected participant(s).*

The primary emphasis of this guide is upon the voluntary and correct assessment of the situation of moral imbalance so that the needed compensation can be provided. Voluntary and correct assessment assumes that (a) the inadvertent negative result of the agent's action is recognized by the responsible agent and (b) the responsible agent's perception is accurate.

However, an agent may not always recognize the inadvertent result of his/her act as breaking the moral equilibrium because he/she may not perceive the act correctly. For example, a defensive basketball player may not perceive that he has hacked, unintentionally, an opponent who is shooting for the basket. He may even perceive that he has blocked the shot legally. Or a volleyball player spiking the ball on the opposite side of the net, on the opponent's second hit, may perceive that the contact was on her side. Or a racquetball or handball player may not perceive that he has hindered an opponent's shot. Or a tennis linesman may perceive that a shot by a player was in court when it was out. These instances illustrate that inadvertent acts which break the moral equilibrium may not be perceived as such by the acting agents. In such cases, the agent whose act has broken the moral equilibrium cannot volunteer to restore it since he/she does not recognize an imbalance. Therefore, if the equilibrium is to be restored other agents must act. Accordingly, a supplement to the guide of voluntary assessment is needed.

## GUIDE XIXa: THE SUPPLEMENTARY GUIDE
## OF VOLUNTARY ASSESSMENT

*When the athletes, coaches, or the contest officials — whose acts inadvertently break the moral equilibrium in the sports contest — do not offer the correct assessment of the situation, then their teammates, coaches, or colleagues shall voluntarily offer the correct assessment of the situation to allow the necessary compensation for the negatively affected participant(s).*

These two guides of voluntary assessment provide a foundation for restoring the moral equilibrium for the class of moderate moral imbalance. The efficacy of such voluntary assessment, first, leads directly to the necessary compensation for the negatively affected agent. Second, and important in the long run, such voluntary assessment — when viewed in relation to adherence to the primary guides and to the guides of supererogation — establishes a quality of human relationship wherein it is very unlikely that the moral equilibrium will be intentionally broken.

Such voluntary assessment does not, by itself, provide the necessary compensation. Neither does it apply to all instances of acts that inadvertently break the moral equilibrium. For example, it could happen that neither one tennis linesman nor another, nor even the umpire, would correctly perceive that a shot lands on the line and thus incorrectly calls it out. Or perhaps neither the defensive basketball player who hacks an offensive player, nor his teammates or coach, may perceive the hack. Or, a racquetball or handball player may not perceive that she has obstructed her opponent. In such instances, neither the offending agent nor his/her partisans or colleagues can volunteer a correct assessment of the situation because they have not perceived it correctly. Any compensation here can be provided in two very different ways.

Nonvoluntary compensation to negatively affected participants most frequently occurs by normal actions of contest officials who provide the compensation specified by the rules. For example, a basketball referee who detects a defensive player inadvertently hacking an offensive player will normally award the offensive player free throws. A racquetball or handball official who detects one player obstructing another will normally call for a replay or call an avoidable hinder as compensation. In such instances, the compensation provided and the responsibility for providing it is determined strictly by the rules. So, assessment of sports situations correctly for prescribing necessary compensation can occur voluntarily by the agents whose actions have the inadvertent negative result, or through contest officials who assess such negative acts when they are not recognized by the acting agent or his/her partisans. With one exception, these two kinds of assessment are all that can be done to restore the moral equilibrium. The exception to such assessments will be established in yet a third kind of voluntary assessment.

### GUIDE XIXb: THE GUIDE OF VOLUNTARY AND DISADVANTAGEOUS ASSESSMENT

*An athlete or coach who perceives an advantage bestowed upon him/her or the team inappropriately, either by an official's error or inability to assess the situation correctly, shall volunteer the correct assessment of the situation if such assessment would help eliminate the inappropriate advantage.*

This guide addresses those instances in which an official's inadvertent error provides an inappropriate advantage to the athlete or his/her team, and that athlete or his/her coach or team perceives the error and its inappropriate advantage. For example, suppose a tennis player can see clearly by the mark on a clay court made by a ball hit by an opponent that a linesman's call of "out" was an error. Or suppose that a football coach can see clearly that a player carrying the ball for his team stepped out-of-bounds, but the officials did not see this and allowed the play to continue and result in an apparent touchdown. Or suppose that a volleyball referee inappropriately charged a spiker with hitting the ball out of bounds when a blocker from the opposing team clearly felt the ball touch his/her hand on its way to out of bounds.

These examples all show that the official's error resulted in the inappropriate advantage; the advantaged athlete or team did not act to break the moral equilibrium. Rather, the official's action broke the moral equilibrium but it was performed in good faith and on the basis of the official's best, though faulty, perception of the situation. Thus, there was an inadvertent result for which the offending official could not provide the correct assessment. In such instances, neither the agent whose error broke the equilibrium nor his/her colleagues can assess the situation correctly and voluntarily and, thus, cannot be responsible for restoring the moral equilibrium. For this reason, agents who gained the inappropriate advantage must assume the responsiblity.

It is important to focus explicitly on how actions of voluntary assessment affect the moral climate in the good sports contest. Such voluntary assessment tends to develop an atmosphere wherein participants all realize that the contest's outcome will be determined by the quality of performance of the positively constitutive skills. Such assessment demonstrates that all participants eschew inappropriate advantage and disadvantage. It is in just such an atmosphere that inappropriate advantage or disadvantage will be unlikely to occur—precisely because responsibility is shared by many participants and is not delegated solely to contest officials.

It is not a romantic delusion to assume that such voluntary assessments can happen. It is fact that in many sports contests that do not have officials, the participants themselves assume responsibility for such voluntary assessment. Self-assessed hinders in handball or racquetball, double hits in badminton, traveling in basketball, and calling balls in court on your side of the net in tennis when they are very close, all illustrate this fact. In fact, even in international and/or professional competition where the rewards for winning are very high, such voluntary assessments do occur. For instance, professional golfer Tom Kite called a one-stroke penalty on himself for an infraction that no one else saw in the 1978 Hall of Fame Golf Classic. That one-stroke penalty cost him a tie for the lead at the end of four rounds and eliminated him from a play-off. That one-stroke penalty resulted in a loss of at least $9,167, and possibly $30,000 if he had won a play-off.[17]

It is a fact, also, that the wicket keeper for the Australian cricket team voluntarily acknowledged that he had trapped a ball off the bat of English batsman Derek Randall rather than catching it on the fly as the official had ruled. This occurred in the Centenary Test Match in Cricket between Australia and England in the spring of 1977; the wicket keeper's voluntary assessment allowed Randall to continue his successful batting rather than being retired.[18] In fact, such voluntary assessments happened regularly in the past in several sports. Tennis players would often deliberately double fault on their next serves if a linesman erred in calling an opponent's ball out when it was in. Volleyball players frequently acknowledged their own net violations by signaling so. The major point in these examples—and many more could be cited—is that voluntary assessment can and does happen and that more widespread practice of such assessment will help to establish a more desirable moral climate in sport. In short, the morality of fairness in the sports contest, if it is to be a morality, is the responsibility of all participants—not just the contest officials.

The clarification of these guides of assessment leads now to the statement that governs compensation to restore the moral equilibrium.

## GUIDE XVIa:
## THE GUIDE OF APPROPRIATE COMPENSATION

*Athletes, coaches, and contest officials, when able, shall provide appropriate compensation when participants have been inadvertently denied equal opportunity for optimal performance, or their performance effectiveness has been inappropriately decreased, or other participants inappropriately increase their own performance effectiveness.*

This second formulation of the guide of appropriate compensation must be stated in general terms like the first. If it is to apply to all instances within this class it must specify all agents who could possibly restore the moral balance, not just the contest officials. Also, appropriate compensation can happen only when some agent perceives correctly that the moral equilibrium has been broken inadvertently. Finally, responsibility for compensatory acts is generalized to all agents to stress that everyone should be involved in restoring the moral equilibrium. If athletes and coaches share responsibility for compensatory action with contest officials, they are acting on a moral principle of action beyond what the rules codify. In fact, not all sports rules specify such general responsibility for compensatory actions. Accordingly, if a contest official who is responsible under the rules does not perceive that an act has broken the moral equilibrium inadvertently, then appropriate compensation could not take place without broadening the responsibility to all other agents.

Like its first formulation, this guide generalizes the compensation to "appropriate compensation." The guide itself must be broad enough to cover all instances; the particular compensation appropriate to this class cannot be specified, but operative standards of compensation can be.

## The Standard of Voluntary Suspension of Contest

When an athlete has been injured seriously, though inadvertently, and substitutions for the injured athlete are not a normal part of the particular sport, the acting agent shall suspend the contest without determining winners and losers. If the acting agent fails to do so the partisans of the acting agent or the contest officials shall suspend the contest.

This standard is limited to situations in which (a) incapacitating injury inadvertently results from a participant's acts, and (b) the sport contest involves one athlete against one opponent or two athletes as partners against two opponents. Examples of this are,

1. A racquetball player, in following through on a shot, inadvertently strikes an opponent and causes an incapacitating injury.
2. A referee in a boxing or wrestling match, unable to get out of the way during the contest, inadvertently trips one athlete and the resulting fall causes an incapacitating injury to the athlete.

This standard does not apply to team sports because team sports normally provide competent substitutes for injured players. Therefore, the team unit is compensated by being allowed to substitute another person for the injured player. No other compensation is needed to restore the moral equilibrium even though the substitute for an injured "star" performer may not be completely comparable.

## The Standard of Voluntary Adjustment of Score

When acts inadvertently but inappropriately decrease or increase a participant's score, the acting agent shall try to adjust the score so that its relationship between opponents will revert to what it was prior to the inappropriate imbalance. If the acting agent fails to do so, then his or her partisans, the contest officials, or the agents given the inappropriate score advantage shall do so.

This standard applies when (a) a change in score relationship between opponents was done inappropriately, and (b) the acting agent did not intend such an inappropriate result. Several examples illustrate this.

1. A spiker in volleyball reaches across the net on the opponent's second hit and spikes the ball for an apparent point or side out.
2. A handball server serves the ball before the opponent is ready and scores an apparent point.
3. A tennis linesman calls a shot out that lands on the line and, thus, a point is awarded to the opposing player.

4. A basketball scorer erroneously scores a point for a team when, after turning away for a moment, sees the ball falling through the basket without realizing that the referee threw the ball through to clear the net.

Each example shows an inappropriate change in the score relationship of contestants and results from other than skillful performance of the sport's positively constitutive skills. In each case, the agent whose act resulted in the changed score relationship may try to adjust the score. The volleyball spiker can signal to the referee that he/she has reached over. The handball server can ask the receiver, "Were you ready?" The tennis linesman can ask the umpire or the advantaged player where the ball landed. The scorer can ask the referee if he/she scored the point correctly.

In all of these cases, if the agent responsible for the inappropriate change in score does not act to correct it, other agents may do so. The volleyball spiker's teammates or coach can acknowledge the inappropriately gained point. The receiver in handball can say, "not ready!" The advantaged tennis player can indicate the shot was in or could fault deliberately on his/her next shot. The basketball players or coach of the advantaged team could recognize the error in scoring. In summary, when all agents share moral responsibility for voluntary assessment, it is quite unlikely that such inappropriate errors will affect the contest. Again, it is important that the moral responsibility of sports agents in assuring appropriate compensation goes beyond the technical legalities codified in the rules.

## The Standard of Voluntary Earned Advantage

When a participant's properly earned advantage has been inappropriately neutralized or reversed, the agent at fault shall try to restore the advantage so long as such restoration does not thereby impose unwarranted disadvantage on other participants. If the agent at fault fails to do so, then his or her partisans or the contest officials shall do so.

This standard applies when (a) a participant's earned advantage is inappropriately neutralized or reversed, (b) unintentionally, (c) the neutralization or reversal is correctable, and (d) correcting the situation would not impose unwarranted disadvantage on other participants. Examples include instances when restoration of advantage may occur immediately, as shown in example 1, and when restoration can occur only after the contest is over, as shown in example 2.

1. A basketball or soccer player has advantage by a clear breakaway for an unhindered shot on goal and is held or tripped accidentally by a defensive player in an attempt to defend legally.

2. A runner in a mile race is pushed or tripped by the runner behind her.

In the first example, the agent at fault can indicate clearly that he has tripped or held the opposing player, and thus halt the contest to allow the advantage to be restored. In the second example, the agent at fault can tell officials that she tripped or pushed the other runner accidentally, thus allowing for an adjustment in the disadvantaged athlete's place in the race. This latter may be done, however, only when it does not lower the placing of other contestants except for the runner who pushed or tripped accidentally. Both illustrate the restoration of an earned advantage. The actual stopping and restarting of the contest with the advantage restored, or the revision of finishing positions, will usually be done by contest officials. However, it is the voluntary assessment of the situation that allows such restoration of the moral equilibrium. In contests having no officials, the assessment and restoration are both performed by the same agent.

### The Standard of Voluntary No Advantage

When a participant's position of no advantage is lowered to one of disadvantage, due to another participant's inadvertent act, the latter shall try to restore the position of no advantage, so long as such restoration does not impose unwarranted disadvantage on other participants. If the agent at fault fails to do so, then his or her partisans or the contest officials shall do so.

This standard, like the preceding one, applies when (a) a participant's position of no advantage is inappropriately changed to disadvantage, (b) unintentionally, (c) the position of disadvantage is correctable, and (d) correcting the situation would not impose unwarranted disadvantage on other participants. Again, sometimes the restoration of no advantage may be immediate, as shown in example 1, but other times restoration can occur only at the end of the contest, as example 2 shows.

1. A golfer steps on an opponent's golf ball accidentally, thus pressing it firmly into the turf.
2. A runner accidentally elbows another runner, who is then tied with her and whose stride is disturbed enough to result in her finishing the race behind the elbowing runner.

The golfer who steps on the ball in the first example can report it to the negatively affected golfer and to tournament officials, thus allowing the restoration of no advantage. If there are no officials the offending agent would assess the situation and restore no advantage by allowing the opponent a free drop. The offending runner in the second example can report it to contest officials so they may assign the negatively affected participant to a tied finish with the elbowing runner, provided it does not lower the finish order of other runners.

Even though these four standards address most instances of appropriate compensation to negatively affected participants, yet another kind of compensation is needed for a special set of cases. This special set includes instances when the inadvertent result of an agent's act is preventing the negatively affected opponent(s) from winning, tying, or placing in a scoring position in the contest. The standards relevant to earned advantage, no advantage, and adjustment of score do not completely cover certain negative effects. For example,

1. A cross-country runner inadvertently takes a short cut when he is leading and finishes ahead of or in a tie with another runner who has run the full course.
2. A golfer in an 18-hole match fails to count one stroke at a time when she is one up in the match and, as a result, ties the hole. Subsequently, the match finishes in a tie.

In neither case does the standard of voluntary earned advantage or the standard of voluntary no advantage apply because the negatively affected participant(s) are already in positions of disadvantage. Besides, the standard of voluntary adjustment of score, if applied, would only return the negatively affected participant(s) to the score relationship they had prior to the negative act. In the first example, all runners would revert to their positions behind the runner who inadvertently short cut the course. And the negatively affected golfer in the second example would revert to a position of one down in the match. Therefore, another standard is needed to provide appropriate compensation in such cases.

**The Standard of Voluntary Disqualification**

When acts inadvertently prevent opponents from winning, tying, or placing in a higher position in the contest, and such inappropriate results cannot be compensated by applying the standards of voluntary earned advantage, voluntary no advantage, or voluntary adjustment of score, the agent at fault shall disqualify himself/herself voluntarily from the contest if such disqualification would place the negatively affected opponents in the finishing positions they would have occupied without the inadvertent act. If the agent at fault fails to disqualify himself/herself, then his/her partisans or the contest officials shall do so.

This standard of voluntary disqualification differs from the guide of disqualification discussed under the class of serious moral imbalance.

**Table 10-3.  SUMMARY OF SECONDARY GUIDES FOR
CLASS OF MODERATE MORAL IMBALANCE**

| Circumstances | Type of Action Necessary for Restoration | Secondary Guides Applicable |
|---|---|---|
| Denial of equal opportunity or inappropriate decrease of performance effectiveness or inappropriate increase of performance effectiveness of participants as a direct inadvertent result of acts by sports agents | Compensation | XIX — Voluntary assessment XIXa — Supplementary guide of voluntary assessment XIXb — Voluntary and disadvantageous assessment XVIa — Appropriate compensation |

In that guide, the disqualification was involuntary whereas in this standard it is voluntary. Also, this is a standard for appropriate compensation whereas the guide of disqualification is a guide of retributive sanctions. Accordingly, since the standard of voluntary disqualification covers instances of voluntary compensation, it has no negative stigma attached.

The secondary guides applicable to the class of moderate moral imbalance, then, are summarized in Table 10-3.

## NOTES

[1] Kurt Baier, *The Moral Point of View* (Ithaca and London: Cornell University Press, 1958), pp. 204-205.

[2] Ibid., p. 205.

[3] David A. J. Richards, *A Theory of Reasons for Action* (Oxford: Oxford University Press, 1971), p. 102.

[4] Francis W. Keenan, "Justice and Sport," *Journal of the Philosophy of Sport* II (September 1975), p. 117.

[5] Baier, *Moral Point of View*, p. 207.

[6] Peter McIntosh, *Fair Play: Ethics in Sport and Education* (London: Heinemann, 1979), p. 124.

[7] Ibid., p. 123.

[8] Kurt Baier, "Responsibility and Action," in Myles Brand, ed., *The Nature of Human Action* (Glenview, IL: Scott Foresman & Co., 1970), p. 103.

[9] Ibid., p. 113.

[10] Ibid., p. 104.

[11]Ibid., p. 105.

[12]Ibid., p. 106. The reader is referred to the cited work for clarification of what the limitations and qualifying conditions are for legitimate exculpatory explanations.

[13]Ibid., p. 107.

[14]Ibid., p. 101.

[15]It must be reiterated here that this book attempts to focus only on moral actions for those directly involved in the sports contest: the athletes, coaches, and trainers. However, some instances require that other sports agents, such as contest officials, be involved because of their functions in the sports. Although this work will not undertake a thorough analysis of guides for the actions of referees, umpires, linesmen, judges, and so on, such agents clearly have a crucial relevance to the secondary guides because they can impose retributive sanctions. The guide of condemnation may also apply to agents not involved directly in the sports contest, such as sports organization officials, sports reporters, sports rulemakers, and fans. But these agents are not obliged to assume responsibility because they have not entered into a social contract as direct participants have.

[16]Eric D'Arcy, *Human Acts: An Essay in Their Moral Evaluation* (Oxford: Oxford University Press, 1963), pp. 125-126.

[17]*Rochester Democrat and Chronicle*, August 28, 1978.

[18]Observed on BBC Television, London, spring 1977.

# PART FOUR

# HOW SPECIFIC
# SPORTS CONTEST SITUATIONS
# RELATE TO THE GENERAL
# GUIDES AND ENDS
# OF RIGHT ACTION

The general guides and ends of right action for the good sports contest have been explained in Part III. We must now sketch out the relationships of specific sports contest situations to the general guides and ends of action. Correct use of the guides in specific problematic situations encountered in the sports contest require as much. Chapters 11 and 12 will address certain problems that occur when sports participants attempt to apply the guides for right action to situations in which the questions are, "What ought I to do?", "What ought to be done?", or "What ought to have been done?" Three kinds of problems arise.

## THE PROBLEM OF APPLICABILITY

If we have many different guides for right action and a sports participant understands and wishes to use them to answer one or more of the "ought" questions, he/she must be able to choose those that apply to each situation correctly. The guides for right action are our general "ought" rules which give specific advice for singular "ought" sentences. As indicated in Chapter 1, when an agent says "I ought to do X," or "X ought to be done," or "X ought to have been done," — and the ought is a moral ought — then that agent is applying a general "ought" rule. We can see that sports participants must answer "Which guides for right action (the general "ought" rules) are the correct ones to apply to this situation to answer my specific 'ought' question?" This is the problem of applicability.


## THE PROBLEM OF PRIORITIES

A second problem concerns priority. If our sports participant, for instance, finds that more than one guide for right action applies to the situation in question, he/she may possibly have a conflict if the applicable guides advise actions that are incompatible. Which guide should have priority?

Another priority problem occurs when a sports participant finds that more than one action in a specific contest intends the same general end and is in accord with the same general guide of right action. Here the participant must be able to assess the multiple actions to determine which, if any, are better. Doing so will require some relevant way of evaluating the many possible actions.


## THE PROBLEM OF ONE ACTION
## DONE BY DIFFERENT AGENTS
## FOR DIFFERENT REASONS

The third problem deals with the reality that different agents in the same situation can perform the same action with the same intended end and which pursues the same general end included in the guides for right action but for different kinds of reasons. We saw in Chapter 2 that people can make the same "ought" statement but for different kinds of reasons. To illustrate once more:

> Person A says: "I ought to play fair in sports."

> Person B asks: "Why ought you to play fair?"

> Person A responds: "Because if I do not play fair I will be penalized." (self-interested reason)

> Person A responds: "Because the regulations of my sports organizations say that playing fair is expected." (conventional reason)

> Person A responds: "Because playing fair fulfills the tacit promise that everybody makes when they agree to play a sport and playing fair is absolutely necessary for everyone to have equal access to the value of sport itself." (moral reason)

This reality presents both an immediate and a long-range problem for the ethics of the sports contest and will be identified in Chapter 12.

# Chapter Eleven

## Problems in Applying Guides for Right Action in Specific Situations in the Sports Contest

The establishment of guides to right action provides, at least in some instances, unequivocal guidance in some specific situations in the sports contest. It was stated in Chapter 2 that the kind of end being sought is necessarily selective in its range of actions that may be used. For one example, the guide of noninjurious action informs the sports participant that one of its general ends is non-injury and that actions which intend otherwise are prohibited. This narrows the range of acceptable actions. Likewise, the guide of effective contesting informs the participant to intend the general end of effective contesting and restricts its range of acceptable actions to those which seek oppositional superiority. Such a restriction thereby eliminates actions that intend the end of trying to tie, where trying to tie is not seeking oppositional superiority.

The illustrations above help us to understand that we do not arrive without help at each situation in which the specific "ought" questions occur. To appraise the possible action options we do not have to return, in each instance, to a systematic consideration of our guides. Rather, in each situation we seek to identify alternative acts as *instances* of a kind of act which is already understood as good, bad, wrong, and so forth.[1] Golfers know, for instance, that not standing along the line of the putt of another golfer is the right thing to do because it is courteous. This example illustrates the idea that sports participants in specific situations often answer their "ought" questions by accepting or eliminating certain alternatives; they know which acts are subsumable under which general guides.

## THE PROBLEM OF APPLICABILITY

In order for a sports participant to select the action for a specific situation, he/she must know what guide applies (the general "ought" rule). If the form, content, and organization of the guides for right action are viewed together, it may be clear that at least in general the appropriate guides and ends of right action are already stated. One way to determine the applicability of the several guides is by seeing which specific possible actions are instances of the general actions subsumed by a certain guide. To illustrate, one of the possible actions in the specific situation of being a defensive basketball player who has been faked out of position by an offensive player is to hold that player intentionally. In this case, the basketball player would know that the act of intentional fouling is subsumed under the guide of nonreversible earned advantage because it is proscribed by the constitutive rules and that guide makes specific reference to avoiding such acts. In the same basketball situation, another possible action is for the defensive player to try to recover and block the shot from behind. That action is subsumable under the guide of effective contesting because it seeks oppositional superiority within the letter and spirit of relevant rules. In that situation the player knows that at least two of the guides apply.

In addition, the form and content of each statement specifies the situations to which it applies. Accordingly, certain differences in applicability to specific circumstances are built into the guides. In one class of applicability, there are no specific situations to which certain guides are not applicable in principle. This means that the ends to be sought under certain guides must always be operative, either by direct actions or by assessment to see that these ends are fulfilled already. These guides are equal opportunity for optimal performance, noninjurious action, nonharassment, mutual respect, and courtesy. To illustrate briefly: Under any circumstances all sports participants must seek and sustain equal opportunity for themselves and for opponents to achieve oppositional superiority within sports contests; no sports participant is ever to attempt to injure another person; and all sports participants are to treat all others with courtesy.

A second class of applicability includes situations of restricted coverage to which certain guides are always applicable. All the guides not mentioned under the first class of applicability fall within this second class. Several illustrations will clarify this class.

1. The guide of effective preparation — applicable to all situations involving the actions of sports participants in preparing for scheduled sports contests;
2. The guide of positive recognition — applicable to all situations in

which other sports participants perform skillfully and effectively;

3. The guide of condemnation — in both formulations, applies to all situations in which sports participants perform actions intended to violate the primary guides;

4. The guide of appropriate compensation — in both formulations, applies to all situations in which a sports participant has been deprived of equal opportunity or has had his/her performance effectiveness decreased inappropriately as a result of an opponent's actions.

5. The guide of appeal to partisans — applies to all situations in which the fans of an athlete or team attempt to interfere inappropriately with the performance effectiveness of opponents.

This second class of applicability specifies the kind of restricted situational relevance each guide has. For example, we know that the guide of positive recognition does not apply to situations where sports participants play poorly; the guide of condemnation does not apply to situations wherein the inadvertent, nonintended results of participants' actions decrease the performance effectiveness of other participants; and the guide of nonreversible earned advantage does not apply when sports participants attempt to negate earned advantage of opponents by the skillful performance of the positively prescribed skills of the sport.

The problem of applicability is also somewhat resolved by the fact that each guide identifies the sport agent or agents to whose actions it applies. For example, we know that the agents responsible in specified kinds of situations under most of the guides described in Chapters 8 and 9 are athletes, coaches, and athletic trainers. On the other hand, we know that the only responsible agent under the guide of voluntary and disadvantageous assessment is the sports participant who knows that he/she has inappropriately benefitted by an official's error. Thus, to understand the applicability we must know to which agent(s) each guide applies. Our guides to right action, when properly understood, specify who is responsible for action, what kinds of actions are to be taken, in which kinds of situations, and the general end being sought.

## THE PROBLEM OF PRIORITIES

Even though our guides to right action, as stated, will help sports participants sort out the kinds of situations to which each applies, it is still possible that more than one guide may apply to a specific situation. This presents still another problem, that is, whenever we have several rules applicable there may be conflict between the action specifications of more than one rule.[2] This leads to the problem of priorities among our guides.

## Priorities in Application of the Guides for Right Action

In the broadest sense, one kind of priority problem is dealt with by the differing functions of primary, supererogatory, and secondary guides and ends. First, as the name indicates, the primary guides and ends and the actions subsumed therein have a certain kind of priority in relation to the moral equilibrium in the sports contest. This is a priority of sequence in time and a priority in terms of the general spread of responsibility of sports agents. The sequence in time priority means that in principle at the beginning of the sports contest, the first necessary kinds of actions are those subsumed under the primary guides and ends. The first efforts are to be directed by the general ends of equal opportunity for optimal performance, noninjurious action, nonharassment, effective preparation, effective scheduling, effective contesting, and nonreversible earned advantage. The priority of general responsibility means that primary guides and ends, when taken as a set, specify wider responsibility among more sports agents than do the supererogatory guides and ends or the secondary guides and ends. Thus, the primary guides and ends specify the required duties of a broad population of sports participants.

In contrast, yet importantly supportive, the supererogatory guides and ends are not first priority in terms of time sequence. The acts subsumed under the guide of positive recognition and positive instruction are contingent upon fulfilling the primary guides. Remember our example of the athlete who devoted so much time to voluntary unrequired instruction of other athletes that he/she neglected his/her own effective preparation for scheduled sports contests. Such voluntary, unrequired instruction is not altogether wrong but, in terms of the good sports contest, it must not assume priority over acts subsumed under the primary guides. Accordingly, the supererogatory acts under the guides of positive recognition and positive instruction are to be performed *after*, and in conjunction with, the acts under the primary guides which have established the conditions necessary for the good sports contest. Supererogatory acts, when supportive of and in conjunction with acts under the primary guides, will increase the probability of maintaining these necessary conditions. Taken by themselves, supererogatory acts will not construct those conditions. However, one should not assume that supererogatory acts are not necessary to the good sports contest — only that their necessity be in proper relation to other acts.

There is yet another relationship of supererogatory acts to the acts specified under other sets of guides. This is the relationship of acts under the guides of mutual respect and of courtesy. First, such acts are not contingent upon fulfilling the acts under the primary guides. For, there is no necessary conflict between acting with mutual respect and courtesy and acting toward the general ends of equal opportunity, noninjurious actions, nonharassment, effective scheduling, effective preparation, effective contesting, and nonreversible earned advantage. All of those primary general ends may be intended without any lack of respect for, or courtesy to, other sports participants. It is clearly possible that any sports participant can treat all other participants with respect and courtesy even if he/she has a strong personal dislike for some of them.

With respect to questions of priority, a similar relationship exists between acts under the guides of mutual respect and of courtesy and acts under those secondary guides which concern themselves with retributive treatment of agents whose acts violate the moral equilibrium. The important aspect of this relationship is that even negative acts of retributive punishment, such as those under the guides of condemnation, warning, expulsion, disqualification, and exclusion, may be done without any lack of respect or of courtesy toward the offending agents. Thus, what appears to be a conflict in acting according to the supererogatory guides of mutual respect and of courtesy—yet at the same time according to the secondary guides requiring punishment—is not a conflict. The use of punishment does not require hostility—as any parent knows very well.

We may generalize, then, that there is no priority conflict between acts under the supererogatory guides of mutual respect and of courtesy and acts under the primary guides or the secondary guides. In short, sports agents are required to do their duties under primary guides, they are required to fulfill their obligations under secondary guides, but they *should* perform these acts of duty and obligation with respect for and courtesy to other sports participants.

As between the applicability of primary guides or of secondary guides, no priority conflict is possible. For actions under the primary guides have the time sequence priority mentioned above. With that priority, acts under the secondary guides do not become a factor until the moral equilibrium has been broken by acts that violate the primary guides. At that point, the time sequence priority reverses itself: Acts required under the secondary guides must be performed, whenever possible, before the contest continues or as soon as possible. Therefore, when a state of moral imbalance exists, the priority is to restore the moral equilibrium.

Another potential priority problem concerns possible conflicts between applicable guides from the same category. What are the priorities between acts under two or more applicable guides within the set of primary guides, within the set of supererogatory guides, or within the set of secondary guides?

The secondary guides have been organized and their form and content is so stated that conflict in their application should not occur. At the most general level, potential conflict is alleviated through the organization of the three classes of moral imbalance: very serious, serious, and moderate. Since the circumstances to which such classes of guides are applicable essentially differ, there is little possibility that guides drawn from more than one class of guides will apply to the same case. Thus, no priority problem occurs.

*Within* each of the three classes of moral imbalance, more than one guide may apply to a specific situation. For instance, it is perfectly possible for a single situation, say, in the class of serious moral imbalance, to require acts under more than one of the guides in that class. Suppose that a defensive player in American football intentionally grabs and holds the jersey of an offensive pass receiver who is eluding him after the receiver has faked the defender out of position. In such an instance, if it is the defender's first intentional violation in that contest, three guides would be applicable: appropriate compensation, condemnation, and warning. However, when the statements of these guides are examined, there is no conflict between the kinds of acts required. In that instance, there can be appropriate compensation to the offensive player or his team along with acts of condemnation and warning to the offender. To generalize, the secondary guides have been so organized and their form and content so stated that, if more than one guide applies, there is no priority conflict and/or the circumstances to which the several guides apply are different so that contradictory guides do not apply to the same circumstances.

In a similar way, acts subsumable under the supererogatory guides and ends should not cause priority problems. The specific set of circumstances to which acts of positive recognition, positive instruction, and sympathetic regard are applicable all differ and, therefore, cannot conflict with one another. Also, there is no real contradiction between acts under the guides of mutual respect and of courtesy, so these acts can apply to the same situation without priority problems arising. Finally, there is no real contradiction between acts of mutual respect and courtesy on the one hand, and acts either of positive instruction, or positive recognition, or sympathetic regard on the other hand. For all the above reasons, the application of several of the guides and ends of supererogation does not in principle cause priority problems.

The possibility of priority problems arising because of the applicability of more than one of the primary guides needs specific attention. The question of priority among the primary guides and ends was discussed in Chapter 8, independently, in relation to each guide. It will be helpful to pull the essentials of priority problems in primary guides and ends together here. First, because the guides of effective preparation, effective scheduling, effective contesting, and nonreversible earned advantage apply to situations having defined and mutually exclusive characteristics, there cannot be a priority problem among the acts subsumable under each. Also, there can be no priority problem between acts subsumable under the guides of equal opportunity for optimal performance, of noninjurious action, and of nonharassment because the latter two situations have specific characteristics and appropriate acts that cannot contradict the more general characteristics and appropriate acts of equal opportunity for optimal performance. Briefly, any act supported by the guides of noninjurious action or of nonharassment also supports the more general specifications of the guide of equal opportunity for optimal performance.

Nonetheless, there are many possibilities of priority conflicts among acts subsumable, on the one hand, under the guides of effective preparation, effective scheduling, effective contesting, nonreversible earned advantage and, on the other hand, of acts subsumable under the guides of equal opportunity for optimal performance, noninjurious action, or of nonharassment. We must clearly establish the priority system that sports participants must use to resolve such conflicts.

First, one should understand that acts subsumable under the first four guides mentioned above are contingent upon fulfillment of the general ends of equal opportunity for optimal performance, of noninjurious action, and of nonharassment. No act of preparation, scheduling, or contesting is acceptable if it contradicts or negates the general ends of equal opportunity, noninjurious action, or nonharassment. Several examples will help clarify this priority relationship, but first it is necessary to be very clear on what is happening in this effort to establish the priority system to use in resolving conflicts.

In dealing with priorities, we attempt to establish their systematic exposition so that they may be applied to particular situations. This means that we do not develop our priorities solely in response to particular situations; rather, we respond consistently to many situations because we have our priority system in hand by the previous systematic exposition. Thus, the three "ought" questions, when involving conflicting answers from different primary guides, can be answered instead by considering the priority system. Consistent answers to such questions cannot occur without some previous consideration of priorities. Consequently, sports participants do not deal with these specific "ought" situations that have conflicting answers without *some* sense of priority.

Second, the three examples used below will illustrate some different conflicts between acts under the primary guides. Each example will describe a specific sports situation and identify two possible acts. Each of the two acts will be the right thing to do under different primary guides, and the right act in each case will be stated in accord with priorities among primary guides.

*Case A: A right act subsumable under the guide of effective scheduling conflicts with a right act subsumable under the guide of noninjurious action.* Suppose that a coach schedules a sports contest between two individuals or teams whose experience and preparation indicate clearly the promise to provide an equal contest. This act of scheduling is the right thing to do under the guide of effective scheduling. But suppose, also, that these two opponents are known to have severe and potentially violent animosity toward one another, making it likely that their opposition in the contest would provoke attempted physical injury. Under the guide of noninjurious action, the right thing to do is to avoid encouraging acts that could injure another person unnecessarily.

The coach arranging the schedule has a clear conflict of two right acts—each right because of a different primary guide. In this case, the avoidance of physical injury has priority over scheduling opponents who promise to provide an equal contest. This priority is already established in the statement of the primary guides and in their discussion. That is, we know already by the specifications of this normative theory for the good sports contest that acts subsumable under the guide of effective scheduling are contingent upon fulfillment of the general end of noninjurious action specified by the guide of noninjurious action. Consequently, the right thing to do here is to avoid the possibility of physical injury by not scheduling the contest.

This particular case is not invented for convenience. In fact, the kind of priority problem it illustrates can and does occur—witness the bloody battle of the Hungarian and Soviet water polo teams in the Olympics following the Soviet invasion of Hungary. In that case political animosity clearly increased the possibility of physical injury to the extent that intentional bloody injury was a feature of the contest.

*Case B: A right act subsumable under the guide of effective contesting conflicts with a right act under the guide of equal opportunity for optimal performance.*      Suppose that a baseball runner on second base, by prior agreement with a batter on his team, attempts to steal the catcher's signs to the opposing pitcher and transmit them to the batter so that he knows what kind of pitch is coming. This is a right act under the guide of effective contesting since it seeks oppositional superiority. Clearly, knowledge of what kind of pitch is coming will facilitate pursuit of oppositional superiority by making it easier to hit the ball. Further, the rules do not prohibit the stealing of signals by players on the field. However, the rules are explicit about prescribed positive skills of pitching and batting.

In this same situation, the right thing to do under the guide of equal opportunity for optimal performance is to seek and sustain like equal opportunity for both sides to achieve oppositional superiority. *Like* equal opportunity in such an instance would be whether or not the batters of both teams, in fact, had prior knowledge of what kind of pitch is coming next—not the opportunity to steal such knowledge. For even if both have like equal opportunity to steal the knowledge, they would both have to be equally successful or unsuccessful in obtaining such knowledge in order to have like equal opportunity for oppositional superiority in batting and pitching. In principle, stealing the catcher's signals cannot guarantee such equal opportunity because equal success or failure for both teams in stealing signals, and in other crucial contest situations, is not predictable. Such equal opportunity would only be possible if all batters would know what pitch is coming next, or if no batters would know what pitch is coming next. Accordingly, under current baseball rules and under the guide of equal opportunity for optimal performance, the right act here is not to steal the catcher's signals.

This conclusion illuminates another priority problem: the priority between positively constituted skills explicitly prescribed by the rules (pitching and hitting) and conventionally used skills not mentioned in the rules (such as stealing a catcher's signals to the pitcher). Beyond the priority of equal opportunity over effective contesting the contention is that, in cases of conflict, equal opportunity to perform the positively prescribed skills has priority over equal opportunity to perform skills not prescribed by the rules when we are pursuing the good sports contest. This conclusion cannot be generalized to say that *all* stealing of signals in baseball is inappropriate. That problem has not been examined here. All that has been examined in this restricted analysis is the contradiction of stealing a catcher's signals to the pitcher with equal opportunity to contest the skills of pitching and batting.

This situation presents still another potential, albeit unpredictable, conflict — that between seeking oppositional superiority by stealing signals and the potential of increasing the possibility of injury by giving the batter incorrect information because of an inadvertent mistake by the runner. For instance, if the runner signaled the batter incorrectly that a curve ball was coming and the pitcher threw a fastball instead, the possibility of the batter being hit by an inside fastball would be increased. The baserunner in this instance would know, on the basis of established priority among the primary guides, that avoiding the possibility of injury to another has priority over the seeking of oppositional superiority. The good sports contest makes right acts subsumable under the guide of effective contesting contingent upon fulfillment of the general end of noninjurious action as specified by that guide.

*Case C: A right act subsumable under the guide of effective preparation conflicts with a right act subsumable under the guide of nonharassment.*     Suppose that a coach in preparing her team for a contest motivates the players to train diligently, and to be prepared to put forth maximum effort during the contest, by characterizing the opponents as ignorant persons of a certain national and religious ancestry to whom it would be a disgrace to lose. In this instance, the coach's act is right under the guide of effective preparation because it helps the athletes become fully prepared for best performance. In the same situation, the right act under the guide of nonharassment is to avoid acts that are intended to insult or derogate the character, intelligence, or ancestry of other persons. In such a case, avoiding acts of harassment would have priority over that type of effective preparation because the guide of effective preparation is contingent upon fulfillment of the general end of nonharassment.

Without such established priorities, our judgment in specific situations becomes subject to influences other than the good sports contest from the moral point of view. For example, in stealing signals in baseball, our judgment of what is most right to do would likely be influenced by our socialization into the view and common practice that stealing signals is part of the game. In fact, a conflict in priorities probably would not even occur without the established guides.

In scheduling contests between opponents who harbor severe animosity toward one another, our judgment might be influenced by such things as economic priorities. Witness, if you will, some current promotions of scheduled sports contests under the phrases "it will be a war!" or "it will be a shoot-out!" In such instances the priority of self-interested reasons of monetary profit predominate. And, any number of motivations could make a coach psych up his/her athletes by disparaging the opposition without any recognition of the primafacie priority of nonmaleficence.

Having discussed the priorities in applying the guides to right action, let us consider other facets of the problem of priority.

## Priorities Among Different Actions
## That Intend the Same General End

Sports agents may know which of the guides of right action apply in each situation, and they may also know what the priorities are among applicable guides, but there is still more to know about possible problems of priorities. For several possible actions in the same situation may each be consistent with the same guide and end of right action. Here we will illustrate and examine a case in a reasonably restricted analysis to highlight how priorities may be established. Our purpose here is not to come to a definitive conclusion on the case, but to illustrate the considerations important to such priority conflicts.

*The Problem of Right Action in the Uneven Contest.*     Chapter 1 described cases to illustrate the kinds of problems facing sports participants. One such case involved the problem of an uneven contest and is repeated here for our analysis.

At times, a thoroughly unequal contest occurs wherein one contestant or team has so completely dominated the other and has attained such a substantial lead in the score that it is almost impossible for the opponent to win. What ought to be done under such circumstances? Should the presently superior contestant or team increase the advantage as far as possible by vigorously using their normal style of play? Should the superior contestant or team play deliberately to the opponents' strength?

To clarify some other situational variables, we must point out that this describes a specific contest occurring between two evenly matched contestants. The unevenness of the contest has not resulted from scheduling unequal opponents, which would violate the guide of effective scheduling. Neither has the unevenness of the contest resulted from injury, illness, equipment failure, or some other unfortunate circumstance for one of the contestants. In short, the uneven contest is a result of one opponent playing well while the other plays poorly in the normative senses established in Chapter 4.

It appears that the secondary guides do not apply here since none of the primary guides has been violated to unbalance the moral equilibrium. The supererogatory guides of mutual respect and courtesy apply and are always appropriate, and such does not contradict the primary guides. Also, the guides of equal opportunity for optimal performance, effective scheduling, and effective preparation have been fulfilled. The guides of noninjurious action and of nonharassment are applicable and inform the contestants in this case of what they *cannot* do. Consequently, we see that the now-ahead contestant faces the problem of what actions, subsumable under the guide of effective contesting, are possible and which is the best action? What are some of the possible actions for the now-ahead contestant?

1. The contestant ahead could attempt to increase the advantage by vigorously using his/her normal style of play.

2. The contestant ahead could play deliberately to the opponents's strength.

3. If in a team sport, the contestant ahead could substitute less competent players.

4. The contestant ahead could deliberately offer little effective defense to the opponent's offense.

5. The contestant ahead could attempt untested tactics and strategy that are within his/her possibility.

Of these five possibilities, the fourth would contradict the guide of effective contesting since it negates seeking oppositional superiority continuously. It would be eliminated. The other four options all appear to seek oppositional superiority, albeit by different means, yet there appear to be some conflicts between them. For instance, the winning contestant cannot, at the same time, attempt to increase the advantage by his/her normal style of play while playing deliberately to the opponent's strength or while using untested tactics and strategy. However, if it is a team sport, the contestant can substitute less competent players and still use his/her normal style of play, or play to the opponent's strength, or use untested tactics and strategy. These possible combinations all appear to be consistent with the guide of effective contesting. Which possible combination is the best action subsumable under the guide of effective contesting? Our described priority system to this juncture does not answer this question.

*Right Action in Relation to Reasons for Action.*    The four possible actions subsumable under the guide of effective contesting are all different ways of intending the general end of effective contesting. Nonetheless, as indicated in Chapter 2, we adopt our intended ends for different kinds of reasons. Moreover, the reasons we give to support actions may be of three different kinds—self-interested, conventional, or moral reasons. Further, we have indicated in Chapter 1 that the best course of action is the one supported by the best reasons and the best kinds of reasons are moral reasons. Thus, if we have four different actions that intend the general end of effective contesting, we can evaluate the priorities among them in relation to the kind(s) of reasons given to support them. We can assess their supportive reasons in relationship to a hierarchy of reasons.

Now, as stated, our sports agents are interested in answering one or more of the three "ought" questions. The first and second are asked before acting, and the third is asked after an uneven contest of the type described has occurred. By each of these "ought" questions, the sports agents attempt to determine which action(s) is supported by the best reasons.

Any agent asking any of the three "ought" questions must now do three things to get his/her answer: First—identify what actions are possible and subsumable under the guide and end of effective contesting in the described kind of uneven contest; second—give reasons to support each of the possible and subsumable actions; and third—evaluate the reasons given in support of each possible and subsumable action in terms of a hierarchy of kinds of reasons.

Given this sequence, it is obvious that the action evaluated as the best is contingent upon the agent's abilities in two ways. First, the asking agent can seek to establish priorities only among those specific actions that he/she can identify as possibilities. This will restrict or expand the possible actions to the agent's own knowledge, creativity, and maturity.

Second, the kinds of reasons the agent is able to provide for the actions will depend, also, on what reasons the agent can cite. And, as indicated in Chapter 2, it is possible to cite reasons of different kinds—self-interested, conventional, or moral—for the same action. Thus, any establishment of priorities among different possible actions, even if informed by a hierarchy of reasons, cannot always arrive at the same answer because different agents bring different competency to the task. In short, any sports agent attempting to answer any of the three "ought" questions must come to his/her own decision, but doing so is no guarantee that the decision is the very best possible. Frankena[3] identifies this reality as follows:

> It remains true...that a man must in the moment of decision, do what he thinks is right. He cannot do otherwise. This does not mean that what he does will be right or even that he will not be worthy of blame or punishment. He simply has no choice, for he cannot at that moment see any discrepancy between what is right and what he thinks is right. He cannot be morally good if he does not do what he finally believes to be right, but even then, what he does may not be what he ought to do. The life of man, even if he would be moral, is not without its risks.

### *Reasons for Possible Actions in the Uneven Contest.*

If sports agents are to determine priorities among different actions that are subsumable under the same guide and end of right action in the uneven contest, they must state the reasons for each action. In our restricted analysis of the uneven contest, we can cite some possible reasons for *some* of the possible actions. This analysis cannot reveal all of the complexities of the case. Because our purpose here is to illustrate the considerations important to such priority conflicts, the analysis will cite several reasons for and against only two of the possible actions in the uneven contest. This analysis does not attempt to reach a final conclusion in such a circumstance since the primary function of this normative ethic is to provide guides to right action and to indicate how such guides are used to reach decisions. The two possible actions will be, first, the ahead contestant attempting to increase his/her advantage by vigorously using his/her normal style of play and, second, the same contestant changing from his/her normal style of play to try new tactics and strategy.

*In the uneven sports contest the ahead contestant should attempt to increase the advantage by vigorously using his/her normal style of play because:*

1. Such action would be consistent with seeking oppositional superiority continuously.
2. It would maintain the oppositional superiority already earned.
3. It would save the alternative tactics and strategies for future contests when they may be needed.

4. It would provide for the continuation of the test, which the behind contestant chose upon entering the contest.

5. It would fulfill the tacit promise, made by the ahead contestant, to try to perform the test better than his/her opponent.

*In the uneven sports contest the ahead contestant should not attempt to increase his/her advantage by vigorously using his/her normal style of play because:*

1. Such action would be viewed by other sports agents and spectators as "running up the score," intentionally, which is a negatively sanctioned act and contrary to courtesy.

2. It would provide an insufficient test of the abilities of the ahead contestant.

*In the uneven sports contest the ahead contestant should change from his/her normal style of play to use untested (for that individual) tactics and strategy that are within his/her possibility because:*

1. Such action would be consistent with seeking oppositional superiority continuously.

2. It would probably maintain the oppositional superiority already earned.

3. It would test, further, the abilities of the ahead contestant.

4. It would provide more fully for the continued test that both contestants chose when they entered the contest.

5. It would fulfill the tacit promise made by the ahead contestant to try to perform the test better than his/her opponent.

*In the uneven sports contest the ahead contestant should not change from his/her normal style of play to use untested tactics and strategy that are within his/her possibility because:*

1. Such action would risk losing the oppositional superiority earned.

2. Such action, if successful, would be viewed by other sports agents and spectators as running up the score which is a negatively sanctioned act.

3. It would reveal to future opponents some unknown tactical and strategic competencies of the ahead contestant.

## THE HIERARCHY OF REASONS FOR ACTION

In establishing our hierarchy, first it is helpful to clarify the *form* of response to the "ought" questions. Note that agents responding to the "ought" questions in the uneven contest situation do two things.

1. They state an action that "ought" to occur or ought not to occur. The ahead contestant (a) ought to try increasing the advantage by vigorously using his/her normal style of play; (b) ought not to try increasing the advantage by such means; (c) ought to change from his/her normal style of play to use untested tactics and strategy; (d) ought not to change to untested tactics and strategy.

2. They follow the statement of the action with the word "because" and then the substance of their thought — their reason — about why that action is supportable. For example, such action (a) would be consistent with seeking oppositional superiority continuously; (b) would maintain the oppositional superiority already earned; (c) would be viewed by other sports agents and spectators as running up the score, which is frowned upon; (d) would provide more fully for the continued test that both contestants chose when they entered the contest.

Next, if we examine the substance of these "ought" responses and their reasons, two things may be noted. (a) The actions that ought to be done show what the agents facing the "ought" questions think are practical ways of pursuing the general end of effective contesting in that particular situation. (b) The reasons stated show different kinds of support for the recommended action. The different kinds of support are composed of two factors, one being the good or bad that the action would bring about, the other being the agent for whom that good or bad would occur.

Finally, when we analyze the differing reasons in support of the same action we find different kinds of support, again composed of the two factors, for that same action. For example: (a) Such action would be consistent with seeking oppositional superiority continuously — the good outcome is consistency with a guide of right action while that good outcome, since it relates to the guide, would be for the good of both contestants. (b) Such action would maintain the oppositional superiority already earned — the good outcome is maintaining oppositional superiority and that good outcome is for the good of the ahead contestant only. (c) Such action would be viewed by other sports agents and spectators as running up the score, which is frowned upon — the bad outcome is running up the score and that bad outcome would be bad for the ahead contestant because of the negative sanction attached. (d) Such action would provide more fully for the continued test that both contestants chose when they entered the contest — the good outcome is providing more fully for the continued test chosen and that good outcome is for both contestants alike.

Now, if we look carefully at the two factors cited as support in the reasons for an action, it seems possible to make two kinds of analysis. The first would be whether the good to be brought about by the action is meant for everybody. The language used in the reason will help determine how widespread the consequent good will be *in the eyes of the agent stating the reason.* That is, how many sports participants does that agent see the good occurring to? The second kind of analysis would be whether the resultant good will be for the good of everyone alike. That is, in the eyes of the agent stating the reason, will the resultant good benefit sports participants *in the same way?* In short, we can analyze the reasons by examining the agent's language carefully in terms of these two characteristics of the moral point of view. After all, if the agent answering any of the "ought" questions gives supportive reasons for his/her proposed actions, we can reasonably assume the agent will provide what he/she considers to be the best reasons.

Let us now analyze the four chosen examples of reasons in relation to these two characteristics, classifying them as moral reasons, self-interested reasons, or conventional reasons. Recall that we are still using the illustration of the uneven contest situation in which one or more "ought" questions is being asked by the ahead contestant.

First, the reason "because such action would be consistent with seeking oppositional superiority consistently" recognizes the same kind of good for both opponents in the sport contest and that the good is alike for each contestant. Accordingly, it would be evaluated as a moral reason.

Second, the reason "because such action would maintain the oppositional superiority already earned" recognizes a good meant only for the ahead contestant and, thus, cannot be the same good for both contestants alike. Since this reason supports action from the standpoint of and is good for the ahead contestant only, it would be classified as a self-interested reason.

Third, the reason "because such action would be viewed by other sports agents and spectators as running up the score, which is frowned upon," recognizes that the act is bad in the eyes of a social group. Its consequence is social disapproval imposed upon the ahead contestant. It may be classified as a conventional reason.

Fourth, the reason "because such action would provide more fully for the continued test that both contestants chose when they entered the contest" recognizes the same kind of good for both contestants alike. It may be evaluated as a moral reason.

Having examined illustrations of the basic form by which reasons for or against certain actions are stated, we can describe different kinds of supportive reasons and, from that description, establish a hierarchy.

## The Hierarchy of Reasons for an Action

*Moral Reasons.*    A moral reason in support of an action is offered by an agent who states that the action is the right thing to do because it has identifiable good consequences for all participants in the sports contest, and those good consequences are good in the same way for all participants.

*Good Reasons.*    A good reason in support of an action is a self-interested or conventional reason offered by an agent who states that the action is the right thing to do because it has identifiable good consequences for some participant(s), but not necessarily for all, and that the good consequences are in that participant's self-interest or are approved by a limited social group.

From the description of a moral reason and a good reason, we can derive the following hierarchy of reasons for an action:

*The best reasons for an action* are present when the action is supported both by moral and good reasons. An action supported by both kinds of reasons is the best because its consequences are good for all participants, and in the same way for all. At the same time the action has good consequences in the self-interest of the agent offering the reason, or for another agent he/she is advising, and/or the good consequences are approved by the agent's limited social group.

*Good reasons for an action* are present when the action is supported only by moral reasons. An action supported by this kind of reason is good because its consequences are good for all participants, including the acting agent, and are good in the same way for all.

*Acceptable reasons for an action* are present when the action is supported by self-interested and/or conventional reasons only. An action supported by one or both such reasons is acceptable because it has known good consequences for some participants, though not necessarily for all, and/or those consequences are approved by the agent's limited social group.

## The Hierarchy of Reasons Against an Action

*Moral Reasons.*    A moral reason against an action is offered by an agent who states that the action is wrong because it has identifiable, nonreversible, bad consequences for another agent. That is, the agent stating the reason recognizes that the bad consequences would be contrary to reason for the negatively affected agent to do to himself/herself, just as they would be for the former agent were the situation reversed.[4]

*Good Reasons.*    A good reason against an action is a self-interested or conventional reason offered by an agent who states that the action is wrong because it has identifiable bad consequences for him/her, those consequences being contrary to his/her own self-interest or negatively sanctioned by a limited social group.

From the descriptions of moral and good reasons we can derive the following hierarchy of reasons against an action:

*The strongest reasons against an action* are present when the action has both moral and good reasons not to commend it. An action with both kinds of reasons against it is the worst thing to do because it has negative, nonreversible consequences that harm another agent. At the same time, it has negative consequences in relation to the self-interest of the agent offering the reason, or for another agent he/she is advising, and/or the bad consequences are negatively sanctioned by the agent's limited social group.

*Strong reasons against an action* are present when that action has only moral reasons against its performance. An action with moral reasons against it is the worse thing to do because it has negative, nonreversible consequences that harm another agent.

*Weaker reasons against an action* are present when the action has only self-interested and/or conventional reasons against its performance. An action with self-interested and/or conventional reasons against it is a bad thing to do because it has negative consequences in relation to the self-interest of the agent stating the reason, and/or those negative consequences, for whomever, are negatively sanctioned by the agent's limited social group.

### Applying the Hierarchy of Reasons
### in the Uneven Sports Contest

When two or more actions are subsumable under the same guide and end of right action, the agent asking the "ought" questions must evaluate all of the actions by examining the reasons for each. This involves applying the two hierarchies of reasons and will be illustrated here. Again, the present emphasis is to understand the use of the guides to right action. This is not an attempt to reach a definitive conclusion on right action in the uneven sports contest.

To evaluate reasons in relation to their hierarchies, the asking agent must first analyze the language of all the reasons cited and determine, for each, if it is a moral or good reason for or against the action. Second, the agent must then see how the combination of reasons for and against an action relates to the two hierarchies; that is, does the action have best, good, or acceptable reasons for it and/or strongest, strong, or weaker reasons against it. Third, to reach a decision, the agent must compare his/her evaluations of the reasons related to each action to determine which action(s) has greatest support by the hierarchy. If two or more actions are subsumable under the same guide and end of right action, this will provide the best answer to the agent's "ought" question. To illustrate this process, we will complete the first two steps in examining one of the possible actions subsumable under the guide and end of effective contesting in the uneven sports contest. Consider the reasons for and against the ahead contestant's changing from his/her normal style of play to use untested tactics and strategy.

Moral reasons for such action are:

1. Such action would be consistent with seeking oppositional superiority continuously.

2. It would provide more fully for the continued test that both contestants chose when they entered the contest.

3. It would fulfill the tacit promise, made by the ahead contestant, to try to perform the test better than his/her opponent.

Good reasons for such actions are:

1. Such action would probably maintain the oppositional superiority already earned — a self-interested reason.

2. It would test further the abilities of the ahead contestant — a self-interested reason.

The combination of reasons cited above in the hierarchy would indicate that the specified action has the best reasons for it because it has three moral and two good reasons of positive support. We turn now to examine reasons against the ahead contestant's changing from his/her normal style of play.

Good reasons against such action are:

1. Such action would risk losing the oppositional superiority earned — a self-interested reason.

2. Such action, if successful, would be viewed by other sports agents and spectators as running up the score, which is a negatively sanctioned act — a conventional reason.

3. It would reveal to future opponents some unknown tactical and strategic competence of the ahead contestant — a self-interested reason.

Since none of the reasons against the action appears to be a moral reason, the combination of reasons against the action would indicate that they add up only to strong reasons (vs. strongest or weaker reasons).

In comparing the ahead contestant's changing his/her normal style of play with other possible actions, the agent asking the "ought" question(s) will know that this action has the best reasons for it and only strong reasons against it. Similar appraisals of other possible actions allow for comparing the evaluations to ascertain which, on balance, have the most positive support. Comparison of the evaluations will allow the agent to decide which action(s) "ought" to be done. The comparison can result in four different kinds of determinative answers.

1. One action has the most positive support over all others; therefore, it is the best option.

2. Two or more actions have the same positive support over the others; therefore, any of those actions may be chosen.

3. None of the actions has more positive support over the others; therefore, any of the options may be chosen.

4. All of the actions have only reasons against them; therefore, agents must find other actions that can be positively supported or must choose the least offensive among the negatives.

## NOTES

[1]Eric D'Arcy, *Human Acts: An Essay in Their Moral Evaluation* (Oxford: Oxford University Press, 1963), p. 24.

[2]William K. Frankena, *Ethics*, 2nd ed. (Englewood Cliffs, NJ: Prentice-Hall, Inc., 1973), p. 25f.

[3]Ibid., p. 60.

[4]Kurt Baier, *The Moral Point of View* (Ithaca and London: Cornell University Press, 1958), p. 202.

# Chapter Twelve

## The Acting Agent, Reasons for Action, and Moral Maturity

Chapter 1 discussed several specific sports situations involving questions of what were the right actions. As indicated there, sports participants are constantly faced with questions about right actions. We stated in Chapter 2 that agents facing the questions of right action do provide answers and, in their own minds, support those answers with reasons. Nonetheless, we find that the answers and the reasons offered by different sports participants in the same situation often conflict. Accordingly, this book has attempted to establish a basis—the description and explanation of the good sports contest—for the guides and ends of right action which, if applied correctly, would provide consistent answers to the questions. Let us now return to the existential status of the sports participant in answering the questions on right action.

When a sports participant responds to any of the "ought" questions, he/she first identifies those particular actions seen as being appropriate and, second, cites the reasons to support the appropriateness of the actions. In so doing, the agent may assume different meanings for the word "ought" as it is used in the question. For example, he/she may assume that:

1. "Ought" asks, "What is the best thing for me to do in order to advance my own interest?" Accordingly, the answer will be stated in the form, "I ought to X because it is in my own interest to do so. It is rational and prudent for me."

2. "Ought" asks, "What is the best thing for me to do in order to be in harmony with my social group?" Accordingly, the answer will be stated in the form, "I ought to X because the sanctions of my group tell me it is the right thing to do."

3. "Ought" asks, "What is the best thing for me to do in terms of a moral imperative?" Accordingly, the answer will be stated in the form, "I ought to X because X is an action consistent with a moral guide that I accept because if everyone always acted in accord with that guide, everyone would be better off."

These illustrations attempt to show in yet another way that agents sometimes come to support different actions, or even the same actions, for different types of reasons. Further, the reasons given in support of action often show that the "ought" is requesting a different response from different agents because each agent presumes "ought" means something very different. But in any case each agent, assuming honest responses, is offering what he/she thinks is the best action for the best reasons he/she understands. To illustrate in another way:

Person A asks person B: "In situation A, should I intentionally foul a player on the other team?"

Person B responds: "You ought not to foul the other player in situation A because you will be penalized if you are caught!"

Person A asks person B: "In situation A, should I intentionally foul a player on the other team?"

Person B responds: "You ought to foul the other player in situation A because it is the smart thing to do and is considered so by most players and coaches of your sport."

Person A asks person B: "In situation A, should I intentionally foul a player on the other team?"

Person B responds: "You ought not to foul the other player in situation A because intentional fouling is not a constitutive skill of the sport, and to do so violates the spirit of the rules you promised, tacitly, to observe when you agreed to contest. Besides, I have just read Fraleigh's Chapter 5 on 'Rules and Their Functions' and his Chapter 8 on 'The Primary Guides and Ends of Right Action,' and intentional fouls in situation A are acts prohibited by the guide of nonreversible earned advantage. I think if everyone acted in accord with that guide, everyone would be better off. Don't you agree?"

The differences in what individual agents presume "ought" is asking of them, and in the kinds of reasons given in response, help us to understand yet another thing about moral reasoning. Concerning the advisability of the intentional foul above, we find that the response against fouling for fear of punishment loses strength if, for instance, there is small chance of being detected. Thus, if the agent presumes that the right thing to do is avoid punishment, and he/she sees no other support for not fouling, then the agent would be aware of no reason not to foul. If the agent presumes that the right thing to do is determined by its social acceptance, and if the intentional foul situation (alike in all relevant aspects) occurs in two different sports, one in which it is socially approved and one in which it is disapproved, then the agent would have the *same reason* (social sanctions) for *contradictory* acts. We can see from these two examples that answers to "ought" questions, in which the "ought" is assumed to mean good for one's self-interest or good according to conventional group sanctions, are not answers to the moral "ought." They are not moral "oughts" because they are not actions whose reasons indicate that we are willing to universalize them.

The point is, unless the acting agent knows and understands that a certain kind of action is required by a moral guide, that person is not aware of any reason supporting that action unless it is a self-interested or conventional reason. Accordingly, if the right action for the moral reason is not also supported by a self-interested or conventional reason, the agent lacks any reason whatsoever to do what he/she ought to do morally.

Because agents identify what they ought to do for reasons which appear to be the most supportive to them, and because these agents assume different meanings for "ought," whether or not any agent's response to the "ought" questions is a moral one depends upon his/her moral maturity. That is, what any agent assumes to be a moral response is conditioned by the agent's level of moral development.

The work of Kohlberg,[1] Rest,[2] and others helps us to understand that moral maturity is a cognitive developmental process having various stages that fall, roughly, within three levels. Although this theory of moral development cannot be discussed in full here, some of its features are related to our discussion of the acting agent and his/her reasons for action. The three levels of development from least mature to most mature have been called "preconventional," "conventional," and "postconventional."[3] Each level has two stages: preconventional includes stages one and two, conventional includes stages three and four, and postconventional comprises stages five and six. In terms of our sports agents and their reasons for action, this theory helps us to see that judgments are made:

> in terms of different kinds of "social perspective": the perspective of an individual considering his own interests (at stages 1 and 2), or the perspective of an individual who sees himself as a participant in a group whose members share expectations (at

stage 3 and 4), or the perspective of a rational moral individual "who has made the moral commitments or holds the standards on which a good or just society must be based" (stages 5 and 6).[4]

Roughly speaking, then, what has been called in this book a self-interested reason corresponds with moral maturity at the preconventional level, while a conventional reason is compatible with the conventional level and a moral reason for action is related to the postconventional level of moral maturity.

As indicated, sports agents reacting to "ought" questions can only identify the actions they think are right and can only supply the reasons they think are the most supportive. Therefore, if a sports agent sees a certain action as being consistent with one of the guides and ends of right action proposed in this normative ethic but he/she has only self-interested or conventional reasons to support the action, then the agent is acting in relation to that guide but not acting on that guide. If the self-interested and/or conventional reasons for acting in accord with a guide and end of right action are removed but a moral reason still applies, then that action is required for a moral reason. If the acting agent sees that the action is required for a moral reason, then he/she is acting on principle. "If one has adopted the moral point of view, then one acts on principle and not merely on rules of thumb designed to promote one's aim. This involves conforming to the rules whether or not doing so favors one's own or anyone else's aim."[5]

We may see that the concept of moral maturity as a developmental process, in relation to the existential situation of the sports agent answering "ought" questions about the sports contest, generates the problem of moral education. That is, if sports agents are to determine whether or not the guides and ends of right action specified here are correct, they must be developmentally able to evaluate them in terms of the moral point of view—at a post-conventional level of moral maturity. Also, if sports agents are to act on such correctly held guides of right action, they must be able to ascertain the moral reasons in support of appropriate action. That there are barriers to such moral education is abundantly clear. For instance, McIntosh[6] cites many difficulties in the institution of sport that can detract from sport contributing to the development of moral maturity. Although there are always hindrances and barriers to the pursuit of any kind of maturity, moral or otherwise, such conditions constitute a hindrance "for" such development—not insurmountable obstacles. Indeed, this entire book has been an attempt to develop a normative ethic for the good sports contest which is a rational exposition of what kinds of guides for action are necessary. The arguments presented here attempt to explicate what ought to guide our sports actions and why those guides are morally mature. Only time and considerable debate can tell whether this normative ethic is totally deficient, or totally correct, or whether it is correct in certain respects but incorrect in others. As a reasonably comprehensive ethic of the sports contest, it represents one contribution to the development of the moral maturity of sports participants. As author, I assure you that completing this task has contributed to the ongoing development of my own moral maturity in sport.

## NOTES

[1]L. Kohlberg, "Stages of Moral Development as a Basis for Moral Education," in C.M. Beck, B.S. Crittenden, and E.V. Sullivan, eds., *Moral Education: Interdisciplinary Approaches*. Toronto: University of Toronto Press, 1971.

[2]James R. Rest, *Development in Judging Moral Issues*. Minneapolis: University of Minnesota Press, 1979.

[3]L. Kohlberg, "From Is to Ought: How to Commit the Naturalistic Fallacy and Get Away With it in the Study of Moral Development," in T. Mischel, ed., *Cognitive Development and Epistemology*. New York: Academic Press, 1971.

[4]James R. Rest, *Development in Judging Moral Issues*, pp. 9-10.

[5]Kurt Baier, *The Moral Point of View* (Ithaca and London: Cornell University Press, 1958), p. 191.

[6]Peter McIntosh, *Fair Play: Ethics in Sport and Education* (London: Heinemann, 1979), Chapter 12.